After the Storm

The World Economy &
Britain's Economic Future

VINCE CABLE

Atlantic Books
London

First published in Great Britain in 2015 by Atlantic Books, an imprint of Atlantic Books Ltd.

This paperback edition published in 2016 by Atlantic Books

10 9 8 7 6 5 4 3 2 1

A CIP catalogue record for this book is available from the British Library.

Paperback ISBN: 978 178 239452 5
E-book ISBN: 978 178 239451 8

Printed in Great Britain by Clays Ltd, St Ives plc

Atlantic Books
An Imprint of Atlantic Books Ltd
Ormond House
26–27 Boswell Street
London
WC1N 3JZ

www.atlantic-books.co.uk

Contents

Introduction

The decision of the US Federal Reserve in December 2015 to raise official interest rates for the first time since 2006, albeit by only 0.25% per cent, was intended to send a powerful signal to the world that the prolonged, debilitating era of financial crisis and its aftermath of austerity was approaching its end. 'Normality' – in the sense that we have known it in rich countries in the post-war period, of steady economic growth and improved living standards, with modest and manageable inflation – was returning, or appeared to be.

A few days earlier, although overshadowed by terrorist atrocities, a global agreement had been reached in Paris on a far-reaching and ambitious agenda of inter-governmental cooperation to address the issue of global warming and climate change. Critics argue that the agreement was not far-reaching or ambitious enough, or that it is precarious or insincere and won't lead to concrete action. Nonetheless, it represents a return to habits of practical internationalism, embracing the big emerging powers such as China and India. This is in stark contrast to the dissonant voices of nationalism and rejection of what has come to be called 'globalization' (closer economic integration) stirred up by the insecurities and resentments of those left behind or hurt by the crisis.

These two events provide an ideal context in which to review the question: is the crisis finally over? Is it correct to discuss *The Storm*, the title of my 2008 book that sought to explain the financial crisis, as an episode that is now in the past: *After the Storm*. Or are we just entering a new and dangerous period of turbulence centring on the big emerging markets, notably China, which powered the world economy after 2008? And are the legacy problems – in particular the 'overhang' of private and public debt – still sufficiently serious to drag Japan and the euro-zone, and even the more strongly growing USA and UK, into stagnation or worse?

I return to these issues after a gap of seven years, when there is a better understanding of the financial crisis and its aftermath. The book also draws on my experience of five years in the UK coali-tion cabinet, responsible for key elements of economic policy as Secretary of State for Business Innovation and Skills and President of the Board of Trade, and, before that, as economic spokesman for my party in opposition during the financial crisis. If I am able to contribute something new and different, it is through having a national and global perspective on the interaction of economics and politics.

The 2015 Election

In the UK, politics has been heavily influenced by the 2008 crisis and the issue of who was responsible and who could be trusted to manage the aftermath. In 2010, the sense of economic crisis provided the impetus and rationale for a coalition government. The 2015 election campaign also had a strong economic thread. In most parts of the country, there was a collective judgement that the coalition government had been broadly successful in securing recovery, and that this should not be put at risk by allow-ing in what was successfully portrayed by the Conservatives as a destabilizing left-wing alternative of Labour and the SNP. One personally painful consequence was that even those of us who had contributed substantially to the economic recovery were swept away. I have described elsewhere (*New Statesman*, 22–28 May 2015) how the Conservatives' ruthlessly effective deploy-ment of the 'politics of fear', combined with disillusionment with the coalition among left-leaning voters, squeezed my party's support to disastrous levels.

The election also exposed a deeper and more alarming undercurrent, as the issues of Scotland, immigration, and Europe generated an emotional reaction more powerful than the traditional class-based tribalism of British party politics. Twenty years ago I wrote for the think-tank Demos about the emerging 'politics of identity'. I described how people were either developing outward-looking 'multiple identities' in response to growing globalization, or were retreating into political or wider social movements built on race, religion, language or national identity. At the time, the pattern fitted the collapsing autocracies of the USSR and Eastern Europe better than the mature Western democracies. But it has spread in the wake of the financial and economic crisis. The practical consequence of the politics of identity is that British politics is now dominated by the issue of the future of the United Kingdom, by debate in the forthcoming referendum campaign about our continued membership of the European Union, and by the perceived threat of Islam. For a country that defines itself by its self-confident openness to ideas and commerce, the dangers of a revival of nationalism and the fear of others are especially acute.

Moreover, this tension between the outward-looking politics of an increasingly globalized world and the inward-looking politics of identity is being experienced much more widely than in the UK. Shortly before the successful Paris summit addressing global warming, France had a regional election that pitted the traditional parties of centre-right and centre-left against the nationalist and racist appeal of the Front National, fired up by popular anger and fear in the wake of terrorist atrocities perpetrated by Islamic militants.

The United States, in the early stages of selecting candidates for the 2016 presidential election, has seen, primarily in the appeal to Republican activists of Donald Trump and Senator Cruz, unqualified hostility towards all Muslims and Mexican immigrants. We do not yet know which forces will dominate. Suffice it to say that the logic of economics and technology, and environmental concerns, are pulling countries into more integrated arrangements, while national politics are generating a powerful force in the opposite direction.

The rest of Europe has been convulsed by the question of how to respond to a wave of Syrian and other refugees, with the generous and liberal response of the German chancellor and many other Germans and Swedes contrasting with the visceral rejection of others, notably in Eastern Europe – a rejection that has put in doubt Europe's achievement of the ree internal movement of people. The whole concept of the European Union and the alternative it has offered to a ghastly history is now being brought into question.

Following the 2015 general election the UK now has a Conservative government unencumbered by coalition, which, despite having a small overall majority and having gained minority support (37 per cent) in the election, is able to pursue most of its policy agenda in the face of a fragmented opposition. Moreover, the bitter discussions within the Labour party following the surprise election of the far-left Jeremy Corbyn as leader have helped to create a fatalistic view that Conservative government is here to stay, for a decade if not for a generation. There is already a sense of an elected dictatorship, a one-party-state in which the vested interests and prejudices of the Conservatives and their associates dominate policy-making and the public discourse. I don't believe in such fatalism and I set out below some approaches and policies that can hopefully inform an alternative.

The Coalition

But before the coalition recedes into history, there is value in recalling the controversies that dominated its inception and existence. These revolved primarily around economics.

Who was to blame for the financial crisis and subsequent

recession? Was austerity, in the form of budget deficit reduction, premature and excessive? These old arguments now obscure more topical, forward-looking questions. How serious are the domestic and overseas risks to recovery? How should residual fiscal deficit reduction objectives best be secured with the least economic and social damage? Is the banking system now secure? How can short-term recovery be translated into long-term sustainable and balanced growth? The backward-looking arguments matter, however, because whoever owns them has legitimacy and the crucial advantage of a reputation for competence.

The Conservatives showed great political skill in winning these arguments, because it involved transcending a succession of negatives: a history of Conservative government characterized by 'boom and bust' and a reputation for mismanagement after Black Wednesday in 1992; a failure to anticipate the 2008 crisis or to offer useful solutions when it happened; complicity in creating a weak system of banking regulation; and close association and affinity with some of those whose greed and folly were at the heart of the financial sector failures. But memories can be short and impressions remoulded.

There are also aspects of that history that reverberate to this day. Was the coalition really necessary? What persuaded my party to take the risk of losing its identity as a minority party in a tie-up with its traditional political foes? And what persuaded the Conservatives to abandon a long antipathy to coalition and to ourselves? There is now a broad understanding, even among the coalition government's critics, that the arithmetic of the 2010 election created its own logic, with no other combination of parties capable of forming a stable government. Numerically a Labour–Lib Dem government or pact could have been formed with the support or acquiescence of Ulster's Democratic Unionists and Nationalists from Scotland, Wales and Northern Ireland, but it would have been precariously dependent on single-issue minorities. The story of how the coalition was formed has been described in detail elsewhere. As my party's deputy leader and shadow Chancellor, obviously I had a heavy responsibility. Whatever my personal aversion to working with the Conservatives, I could see no alternative.

During the negotiations, I had several conversations with Gordon Brown, exploring the alternative of a centre-left coalition. He was as aware as anyone of the dangers posed by international financial turbulence and he wanted a strong government that could take a leadership role in Europe, continuing the work he had done to help stabilize the world economy two years earlier. I personally had – and have – a high regard and liking for Gordon Brown and I believe the history books will be kinder to him than contemporary judgements. But it was clear, despite his own commitment to making a coalition work, that the parliamentary arithmetic was not there. I am sure it was true, too, that the Cameron–Clegg talks were too well advanced by that stage, and that Gordon Brown's wish to continue in office was regarded by my colleagues as an obstacle rather than an alternative. In any event, the precariousness of the country's economic position meant that there was a sense of urgency about creating an agreed, substantial plan of action, rather than a temporary sticking-plaster solution. What is perhaps not so readily understood, by a public inclined to believe that most politicians are thieves and knaves, is that my party colleagues and I believed we were doing the right thing for the country.

This sense of urgency and importance was enhanced by the personal briefings that I and others received by phone during the coalition negotiations from the Cabinet Secretary and the permanent secretary to the Treasury, reflecting, at one remove, the views of the Governor of the Bank of England. The formation of the coalition coincided with the first major crisis of confidence in Greek government bonds and the euro. The government's top officials expressed the fear that, as the country most exposed to the banking crisis and with the largest fiscal deficit of any major country, the contagion could easily spread to the UK. Since the UK had its own currency, which can float, the fear was not of a classic currency crisis, but that it would be difficult to sell British government debt, which would have driven down the price of bonds and driven up their yield – that is, driven up the cost of borrowing. While they were speaking within civil service constraints, they made it clear that the politicians had a key role – to establish confidence – and that it required a stable government with a commitment to improve the public finances.

There was little disagreement either then or during the early stages of the coalition government about the necessity for such action. At that stage there was a broad understanding among all three parties that spending cuts and tax rises were inevitable – though there was a marked absence of specifics. I had written a pamphlet nine months before the 2010 general election detailing a programme of consolidation, setting out some difficult possible spending cuts, and proposing a schedule close to that later adopted by the coalition. The view prevailed, however (and not only among the Lib Dems) that talk of cuts repelled voters while spending commitments attracted them, and this led us into the disaster of the tuition fees pledge. Even the Conservatives, anxious to appear as the leading fiscal hawks, had said little beyond the need for 'efficiency savings' and 'tackling waste', and one of their main commitments – hailed by much of the press as a political masterstroke – was a promise to sacrifice revenue by cutting inheritance tax. But whichever party was in government would have faced the need for difficult, unpopular cuts and tax rises.

The new element introduced by the eurozone drama and agreed during the subsequent coalition negotiations was a Conservative-led commitment to bring forward a first round of £11 billion of fiscal consolidation. Much was made of this change of emphasis by the Lib Dems at the time, but it seemed a sensible and modest response to what was happening in the real world. The fact that, five years later, the coalition government had reached roughly the mid-point in its programme of fiscal consolidation is eloquent testimony to the flexibility that was employed in practice and also to the practical difficulties of proceeding any faster.

Despite the sound and fury around fiscal policy – the austerity debate – I do not believe that any plausible government would have pursued radically different policies or achieved a radically different outcome. The outgoing Labour government had, in fact, already initiated cuts, as I discovered when I entered ministerial office, in areas such as further education. Moreover, by launching the Browne review of university tuition fees it was preparing the ground for unpopular decisions that the next government would have to take.

The more potent and lingering disagreement has been over who was to blame for the financial crisis and the legacy of budget deficits. The search for the 'guilty men' was, explicitly or implicitly, a theme of almost every speech during the 2015 election campaign – and, I suspect, will reverberate for a generation to come. For the Conservatives, it was crucial to establish that the crisis was caused by a fiscally incontinent Labour government which spent too much, rather than by the financial markets that they had let off the in the 1980s and where they retained close and lucrative relationships with party donors. This political battle the Conservatives won hands-down, despite there being only weak evidence to support their argument. A combination of Tory triumphalism and Labour embarrassment has led to a rewriting of history. As I show in chapter seven, the fiscal position before 2008 was heading in the wrong direction but was basically sound and better than that which Labour had inherited in 1997.

For the angry populist fringes of left or right, however, these nuances are of little interest. They see crisis as a failure of a corrupt, complacent ruling class of politicians who had allowed greedy bankers to run amok and then escape, and who were abetted by a variety of other pantomime villains, from Brussels bureaucrats to multinational companies. The populist fringes made only limited inroads in the 2015 election (outside Scotland, where there has been a different dynamic). But the Labour party has now been captured by the far left. And the coming European referendum will provide a stage for anti-EU populism.

In *The Storm* I argued that there was no politically conveni-ent, simple explanation for what happened during the crisis. Responsibility was widely spread. The banking crisis was global in character, but it struck the UK particularly hard because of the scale of the UK banking sector. For that, the excesses of the bank-ing industry and poor supervision of it were largely to blame. The Labour government can reasonably be criticized for being asleep at the wheel and failing to spot the warning signs of an uncon-trolled credit and housing boom and an inflated banking sector, and for reacting too late. But when disaster struck, the govern-ment and the Bank of England, along with the US authorities, dealt with the consequences in a commendably rational way. The large fiscal hole inherited by the coalition government was mainly the consequence of the financial crisis itself, rather than a previous history of structural deficits, which were real but small.

However unfairly, the Conservatives have won the political argument about historic responsibility, and they had the support of the coalition to take difficult decisions after 2010. But in future, their approach to dealing with the residual fiscal legacy may be judged more harshly, since, beyond the rhetoric about a 'long-term economic plan' and 'financial responsibility', the public has not been properly prepared for continued austerity, which no longer has the endorsement of a consensus-based coalition and has a weaker economic rationale. The proposed £12 billion in welfare cuts, for example, advocated before the 2015 election by George Osborne, appears to have been formulated without much forethought and on the basis that the Liberal Democrats would be around to dilute them.

The subsequent furore over deep cuts to tax credits was very badly received and the Chancellor had to abandon the policy. The 2015 Autumn Statement proved to involve less draconian public spending cuts than had been foreshadowed, due to opti-mistic forecasts from the Office for Budget Responsibility (OBR). But they are still severe, and if sustained they will have major cumulative impacts on the scale and shape of the public sector.

With economic policy now having an increasingly ideological edge, it is useful to contrast it with the style and content of the coalition.

The Workings of the Coalition Government

After five years of coalition government, there is a lot to be written about who said what and to whom and when. There will come a time when the life of the coalition is told in full. This book has no such pretensions. I was involved in some of the high-profile dramas of the government – around the Murdochs and Leveson, the scale of spending cuts, the Lib Dems' tuition fees disaster, clashes over immigration and Europe – but more peripherally in many others. I will use the discussion of my time in government primarily as a backdrop to considering the economy, past and future.

It may come as a surprise to many that the government worked much more smoothly and that relations were much better than the daily reports of rows, feuds, splits, leaks and plots would suggest. What the public actually sees is somewhat like professional wrestling: a confusing mixture of play-acting and genuine combat. For the most part, my experience of coalition government was that, when it mattered, it was professional and surprisingly collegiate. Messrs Cameron and Clegg deserve credit for that.

Critics of the Lib Dems (who clearly include large numbers of former supporters) have argued that the party, and Nick Clegg in particular, were culpable and perhaps naive in mistaking civility as signalling empathy and, especially in the early stages as symbolized by the Rose Garden press conference, something more intimate than a business-like relationship. I would defend Nick Clegg, though my own instincts were different, more suspicious and conditioned by decades fighting the Conservatives. He believed that displays of common style and purpose were important in persuading a sceptical public of the value of coalition government, that there was a constituency for parties that could rise above petty, tribal politics, and that European politics, which he understood well, offered successful role models for centrist parties in coalition (that was before the demise of the German FDP).

For their part, the Conservatives, no doubt taking a lead from the top, operated with personal courtesy and good manners. Some, perhaps even Cameron himself, genuinely believed, at least for a while, that the country had stumbled into a better model of government. Any illusions on that score were stripped away during the Alternative Vote referendum. With deep cynicism the Conservatives colluded with Labour critics of AV to target Nick Clegg, exploiting his personal unpopularity. The nastiness may have been outsourced, but we knew that it coexisted with surface charm. Labour was always less subtle. From day one of the Coalition, they directed aggressive and very personal hostility towards Nick Clegg in particular. The abuse he encountered from Labour activists, especially in Sheffield, almost certainly had the effect of reinforcing our close working relationship with the Tories.

In my own corner of government, sometimes portrayed in the press as an ideological battleground between a grumpy, left-wing secretary of state and various true-blue Tory ministers, relations were always business-like and often cordial. In some cases, as with the universities minister, David Willetts, there was a real sense of partnership. I took the view from the outset that we should leave our ideological weapons at the door and work as a team on issues where we had common ground. Our shifting cast of two Lib Dems and up to six full-time or shared Tory ministers, with a small team of special advisers to broker agreements, largely functioned in this cooperative way. Towards the end there were spats about who should claim the credit for various achievements, though I take satisfaction from the fact that there were achievements to fight over rather than disasters for which to apportion blame.

As in other areas of government, I and my Lib Dem colleagues wanted what we regarded as progressive reforms, which we had to barter for things the Tories wanted. I sought to block what I regarded as ideologically driven spending cuts beyond what had been agreed as necessary for fiscal stability, especially in capital spending. And I carried out a five-year rearguard action to prevent high-flying Treasury graduates demolishing adult and further education, which I felt they neither understood nor respected. I did block 'hire and fire' labour market legislation as recommended in the Beecroft Report, as well as the more extreme proposals to tighten immigration rules on overseas students and non-EU skilled workers, attempts to stop free speech in universities, and unnecessary and provocative reforms to trade unions. I also referred the News Corp–BSkyB takeover to the competition authorities, which helped ensure that it did not happen. I see that the post-2015 Conservative government has quickly moved its tanks on to most of these now unprotected corners of the battlefield. Under the coalition it was possible to mobilize my party leader when the Conservatives would not take 'no' for an answer, so as to weave particular disputes into the wider tapestry of the coalition agreement.

Not all the disagreements were between the coalition parties. Although I had difficult exchanges with the Home Secretary and prime minister over immigration controls on non-EU students and skilled workers, almost all my Conservative colleagues and ministers agreed, at least privately, that those policies were seriously damaging to business, universities and the wider national economic interest. As a Lib Dem, I was able to speak publicly about the way that the government's claim to be 'open for business' was being undermined. But I was struck by the inability of powerful Conservatives like the Chancellor, or even the prime minister, to move the Home Secretary an inch. It is one of the more bizarre outcomes of the election that the Conservatives, having freed themselves of the inhibitions of coalition, should shackle themselves once again to a pledge to reduce net immigration from over 300,000 per annum to under 100,000, a pledge that could only be achieved by inflicting considerable harm on the economy.

Most of the time and energy of my Lib Dem team of two, and my two special advisers, was devoted to finding common ground with the Conservatives and delivering positive results. These included the launching of an industrial strategy and the boosting of advanced manufacturing and creative industries; an unpopular but necessary overhaul of university and student finances, and a liberalization of the sector; the resurrection and reform of apprenticeships; bank restructuring and 'ring-fencing', and the successful launch of the British Business Bank and the Green Investment Bank; corporate governance reform, including executive pay and a register of beneficial ownership; a chain of new industry-led innovation centres, known as Catapults; shared parental leave and flexible working; better gender balance on company boards; the introduction of private and worker ownership of the Royal Mail and the rescue of the Post Office network; an overhaul of the competition regime and the Takeover Code; protection for supermarket suppliers and pubs from market abuse; expansion of the role of adult education into mental health; copyright reform; and much else besides. Sometimes, an explicit deal was involved. I obtained the Chancellor's backing for the British Business Bank in return for not opposing his controversial scheme to create a new form of worker ownership with fewer rights (on the assumption that it wouldn't fly, as it didn't). In short, the coalition was not a zero-sum game. It did many useful things, but usually at the price of a messy compromise.

With the benefit of hindsight, it is clear that the Lib Dems singularly failed to communicate and claim ownership of the very real achievements of government. We were, of course, heavily outnumbered, five to one across government, and we did not have the same depth of support in the media. But we never found a formula for translating achievement in government into public support.

Indeed, the dilemma for me as a Lib Dem secretary of state was that I could gain a distinctive identity for my party by opposing and blocking, or I could achieve results by gaining Tory acquiescence and support for my own proposals, which often meant risking losing ownership of the issue. A typical example was apprenticeships. In the tough bargaining around the 2010 spending round I had managed to ease some of the political pain of increasing student tuition fees by channelling more resources into apprenticeships, which subsequently expanded rapidly. The Conservatives were quick to spot the appeal of the apprenticeship brand and never ceased to claim ownership of the policy. A similar fate awaited the Lib Dem commitment to raise income tax thresholds, which the Conservatives initially disdained, or the strengthening of the state pension and pension reforms. This battle for ownership was at the heart of the coalition.

Whatever external impression may have been created, I was primarily interested in making things happen rather than stopping things happening. Moreover, I had the benefit of some impressive and enthusiastic civil servants and a generally harmonious ministerial team. Whitehall gossip had it that the Department for Business, Innovation and Skills (BIS) was one department where coalition worked, with genuine give and take. Others included Work and Pensions under Iain Duncan Smith (IDS), Health under both Andrew Lansley and Jeremy Hunt, and Transport under Patrick McLoughlin. Others were notoriously factional. The experience of Nick Harvey at Defence and Norman Baker at the Home Office was altogether less happy. We also had to work across government, through Cabinet committees, as well as in Cabinet and in direct relationships with the prime minister and Chancellor. I was left with very ambivalent feelings. The Tories collectively could be appalling, with some ugly tribal prejudices, and when their party interests were directly challenged they could be vicious. But as individuals they were invariably courteous and professional, and often likeable and considerate.

This ability to operate on different levels is part of the *modus operandi* of all successful politicians and can be seen in the way the House of Commons constantly switches mood between elaborate good manners and boorishness, between real or synthetic anger and bonhomie. But the Tories appeared to have an exceptional ability to compartmentalize, to commit political murder with a charming smile. By contrast, in its rapid ascent from the Championship to the Premier League, my party hadn't acquired this ruthlessness, and it has paid the price.

There was, however, in economic policy an underlying tension that was not simply between Lib Dems and Conservatives, or between George Osborne and myself. I believe that the structure of economic policy-making in government is badly flawed. I am far from being the first minister to lament the overarching power of the Treasury, full of highly intelligent and personable individuals, but institutionally arrogant, obsessively short-termist and deeply conservative. The creation of a powerful independent central bank, and other institutions like the OBR, has diluted its influence. But the Treasury is still a powerful agency for short-term cash management – a continental finance ministry writ large, but without a compensating mechanism for mobilizing long-term investment and planning. I tried, like Michael Heseltine and Peter Mandelson before me, to create such a mechanism in the form of a strong and respected Business Department (previously the DTI), but my successors will have their work cut out to preserve and strengthen it – if they want to. All the signs are that since the general election, BIS has been brought very firmly back under the control of the Treasury. My undoubtedly able successor has stepped back from an interventionist role and lauds financial services rather than manufacturing and creative industries as the main source of wealth creation.

One of the weaknesses in the workings of the coalition was that it accentuated the structural flaw of Treasury dominance. A key mechanism for resolving disputes between the coalition parties was the 'Quad'. It was an achievement of Nick Clegg to have created a mechanism in which the two parties had equal status, and he was able to use it to good effect on many issues. And I understand why he wanted his close friend and confidant Danny Alexander alongside him. (I was told that David Cameron would not have tolerated my being the fourth member of the Quad in any event.) The upshot was that there were two Treasury ministers and no one from elsewhere in government. Whatever their other admirable qualities, Nick and Danny seemed convinced of Treasury orthodoxy on matters of economic policy. Indeed, I think they genuinely believed that our party should accept the received wisdom of the Treasury over deficits and debt as part of the party's 'Strong Economy–Fair Society' message. I didn't agree, and areas of disagreement are apparent in the text below. But the consequence was that Osborne and the Treasury had effective control over the government machine, with political cover often provided by the Quad.

I was better insulated than some from the Treasury's influence by having a strong, well-run department with a sense of purpose and some economically literate officials. This was boosted by recruiting some of the brightest and best Treasury officials and promoting them from junior gamekeepers to senior poachers. Since I was considered difficult to sack, I could be bloody-minded, and was. But the Treasury was able to intimidate weaker departments like Culture, Media and Sport, DEFRA and Justice, whose Tory ministers could not afford to offend the Chancellor. Some of the greatest pressure came on IDS at the Department for Work and Pensions whose poor, disabled, unemployed and otherwise vulnerable clients were seen as easy targets for cuts. IDS was a significant political figure, a former leader on the right who couldn't be trifled with, and a fundamentally decent man, but he spent much of his time fighting off pubescent Treasury advisers and officials with brilliant but wacky or cruel ideas for saving money.

My own relations with the Treasury were forged in the negotiations around the spending review in 2010. I believed at the time that we had given too much ground and in the process had compromised some good programmes which gave excellent value for money. My officials, however, felt we had, if anything, got off lightly, and the agreed cuts to current spending (the Departmental Expenditure Limits, or DEL, in the jargon of Whitehall) of 25 per cent had already been agreed in principle by my Labour pre-decessors. I compensated by being more aggressive subsequently and this, no doubt, contributed to a steady distancing from the Chancellor. My relations with him had initially been very affable, as we jointly defended government economy policy in the tough-est early period of office. But our instincts and world-views were very different. I believed in the need for government to be disci-plined in its management of public money and delivered large savings, especially in administration. However, I also believed that government could be a force for good and that it should intervene to counter market failures and promote sustainable growth. The Chancellor had an ideological belief in a small state, which I didn't share, as well as a ruthless eye for party advantage.

A Global Perspective

In the chapters that follow I try to deal with a forward-looking agenda. A forward-looking prognosis is easier to write if the back-ground is one of clear failure and obvious solutions. But in reality we are dealing with a world of glasses half-full or half-empty. In contrast to the last major global economic crisis, during the inter-war period, governments have proved collectively more rational, cooperative and economically literate. World trade has contin-ued to expand, albeit less exuberantly. Global growth has slowed a little, but not dramatically. Yet there remains, as discussed in chapters one to six, persistent threats, most obviously in the euro-zone. The eurozone has confounded the critics who expected it to implode, but there is a lingering malaise and the possibility of a major crisis resulting from Greek default and a Greek withdrawal from the single currency remains very real.

Even in the more successful developed economies, like the United States, there is pessimistic talk of 'secular stagnation'. It is not at all clear how Western economies can escape from the legacy of abnormal monetary policy deriving from an overhang of pri-vate and public debt, and from a destabilizing cycle of boom and bust in asset markets. There is also a high level of uncertainty over whether the slowdown in growth in China – to rates of expansion (around 6 or 7 per cent) still inconceivable in the developed economies – will be managed in an orderly manner. The knock-on effects of the slowdown on commodity markets are having a serious impact on African and Latin American countries highly dependent on exports of materials, oil and other raw materials. Taken in conjunction with the move to higher interest rates in the USA, attracting mobile capital from emerging markets, there is a likelihood of serious adjustment problems and slower growth in the emerging markets that have helped power the world economy since the financial crisis.

The large financial institutions are more secure and richer in capital, as described in chapter two, but it is doubtful whether they are robust enough to deal with some of the potential threats to financial stability. In general, governments have acted prudently to reduce systemic risk from the known unknowns in financial markets through regulatory reforms – but the unknown unknowns may be more dangerous than we appreciate.

In terms of the conduct of UK policy, I have set out analyses and recommendations below. I do so with the specific aim of contributing to the beginnings of a serious debate about the currently fragmented and demoralized centre and left. The context of the debate is the challenge to the two dominant political traditions of the post-war era. One is what can loosely be called the centre-right: traditional American Republicans, British Conservatives and European Christian Democrats, and one strand of European liberalism, as in the German Free Democrats. These parties and individuals fully embraced globalization and free markets, including financial markets, and were seen to have been vindicated by the collapse of communism and the evident success of capitalist economies. But the crisis and its aftermath have shattered these illusions. Leading capitalist economies have barely recaptured the living standards that they enjoyed before the crisis and are falling behind the more directed state capitalism of China and the emerging economies. Many people, especially the young, have been badly hurt – excluded from the housing market in the UK and from employment in some continental EU countries. There is still a lot of anger directed at banks in particular and at business in general, and at the elites who presided over the crisis. Most damagingly, the connection between rewards and talent – the moral basis of capitalism – has been lost. Extraordinary rewards for a narrow area of employment, encouraging risk-taking that has damaging social consequences, has changed the sense of what is useful work.

Pragmatic adaptation and skilled leadership have so far helped centre-right parties to do well politically, especially in Germany, the UK and Japan. A period of insecurity and instability has, paradoxically, increased the appeal of 'the devil we know'. But a protracted sense of crisis could pull them apart, with a reversion to more atavistic politics: disengagement from Europe and the possible disintegration of the UK; a retreat from the European project in continental Europe; aggressive nationalism in Asia, including growing assertiveness by China and India in particular.

There are challenges also to those in the social democratic tradition. In the good times, parties and individuals of the centre-left coasted along, accepting the benefits of open-market economies along with the promise that they could be reconciled with a sense of social solidarity, redistributive fiscal measures, and strong social services and public goods. In the UK there was a Faustian pact between the City and a social democratic government that traded light regulation for tax revenue. In their different ways, Labour under Blair and Brown, Scandinavian and German social democrats, Australian Labour, and their emerging equivalents in Brazil, India and South Africa, all succeeded politically by offering this beguiling cocktail of the best in capitalism and the best in socialism. The crisis should have reinforced their appeal by underlining the need for state intervention and regulation, not least in the financial sector: action to curb the greed of incompetent and reckless financiers; measures to cushion the impact of the crisis on the vulnerable; and inter-governmental cooperation to uphold rules and prevent contagious collapse.

Moreover, the crisis has brought to the fore one issue on which parties of the left have fed throughout the nineteenth and twentieth centuries: the concern that income and wealth inequalities are becoming too extreme. On one level, the world is becoming a more equal place, as many poor countries, especially the giant Asian economies, are growing much faster than rich ones, and the numbers in absolute poverty are falling fast. But governments are national, not global, and within countries there appears to be a widening of inequality. The share of labour in national income has, in general, fallen over the last few decades. The income share of the top 1 per cent has risen strikingly. In terms of the stock of wealth, rather than the flow of income, the richest 1 per cent have a third of all wealth in the USA, and a quarter in the EU, with both figures rising. Such inequalities are not just intrinsically offensive but economically damaging, because they drain demand and reward rent-seeking behaviour and the accumulation of assets, mainly property, rather than innovation and wealth creation. There is undoubtedly resentment that much of this wealth has accrued to financiers and others whose activities were at best socially useless and at worst contributed directly to the crisis and the misery that followed it. At first sight, there was never a better time for progressive politics.

In practice, this hasn't happened. In general, politicians rather than bankers have paid the price for allowing the crash to happen. In particular, governments of the traditional centre-left, as in the UK and Spain, were seen to be overwhelmed by a crisis they hadn't anticipated or prepared for, or, as in France, were seemingly unable to offer more than rhetoric and good intentions in the face of forces over which they had little control. Instead, the political beneficiaries of the crisis have been not just traditional conservative parties but those on the populist fringe: right-wing parties of a nationalistic or even racist bent, feeding off the politics of identity (in France, Holland, Belgium, Sweden, Denmark,

Norway and Finland and parts of Eastern Europe such as Hungary and Slovakia, plus UKIP in the UK); some on the left based on anti-austerity platforms (Spain, Greece, Ireland, plus Sinn Fein and the SNP); some simply anti-establishment (Italy); and some based on a reaction against globalization (the Greens). In some instances, these parties are putting forward worthwhile ideas that should form part of any policy response: the demand for debt restructuring by Syriza in Greece and Podemos in Spain; the environmental imperative of the Greens; the pressure for decentralized, federal structures of government in Scotland and Catalonia. But the political adrenalin that sustains these moments is essentially a negative one of anger and protest.

There is thus a gaping hole which used to be filled by those of the centre and centre-left, the 'progressive' parties drawing in varying degrees on social democratic and politically liberal traditions. Their purpose was to combine idealism and practicality in office. But, as with Labour and the Lib Dems in the UK, and the Democrats in the USA, and in countries like Canada and Australia where such parties used to flourish, as well as in Scandinavia and in much of continental Europe, and in the democracies of the emerging economies, such as India, there is a sense of weakness and retreat – demoralisation, too, from having been seen to be complicit in a consensus that became discredited.

The position is by no means uniformly bleak. One beacon of encouragement has been the election and re-election of America's first black president, who has accumulated a body of legislative reform in health and financial services in the face of a hostile Congress, has presided over economic recovery, and has maintained a calm and rational approach to foreign policy in the face of extreme provocation. Another is the return to power, from a seemingly hopeless position, of the Canadian Liberals.

Yet there is a new agenda that urgently requires convincing answers from those who identify with this tradition: how to constrain and manage the financial sector without destroying it; how to build public support for an open economy and international rules in the face of domestic economic insecurity and fears of terrorism and ouncontrolled immigration when there is also a weakening sense of social solidarity; how to reconcile financial discipline with the growing demands on government, particularly from the health needs of an ageing population; how to reconcile environmentalism with growth and jobs; how to provide a framework for long-term decision-making through business and personal security while embracing the speed of digital and other innovation; how to redistribute income and wealth progressively in a world of great porosity and without destroying incentives to work and to invest. I hope that my own analysis and practical experience of office will at least point to some answers.

What is to be done?

I have been an elected decision-maker as well as an analyst and commentator, and consequently I know that the first is more difficult. Policy-makers have to face the question, 'what do I do next?' And do it. And be judged on the outcomes. So, while this book is primarily analysis and commentary, I have tried to answer the questions, 'what would you do?' and 'what would you have done differently?' and occasionally, 'why did you do what you did?' Here, I try to bring the policy conclusions together.

I do so largely from the standpoint of the UK and the British policy-making of which I have experience, recognizing that the UK has a 2 per cent and diminishing share of the world economy and that national action is heavily constrained by the forces of international economic integration and, more narrowly, by European commitments and rules.

Economic policy-makers normally have an acknowledged and important set of principles on which they draw. Economics, however, has not weathered the financial crisis well. Substantial areas of theory built around 'efficient financial markets' have had to be ditched. It has been necessary to disinter forgotten thinkers like Hyman Minsky, or economic historians like Charles Kindleberger, who understood and wrote about financial bubbles, speculative manias and panics. University syllabuses are having to be rewritten to reflect the new awareness. There is still a distinct lack of clarity. The 2013 Nobel Prize for economics was awarded to authors of two contrasting explanations of asset market behaviour that directly contradicted one another.

In practice, no single unified theory forged by the crisis has emerged. Governments, notably in the USA, the UK and Japan, have followed a somewhat eclectic approach to economic policy, drawing on three different strands of thinking: the Austrian approach, which emphasizes deep structural problems around private and public debt, insolvent or malfunctioning banks and corporate profitability; the Friedmanite monetarist school which, based on experience of the Great Depression in the 1930s, emphasizes adequate money supply and unorthodox monetary policy to support demand; and the Keynesians, also based on experience of the 1930s, arguing for flexible and expansive fiscal policy to support demand. Much heat and emotion has been generated by protagonists of these different approaches. But in practice, governments and central banks have been refreshingly non-ideological, whatever the political rhetoric deployed, and have been broadly successful so far in averting a 1930s-style disaster. The one major exception is in the eurozone where dogma, as well as the difficulties of intergovernmental coordination, has stood in the way of rational demand management and debt restructuring.

My own prejudices inevitably influence my conclusions. I draw on both liberal and social democratic traditions. Looking forward, parties and leaders within those traditions face a major constraint and a major opportunity. The constraint is that since the fall of Soviet communism there is no serious alternative model to what the left calls 'global capitalism', a system of close integration between market economies within sets of regional or global rules. Contrary to many predictions and historical precedents, and some continuing doubts, this system has weathered the storm so far. Protest movements from left and right or the environmental movement have identified injustices and weaknesses but, so far, have provided no coherent alternative. It could be argued that the nationally based state capitalism of China, India, Brazil, Russia, Indonesia or Turkey represents something fundamentally different, but (perhaps excepting Russia) those countries are adapting their economies in ways that are still broadly liberalizing and integrated with the world economy. The comprehensive rejection of Western ideas of all kinds by the growing Islamic insurgency does not purport to offer economic as opposed to spiritual salvation. So, political programmes have to start from where we are, rather than from hypothetical alternatives.

The opportunity is that, within this set of constraints, there is a market for active government (local, national or multinational) based on attacking monopolistic concentrations of economic and political power; fostering public goods, from parks, libraries and common culture to transport and communication networks, education and security, the planning of cities and protection of areas of natural beauty; pooling risks surrounding healthcare or economic uncertainty; developing a capacity to deal with market failures, the short-termism of capital markets, the under-provision of training and long-term scientific research, and dysfunctional land and housing markets; encouraging different forms of capitalism, from private family enterprises to publicly quoted limited companies, domestic or foreign-owned, and mutual models involving customer or worker shares; and creating a system of financial rewards seen to be fair because they reflect hard work, creativity or entrepreneurship rather than extortion, luck or inheritance. These are, of course, massive subjects that range far beyond this text – suffice to say that my own biases are based on a belief that the pendulum has now swung too far, emphasizing the failures of governments rather than the failures of markets.

I also make some assumptions about the future within which policy will have to be framed. Assumptions are not predictions. I have no better knowledge than anyone else about the future. There are clearly risks and the value of scenario planning is to avoid the trap of believing that trends are inexorable or that the conventional wisdom must be right. Many distinguished people made fools of themselves predicting in the 1990s that Japan was set to become the world's leading economic power; or, in the first decade of the century, that clever financiers had found new mechanisms to support ever-growing credit and ever-rising house prices; or, until very recently, that oil prices must continue to rise. But any forward view has to make some working assumptions. I am assuming that, despite some considerable risks, economic Armageddon is not around the corner, that China and the USA will continue to dominate the world economy, the former increasingly so despite its current slowdown, and that Britain's troubled neighbours will manage to make the eurozone work, albeit with poor growth prospects. But the legacies of the storm in the main economies of the West are real and burdensome: exceptional levels of household and public debt; unresolved problems of restoring more normal monetary policy and managing house price bubbles; a dearth of investment to absorb savings at a global level; and a decline in productivity growth and innovation. I broadly support the view that these factors together are contributing to so-called secular stagnation. The UK itself has these negative features and will also be affected by negative developments elsewhere.

I have set out ten broad areas where I believe action is required.

Banks

This is where the financial crisis started. As discussed in chapters two and ten, Britain's mainstream banks are now safer and better capitalized, which is clearly welcome. The big British global banks were too big for their own good and for the British economy, and the reaction of Lloyds and Barclays in particular to move towards more traditional lending and a domestic focus is also welcome. Despite the apparent attractions of a large, exporting, tax-generating financial services industry, international research as well as

experience tell us that a bloated financial industry is a net negative. Relative contraction is welcome, though painful for many
individuals. So what remains to be done?

First, the regulatory reforms separating traditional and 'casino'
banking through ring-fencing are a major step forward and
must be protected from backsliding and industry lobbying. The
banks have still to establish that they are no longer too-big-to-
fail, through 'living wills' and adequate capital, and the more the
financial crisis recedes into history the greater will be the need to
ensure that regulatory standards are maintained both domestically and internationally.

Second, small business lending has been a disaster area, with
net lending still negative seven years after the crash. Post-crisis
risk aversion has reinforced pre-crisis habits of failure to support
entrepreneurial business, especially companies unable to offer
strong property collateral. Progress has been made via the publicly
owned British Business Bank, acting as a catalyst in developing
new forms of credit (like peer-to-peer lending) and, with the private Business Growth Fund, in supporting equity investment in
medium-sized companies. But much remains to be done, including by expanding these institutions.

Third, bank lending remains highly concentrated, for business
especially, but also for personal customers. Under the coalition,
healthy competition had started to emerge thanks to challenger
banks, helped by a less bureaucratic licensing regime and the British Business Bank. One particular lacuna, relative to Germany or
the USA, is the dearth of local community banking, other than
the remaining small building societies. Regulators should ensure
that red tape is minimized in order that new small-scale technology platforms can flourish and new local banks emerge.

Fourth, the elephant in the room is RBS. I believe the Labour
and coalition governments were remiss in parking RBS in an
arm's-length body for seven years, rather than using it to promote
small business lending and to create more diversity and competition in the sector. There has never been any urgency about

privatizing RBS, though it should happen in due course. It is not too late to make further divestments beyond the planned, but enormously protracted, Williams and Glyn's carve-out, so as to increase competition and diversity. One model would be to restructure the bank's very centralized operation so as to create a semi-autonomous, community-based structure along the lines of Handelsbanken, with a particular emphasis on small business lending.

Lastly, the endless scandals resulting in 'regulatory revenge' – imposing fines on the banks themselves, with minimal sanctions on the individuals responsible – has been a continuing source of public cynicism. While petty benefit cheats face jail, it seems unlikely that the architects of the 2008 disaster will suffer any sanction beyond criticism. The Parliamentary Commission on Banking Standards has produced a sensible set of recommendations for creating professional standards around banking which must be followed through, along with legislation, now passed, criminalizing recklessness. A key test will be Governor Carney's proposed Fair and Effective Markets Review, which rightly seeks to establish senior bank executives' personal responsibility for their banks, but leaves oversight to a panel of market participants, which could easily become a cosy, self-serving as well as self-regulating, process. The removal of the tough Mr Martin Wheatley from the leadership of the regulator, the Financial Conduct Authority, a succession of concessions to bank lobbying and the rhetoric of a 'new settlement' with the banks, all suggest that the Conservative government wishes to weaken the post-crisis regulatory framework.

Deficits and Debt

The bitter, highly polarized debate about austerity has disguised some rather mundane realities, as I argue in chapters seven and eight. It is not true that the Labour government grossly mismanaged the public finances in the run-up to the 2008 crisis. There was a small structural deficit, but the Conservative narrative of spendthrift incompetents is simply wrong. The left has been equally dishonest in attacking the coalition for unnecessarily causing the slow post-crisis recovery through aggressive deficit cutting. In practice, structural deficit reduction has been measured and pragmatic – indeed, Keynesian – and aggregate demand has been systemically supported through monetary policy.

The forward-looking debate is about how to manage the residual structural deficit and the legacy of public debt. First, the residual cyclically adjusted structural current deficit – the central policy objective of the coalition – is highly uncertain because of massive statistical disparities in measurement of the 'output gap'. It was cavalier of both coalition parties to promise a crash deficit reduction over three years after 2015. That was over-ambitious and the post-election Chancellor has extended the period for an extra year. It still represents a faster pace of fiscal consolidation than under the coalition. It may well have to be extended again if the economy slows, as it could well do when tighter monetary policy takes effect.

A bigger issue is the government's inclusion in the deficit, which it plans to eliminate by 2019/20, of capital spending. The practical consequence is that the Conservative government's planned deficit reduction is around 2.5 per cent of GDP greater than that planned by the coalition. Ideology rather than economics is driving this. Deep cuts in public investment under both the coalition and Labour have been damaging and unnecessary, greatly aggravating the recession in the construction sector. Income and employment multipliers are much higher for capital than current spending. A major opportunity continues to be missed to borrow at negligible interest rates for capital projects, renewing the country's infrastructure and supplementing social housing.

The Treasury's hostility to public sector capital investment is long-standing – it led to PFI and other expensive alternatives – but it has been intensified by worries over the level of public debt to GDP. The ratio is high compared to pre-crisis levels, having doubled to around 80 per cent, though these are not historically abnormal levels and debt service costs are at a historic low. The USA has very similar levels of public debt and some countries (Japan, Italy, Portugal) have much higher levels. Attempts to force down the deficit debt ratio by curbing investment or otherwise sacrificing growth will be counterproductive, because they depress the denominator while trying to reduce the numerator. The IMF has wisely advised that the debt ratio come down by 'organic growth', not by curbing public investment. Even Kenneth Rogoff, whose analytical work on debt ratios was often cited as evidence of the dangers of public borrowing, now argues for more UK (and German) borrowing for investment. In the face of Treasury scepticism about capital investment there needs also to be an institutional innovation – a National Investment or Infrastructure Bank – modelled on the Green Investment Bank to prepare a pipeline of sound, feasible projects with the prospect of good returns.

The continued resistance of the Treasury is due to lingering fears that Britain is close to a 'cliff edge', losing its creditworthiness and leading to much higher borrowing costs. The 'cliff edge' theory had some plausibility back in 2010, but now borders on the absurd. Even after losing its AAA status, the UK continues to borrow at historically low rates (just over 2 per cent on ten-year bonds), less than the USA and, after inflation, close to zero. To underline the absurdity of the 'cliff edge' argument, Britain's bond yields happen to be higher than, for example, those of Italy, let alone Japan, which have far higher levels of government debt. What the government should be worrying about more is the ratio of household debt to GDP, which is predicted by the OBR to be approaching pre-crisis levels of 170 per cent by the end of the decade, when the public debt will have fallen to 60 per cent.

To date, deficit reduction has primarily centred on cuts in public spending rather than increased tax, and the Conservative government also has a clear objective to shrink the share of the state – though the 2015 post-election budget, sensibly if surprisingly, rebalanced future fiscal balancing towards tax. For parties to the left of the present government the challenge is that the British public appears to have a North American rather than a Scandinavian approach to tax, while retaining a European approach to most forms of public spending. There is little public appetite for substantial increases in taxes on income and, though I don't agree with the Chancellor's efforts to lead a global bidding war on corporation tax, it is unrealistic to aim for large increases in revenue from internationally mobile companies and individuals. Therefore, the tax base will have to centre on consumption, particularly where environmental costs are involved, and immovable property and land.

It should be one of the main tasks of opposition parties to redesign the archaic, inequitable and unpopular system of property taxation (council tax, inheritance tax and capital gains tax). One basic step would be to make council tax more closely proportional to the value of property. A more radical and far-reaching reform would be to give practical substance to long-mooted ideas for the taxation of land, not least to encourage more efficient use. The practical problems of valuation and making the transition from a land market massively distorted by planning have so far frightened away reformers. But such a reform is now long overdue.

On the spending side, politicians of all parties have sought to protect public spending on sectors of the population who can be relied upon to vote (the elderly rather than the young) or on valued areas like the NHS and schools, at the expense of, say, local authority services, social housing and science and innovation. I was, I believe, the only minister to oppose consistently the ring-fencing of departmental budgets. But the further deep cuts in spending agreed in the 2015 spending review will undoubtedly lead to a serious deterioration in important services, including some of economic importance. To change priorities in future means finding new ways of funding universal public services, limiting some non-means-tested benefits such as the winter fuel allowance, and being more creative about public sector delivery – good examples from the coalition being the growth of mutual health and social service providers and a reformed Post Office network.

Money

One of the biggest economic policy issues in the next few years will be the gradual disconnection of the life-support system of cheap money: a move to higher short-term interest rates and the ending and reversal of quantitative easing (QE), at least in recovering economies like the USA and the UK. The potential for major destabilizing shocks – large currency appreciations, distress in highly indebted households – is all too real and in some areas, notably the eurozone, the need for monetary stimulus may well grow rather than diminish.

The fact that monetary authorities are operationally independent makes this transition easier than if it were politicized. But there are several complications for the UK, as I discuss in chapter nine. The first is that asset bubbles are already building up and one of the major innovations of the post-crisis period, macroprudential policies, will need to be used actively (dampening housing markets in particular) if the move to more normal interest rates is slow. The second is that the inflation mandates set for the Bank of England look increasingly archaic and redolent of a bygone era. In practice, the Bank has been pursuing growth and anti-deflation objectives, and that should be formalized into a forward-looking nominal target.

The third complication is that crisis conditions could return, especially if the eurozone problems deteriorate and help to drag the UK back into recession and the risk of deflation. Unorthodox monetary policy was one of the big success stories of the post-crisis era. But QE and ultra-low interest rates have had undesirable side effects, and in any event appear to have diminishing effectiveness. The next step would be to finance public spending directly from central banks (or to cancel government liabilities on the central banks' balance sheets, which amounts to the same thing). Japan may well lead the way in the next few years. In the UK the idea has been unhelpfully politicized as 'people's quantitative easing'. But an economically responsible and depoliticized version has been described by Lord Turner, *inter alia*, for use in another emergency, perhaps by targeting priority areas such as infrastructure investment and small business lending.

Inequality

The use of unorthodox monetary policy has had the side effect of boosting asset prices and the wealth of individuals, thereby widening inequalities. As I discuss in chapter eleven, the evidence is not as clear-cut as some of the more ideologically charged arguments suggest, but there has undoubtedly been a drift towards growing inequality of income (in respect of the top 1 per cent, as opposed to the top 10 or 20 per cent) and wealth. Britain is at the upper end of the more unequal societies, at least in the developed world. Quite apart from any discomfort that these inequalities may bring, there is clear international evidence that inequality harms growth. While some inequality in income and capital gains may be the result of rewards for hard work, investment and productive risk-taking, much is also down to the luck of inheritance, fortuitous investments in property, malfunctioning markets in executive pay, and economically unproductive reward systems in financial institutions.

If parties of the left have anything useful to say on inequality, it should be on how to preserve the right kind of incentives while dealing with the gross abuses. The housing market and property tax are an obvious place to start and I return to this below. Second, I introduced reforms in executive pay, establishing shareholder responsibility more clearly through binding votes, but there is a strong case for going further to embed employees in the decision-making process.

A key area of policy is in relation to labour markets and the setting of wages and conditions. Britain has evolved a highly flexible labour market – in some ways too flexible, where there is serious insecurity and neglect of investment in the labour force – giving the lie to those who have demanded 'hire and fire' labour laws. But near-full employment has been achieved through low wages.

George Osborne's adoption of a mandatory living wage substantially higher than the minimum wage is a bold experiment. We cannot predict what difference it will make. But my instinct is that it is a clever political gesture that will do harm to jobs growth if parallel cuts in tax credits are enacted as originally planned, and would leave poor working families substantially worse off. The approach originally adopted by Gordon Brown, which I continued, of a more cautious, evidence-based approach to the minimum wage, supported by in-work tax credits (a form of negative income tax for those below the tax thresholds) is a better way of reconciling employment and returns to work. Osborne's approach will work only if British business responds by means of a surge in productivity, raising investment in machinery and skills training, rather than simply contracting employment opportunities.

The issues of inequality relate to a deeper sense of what kind of society we belong to. What is clear is that it is simply not sustainable for a country to function when the rewards are seen to accrue overwhelmingly to property owners and financiers in one corner of it.

Rebalancing and Productivity

A key objective of post-crisis economic policy was to achieve the 'right kind of recovery', to avoid the past over-reliance on financial services, especially banking, debt-based domestic consumption, and the stimulating effect of rising house prices. It aimed to address some of the long-standing impediments to export growth, business investment and innovation, where Britain has underperformed. The record, so far, is mixed. Export growth has been poor, despite a major effort to promote exports in emerging markets; manufacturing output has yet to achieve previous levels; and business investment has not fully recovered, either. There was progress during the coalition in addressing these issues, but the commitment has diminished after the change in government.

I urge, in chapter eleven, that the government maintain the broad consensus that has been built up around an industrial strategy (the vocabulary is unimportant; it is the concept of a long-term partnership between business and government, including local government, that is important). I sought to draw on the positive lessons of Conservative government, with Michael Heseltine, and of Labour, with Peter Mandelson and David Sainsbury, but rather more to extract some transferable experience from other countries, notably Germany. The industrial strategy was built around cooperative initiatives in key industries such as automotive, aerospace, life sciences, creative industries, professional services, construction and energy, and transport supply chains. These did not follow the usual manufacturing versus services dichotomy, but aimed to capture the importance of innovation and knowledge. Above all, modern industrial strategy needs to be located in the digital age with creative and IT industries at its core.

The industrial strategy requires business buy-in and, preferably, business leadership, in order to succeed. It is different from the top-down 'picking winners' approach of the 1970s. There are, however, some interventions that I believe are necessary. I was persuaded by the failed Pfizer bid for AstraZeneca that government must intervene in takeovers if the country's science base in R&D-intensive industries is put at risk. A further need is to address market failures in innovation by strengthening the new chain of Catapult centres and specific support for R&D, as in aerospace and automotive. It is reassuring that these programmes survived the 2015 spending review. Another priority is to rebuild the UK supply chain network, badly shot to pieces during the financial crisis and over the preceding decade.

A crucial area, and a growing problem, is training and skills. The coalition began to rebuild the apprenticeship framework and brand. I welcome in principle the proposed employers' levy, provided it is used as an incentive to companies to train rather than (as seems to be the case) as a covert business tax. When I left office there was a growing focus on higher-level skills, where the traditional British distinction between high-status academic universities and low-status non-academic training is a stumbling block that has to be removed.

An even deeper problem is the culture of short-termism in business, engendered by capital markets and the mechanisms for business financing. Following the Kay Review, which I initiated, there is a substantial programme of reform in train. Regulatory bodies like the Takeover Panel and the Competition and Markets Authority (CMA) now have an explicit long-term mandate, and company law has been clarified to underline the long-term duties of directors to their shareholders. But short-term behaviour is still endemic and it will require tax and regulatory measures to change it.

Housing and the Property Market

One of the biggest areas of policy failure under successive governments, including the coalition, has been housing. To a remarkable and quite unhealthy degree, the housing market, and in particular rising house prices, drives the UK economy. The financial crisis was incubated in the mortgage market. Banks are heavily biased towards property-based lending. Major personal and regional wealth inequalities have stemmed from house price expansion in the south-east of England. A significant generational gap is opening up between young renters and older owner-occupiers. While demand rises, supply has badly failed to rise to meet it, due to a complex mixture of issues around land use, planning, credit availability, industrial structure and unbalanced tenure.

I seek in chapter nine to disentangle some of the policy elements and I make it clear, as I did in government, that perhaps more than in any other area the Conservatives' instincts are seriously damaging here: fuelling demand through Help to Buy; undermining affordable housing provision by weakening social housing obligations on developers and imposing on housing associations Right to Buy duties and rent reductions; suppressing local authorities' capacity to borrow for housing development; tax measures, such as inheritance tax rewarding existing owners, and resistance to reform of property taxation; and piecemeal planning reforms which have, for example, generated some new housing but only at the expense of office accommodation for small businesses. I fundamentally disagreed with my Conservative Cabinet colleagues who took a relaxed view of housing inflation, believing that it helps to stimulate the wider economy. It no doubt also strengthened their political support among the 50 per cent of households who are owner-occupiers.

I don't pretend that there are simple silver-bullet solutions and I recognize from my years as an MP that anything that encroaches on the property values of existing homeowners will be politically difficult. But change is badly needed in several areas: planning reform to free up those elements of the so-called green belt outside cities that are of little public amenity (much better than encroaching on the limited green space enjoyed by city dwellers); a reform of capital, property and land taxation in ways that do not simply reward the acquisition and ownership of property but encourage new supply; giving priority in public spending to increasing affordable housing provision (a much better use of funds than subsidizing landlords via housing benefit); empowering local authorities and development agencies to assemble land for development through auctioning or, in some cases, compulsory purchase; using the industrial strategy to drive improved productivity and training practices; ensuring that small builders can get access to credit. Getting the balance of market forces and intervention right will be difficult, but essential. Otherwise, malfunctioning land and property markets will continue to deliver far fewer homes than rising demand requires and will drive widening inequalities between generations and between regions.

Immigration

One of the key demographic factors driving housing demand has been net immigration, and the immigration issue sits at the centre of other issues, too: the supply of skills, our membership of the EU, and the increasingly pervasive issue of identity. As will be clear from my discussion of globalization in chapter six and of long-term economic growth in chapter eleven, my instincts are essentially, but not uncritically, liberal. I buy the broad economic argument that immigration has, overall, been good for the economy, raising not just output but productivity. And I was publicly critical throughout the coalition of the Conservatives' net immigration target as impractical, when some key elements like UK emigration and immigration from the EU are outside of government control (which hasn't stopped them reintroducing the target). Controls have been damaging, by interrupting flows of the very people who make the biggest contribution to the UK – highly skilled workers from outside the EU, entrepreneurs and overseas students – and by sending a signal that Britain is 'closed for business'. It is also easily forgotten that those who for decades have warned about the impact of immigration on our 'overcrowded island' cheerfully ignore the fact that net immigration has been negative for most of the post-war period, until the recent surge of migration from continental Europe.

Yet there are genuine concerns about localized impacts. And there are few who would be brave enough to advocate unrestricted immigration from all sources. The supply is, in practical terms, infinite and there is, as we have recently seen around the Mediterranean, no shortage of people who regard the UK as a highly desirable place to live and work. It is entirely legitimate to want to ensure that borders are policed and laws enforced, and that entitlements to public services and benefits are linked to citizenship or some defined contribution. For that reason, it is right to want to negotiate the terms of admission within the EU on these grounds. I also believe that some attempt has to be made to link the costs and benefits of immigration more explicitly in the public mind: for example, by using visa revenue to fund localized programmes to ease pressure on services. The USA has a system of trade adjustment pay-outs designed to reassure a protectionist Congress that workers affected by imports can be helped to retrain. The scheme is, frankly, gimmicky and difficult to justify in rigorous economic terms – but politics also matters.

It is important to create an environment in which it is possible to liberalize some of the more damaging restrictions on visitors from overseas. The Tier 2 visa system is becoming seriously restrictive and affecting the willingness of companies to invest in the UK – it needs to be more flexible. Overseas students should be removed from the net immigration target – subject, of course, to visa rules being complied with. And there are some overseas students – high-quality engineering and science graduates from India and China, for example – whom we should be encouraging to stay on and work, and, in time, to acquire citizenship.

Immigration has been the main issue fuelling the politics of identity (rather than trade or foreign investment) and there is the capacity for dangerous polarization unless politicians can make the case for a broadly liberal but managed regime.

Europe

At the time of writing, the future of the eurozone is uncertain, with a Greek exit prevented by a new bail-out, at least for now, and the eurozone's economic weaknesses exposed but not repaired. The prolonged Greek crisis has highlighted the current weaknesses: the lack of a large, automatic transfer mechanism, as occurs in federal states, to help weaker members; the lack of an effective mechanism for ensuring that obligations are met, short of forced exit or expulsion; the lack of a common system of public financing (eurobonds) whereby risk is shared; the lack of an agreed approach to fiscal and monetary policy that is supportive of growth and adjustment in the weaker states. It is clear that there are some fundamental disagreements between those who emphasize solidarity with weaker and poorer members and those who emphasize common discipline. There is a risk of fracture and breakdown. The consequences of breakdown for the UK, let alone eurozone members, are potentially huge and largely negative.

Those critics and advocates of closer union are both right to say that the eurozone can only survive as a more tightly integrated group, increasingly approximating to a federal state. In that case, there will be the issue of what happens to those states, like Sweden, that favour membership of the eurozone, but not yet; and those, like the UK, that are firmly on the outside but could see many of the existing EU rules concerning the single market migrate to the inside. The almost universal assumption is that Britain will never join. That is indeed likely, but the word 'never' is dangerous. It is possible that, were the eurozone to succeed, and were the UK to revert to being a poorly performing economy trapped in boom and bust property cycles, we could again be faced with the question of joining.

The immediate issue of UK membership of the EU is now to be subject to a referendum. It is likely, though not certain, to be won, given the broad base of support for continued membership. The exercise is, however, also likely to be unsatisfactory, because only very modest reforms are likely to be achieved in the time period available, the future direction of the EU itself is highly uncertain, and many critics will remain unreconciled.

This is not the place to rehearse all the arguments that will be heard ad nauseam over the coming months, and which will be exaggerated on both sides and confusingly advanced by people on the same side of the argument but with quite different objectives. It is likely that the Conservative leadership will campaign on the basis that membership should continue, albeit with 'less

Europe', and some will vote 'no' on the basis that there isn't 'enough Europe', especially if the provisions of the Social Chapter are to be diluted.

A more plausible position is to recognize that in some areas there needs to be more liberalization of regulation and subsidiarity of function, but that in others there should be 'more Europe', especially if the single market is deepened to include e-commerce, professional services and energy; some degree of tax harmonization around a common company tax base; more cooperation on security and defence issues, including defence procurement, as the USA detaches itself from European and Mediterranean issues and shifts towards Asia; a stronger common position on climate change as part of global negotiations; and some degree of common industrial policy, as in aerospace and industries with a strong R&D component. A generation ago, phrases like 'variable geometry' were common currency, and that is where we should be heading again rather than towards rigid ideological positions.

Reforming Politics and the Structure of Government

I believe that the coalition government will in due course be regarded as a major success story, though it may need a few years of deepening alienation from a single-party administration with minority and regionally concentrated public support for that verdict to become widely accepted. The coalition was, however, a product of particular circumstances: the perceived need for parties to work together in the common interest at a time of economic emergency; the numbers thrown up in a Westminster election and the personalities involved. The electoral outcome in 2015 will deter minority parties like mine from ever again entering into such an arrangement unless it is part of a different political architecture. That architecture will have to have several components.

The first is voting reform. The contrasting experience of minority parties in the 2015 election has highlighted the absurd and arbitrary way that first-past-the-post operates: the virtual clean sweep of the SNP in Scotland giving it fifty-six MPs from 5 per cent of the UK vote, contrasted with derisory representation for the Greens, UKIP and Lib Dems, which collectively achieved ten MPs with 25 per cent of the UK vote. I would be surprised if the case for reform does not now escalate from being the hobby-horse of the Lib Dems and a few anoraks to a widespread movement. Germany and, within the UK, the Scottish Parliament have shown how more representative but equally effective systems can work. Meanwhile, the current revival of interest in local government underlines the case for more representative councils – again, the Scottish model works well – rather than one-party states.

Second, the Scottish independence issue will not go away and will in all likelihood become seriously inflamed as specific issues (a revived oil price? benefit reform? the EU referendum?) provide a *casus belli*. It would be better to grasp now the necessity for a genuinely federal arrangement with Scotland whereby revenue-raising as well as spending are fully devolved, and federal arrangements are preserved through common services and a financial transfer mechanism more balanced and less one-sided than the so-called Barnett formula.

Third, federation should be part of a more radical move towards devolution within the UK and specifically to English local government, which means genuine freedom to raise revenue and greater freedom to raise capital in markets. I was part of earlier halting steps to create 'city' or 'local' deals, and the Chancellor rightly wants to go much further. I would like to think that one of the legacies of the coalition government is the beginning of a fundamental reshaping of democratic institutions that have ossified with age.

Global Reach

I deliberately framed this book within a global economic context. Our politics is so parochial that it is often overlooked that the UK is a small and diminishing part of the world economy: 2 per cent of GDP; under 1 per cent of population. To the extent that wider economic linkages are considered, these relate primarily to the European Union and the problems of the eurozone. These are, of course, very important, but I suspect that not many individuals or businesses have yet taken on board that China is becoming, or may even have become, the world's biggest economy, with India the third. These, along with other emerging economies, are not merely markets of growing importance, but heavily influence the world price of food and raw materials, cross-border flows of investment, and global environmental pressures. It is partly because the main Western economies and Japan are of diminished relative importance that the global crisis had far less impact than the inter-war crash. China and India, for example, were barely affected.

There are several practical implications for the UK. The first is that the focus of trade and inward investment promotion has to shift towards these countries. The coalition government did important work in that area, though we are still making up for many years of neglect. A second is that as a member of the G7 and a key member of organizations like the Bank for International Settlements, the IMF, the OECD and the UN Security Council – and at one remove, via the EU, the WTO – the UK has an important role in shaping new international economic arrangements. The rather fragile structure of governance has so far survived big changes in the centre of gravity of the world economy and the threats of economic nationalism and protectionism that destroyed the pre-1914 global system. The creation of the G20 is a formal recognition of these shifts. More importantly, China in particular shows every sign of wanting to be a constructive global economic player, provided it is given appropriate recognition – as do Brazil, India, Mexico, Korea and Indonesia, to varying degrees.

Third, as one of the few major members of the European Union to have a genuinely global rather than a continental perspective, the UK should be in a position to give leadership on some of the tricky international economic issues that are emerging: the apparent glut of savings at a global level and the drift into 'secular stagnation' (though that would also require some rethinking of the current, very conservative UK approach to public investment); the inability of the WTO to make serious progress, leading to a potentially fragmented system of regionalism; the potential threats to the global financial system from partially reformed banks and shadow banks; and, building on the cooperative approach outlined at the Paris Conference in 2015, the climate change issue. Being able to play such a role will, however, depend on sustained recovery in an economy that is better balanced and on our ability to transcend the politics of identity which is putting at risk the unity of the UK and our membership of the EU.

Conclusion

The storm of 2008 has long since passed, though we are still dealing with its destructive legacy: damaged banks, large government deficits and debt, and highly abnormal monetary policy. There are also some ominous clouds on the horizon: the continued unresolved tensions in the eurozone; evidence of 'secular stagnation' setting in; a slowdown in hitherto booming emerging economies, especially China.

In the UK the coalition presided over a strong recovery and the new Conservative government has got off to a confident start. It is, however, all too easy to see how this could unravel. A switch from 'cheap money' will coincide with some aggressive and ideologically driven fiscal tightening, slowing the economy. There are some deep structural weaknesses that will take many years of consistent policy to deal with: poor productivity performance; large trade deficits; low business investment; lagging innovation and regional imbalances. Housing is a disaster area which the new government is making worse. The banking sector is being let off the leash prematurely. Big inequalities, including that between generations, are becoming acute. There is worrying uncertainty over Britain's future in Europe and over the unity of the United Kingdom itself.

Crisis conditions could return sooner rather than later. For that reason, there is a crying need for alternatives to the present policies that are more positive than fatalistic resignation or nihilistic protest. It is time for those who subscribe to the progressive tradition of politics to snap out of the current mood of defeatism and division and cooperate to produce a forward-looking programme for government.

Part One
The Global Context

1

After the Storm

I wrote *The Storm* during the summer and autumn of 2008, during the most severe financial and economic crisis of my lifetime. In the UK we saw the failure and semi-nationalization of RBS, Lloyds-HBOS and several smaller mortgage-lenders, followed by a severe contraction in production and living standards. There was, of course, a much wider global crisis, which was short-lived in the main emerging economies but has left deep wounds in most developed economies.

I return to the subject five years later, in a climate of guarded optimism, after five years in government as a decision-maker, when an economic recovery is in train – at least in the UK and the USA – and banks appear more stable. Cynics could say 'Storm? What Storm?' Consensus estimates for the world economy are of 2.6 per cent growth in 2015, followed by gradual recovery in 2016 to 2.8 per cent. The countries that were at the epicentre of the banking crisis, the USA and the UK, were each estimated to record 2.5 per cent growth and are 'reasonably robust'. By any standards other than those of the pre-crash boom, these are good figures which promise increased living standards.

But there are serious economic problems in the eurozone and Japan (respectively 0.66 and 1.56 growth in 2015, increasing slightly in 2016), and in important emerging economies, led by China (slowing to 0.5 per cent growth), with sharp falls in GDP in Russia, Brazil and Nigeria. Even the successful Anglo-Saxon countries have yet to see much recovery in living standards, which fell sharply in the post-crash recession and have hardly recovered since. It is also clear that major issues remain unaddressed, and some of the mistakes that led to the financial crisis are being repeated. Pessimists talk about a recurring cycle of credit boom and bust. Others predict 'secular stagnation' – a period of much slower growth, of economies running well below their potential. Some even predict both, as governments frustrated by economic stagnation, or worse, react by fuelling new credit booms.

The original climatic metaphor was, in some respects, misleading. Storms blow over. Damage is cleared up. Normality returns. Would it were that simple. Another metaphor would have been a heart attack which proved not to be terminal thanks to the prompt intervention of central bankers and governments, but which has done long-term damage to government budgets and to business lending, and which requires continuing life-support. This rather better conveys the sense of continuing damage and fragility. But 'the storm' conveys something else: disaster returning. Without stronger defences, the next storm could be as damaging as the last, or even worse.

In *The Storm* I sought to explain the crisis in terms of comparative experience. The major banking disasters in UK history – as opposed to the severe recessions of the 1920s and 1930s – occurred in the early nineteenth century and, before that, during the South Sea Bubble. There are uncomfortable parallels, despite the vast increase in scale and sophistication since those days. There is more contemporary insight to be gained from recent banking crises: in Scandinavia and Japan in the early 1990s, the latter leading to prolonged stagnation and the threat of deflation; and the Asian financial crisis of 1998/9. But all of these were localized and, except in Japan, involved temporary, albeit severe, impacts. The common thread is one of boom and bust credit cycles.

———

A historical approach helps to identify the best conceptual framework for explaining the crisis and its aftermath of chronic instability. As I argued in *The Storm*, understanding is to be found in the neglected work of Minsky and economic historians like Charles P. Kindleberger, who described cycles of speculative excess, 'bubbles', made possible by an accumulation of debt-leverage, offset by inflated and largely fictional asset values. In due course, the bubble bursts, causing panic, debt default, distress and economic contraction as individuals, companies or banks try to reduce their exposure by deleveraging. The economic consequences of such contraction in the wake of a financial sector collapse were described two centuries ago by J. S. Mill, but were formalized much later by Irving Fisher as 'debt deflation', or by Knut Wicksell in his theories of credit cycles. Richard Koo has described the contemporary variant as 'balance sheet recession' – based on a wider application of contemporary Japanese experience. The burden of debt – personal, government, corporate – makes for a reluctance to spend and invest, and a resultant downward spiral of recession or deflation. The cycle is completed when, in order to offset recession, monetary authorities run expansionary, low interest rate policies, which in turn create and feed the next asset bubble. There is plenty of evidence of that cycle at work today. The Bank for International Settlements, in its 2015 annual report, warns that there is a real danger of 'entrenching instability' and 'chronic weakness' in a world of abnormally low interest rates.

The problem, of course, with the big global picture is that it obscures the many particularities. The concept of 'debt deflation' or 'balance sheet recession' describes accurately and meaningfully today's policy problems in Japan and (much of) the eurozone. It is potentially, but not yet actually, an issue in the big Anglo-Saxon economies – were the recovery in the USA and UK to falter and were the current experience of zero inflation caused by falling commodity prices to become a sustained general decline in the overall price level. And it is a risk, though not current reality, in China, where high levels of corporate debt and price deflation currently coexist with rapid, albeit declining, growth.

The various economic philosophies that have been developed, or revived, in response to the crisis reflect these particular circumstances. For many commentators and policy-makers, the main reference point is still the inter-war depression and the ideas of Keynes and Milton Friedman developed in response to events in the USA and the UK. Keynes is frequently invoked as offering an alternative economic model to austerity, meaning falling living standards and job insecurity. To be sure, there are key elements of Keynesian economics that are relevant to conditions of weak demand and high unemployment, as have been experienced in the recent past. There are also surpluses of planned savings over investment on a global scale. The Keynesian approach points legitimately to limitations in aggressive monetary policy of the kind used today to support demand, and to the need for a better mix of monetary and fiscal policy. But monetary policy, building on the insights of Friedman and others from the 1930s, has been successful, at least in the short run, in staving off disaster in the USA, the UK, Japan and, more tentatively, the eurozone. And the Keynesian model was not developed in response to a banking collapse, with its impact on government finances and the accumulation of debt – so it is of some, but only limited, use in resolving our current problems. Moreover, the Keynesian and monetarist approaches are complementary and have the same preoccupation with weak demand.

In terms of fundamentally different approaches, the real alternative is the so-called Austrian school, which regards expansionary fiscal or monetary policies as pointless or dangerous, and relies instead on aggressive structural reforms and market forces – liquidating weak firms and banks – to make business investment more profitable. That is not to say that structural reform is exclusive to this branch of economic thinking. A belief in trade liberalization, or creating a favourable environment for private investment, or radical bank restructuring, can be seen as a third pillar of post-crisis policy, alongside expansionary monetary and fiscal policy. Indeed, the concept of 'balance sheet recession' or 'debt deflation' invites a combination of stimulating overall demand and measures to restructure or write down debt. In its more radical forms, the Austrian approach, derived from Hayek, Schumpeter and others, converges with a Marxist view of economic history: that modern capitalism faces a deep structural crisis which requires a purging of bad investment and debt – albeit through an entrepreneurial, not a workers', revolution.

One of the biggest casualties of the storm has been the theoretical underpinning of modern financial capitalism. The collapse of communism as an alternative model of economic organization led to a period of hubristic self-congratulation, even arrogance: an unwillingness to question the assumptions underlying the Western financial system. These included the belief that financial as well as other markets were essentially rational and self-stabilizing, together with a poor understanding, even on the part of their users, of the complex products being created. Standard economic models, still widely taught and widely used by policy-makers, have at their heart concepts of macroeconomic equilibrium and rational behaviour that have been denied in the real world. Not just free-market ideologues, but many social democratic advocates of a regulated and mixed economy, in the USA and the UK especially, accepted this comforting set of assumptions. In the event, they were wrong.

Those countries whose financial systems were insulated from world financial markets, and tightly regulated, as in China and India, escaped quite lightly. That, however, might simply reflect a stage of development rather than the discovery of a superior, state-capitalist, model. One of the questions posed by the storm is how to ensure that the benefits of liberalized financial markets in allocating resources in an efficient way can be reconciled with systemic stability. In other words, how much financial regulation is needed, and of what kind, globally and nationally? The question remains open. There have been some significant moves to regulate and reform banks, reviewed in chapter two, but these have been essentially national and only loosely coordinated. Large areas of financial activity, such as shadow banking, remain largely untouched by regulation: ticking bombs yet to be defused or, possibly, detonated.

———

There has obviously been much local colour and variety of experience within the global financial crisis. But there are several broad features that have defined this particular crisis.

The first is the importance of asset bubbles, based in particular on inflated property markets in Japan, the USA and the UK (and Ireland and Spain in the eurozone). The institutions that were in the eye of the storm were mortgage-lenders, like Britain's Northern Rock and the Fannie Mae and Freddie Mac in the USA. The toxic products that contaminated financial intermediaries were securitized loans, mainly built up by combining residential mortgages into new products. In the USA, Spain and Ireland, but not the UK, property price bubbles have fully, and painfully, burst, returning property values to pre-boom levels. In the UK, however, there has been fresh house price inflation, especially in London and the south-east, superimposed on an already inflated market. I will argue later that housing inflation in the UK is not merely an issue for financial stability but is also creating great social tensions and inequalities. Serious property-based asset bubbles are now also emerging in Asia, including China. One of the legacies of the crisis is a better understanding of 'macro-prudential' policies to govern the lending policies of banks and other institutions, so as to manage asset bubbles independently of wider inflation. Arguably, these will represent a key new pillar of economic policy. But these mechanisms have yet to be tested in earnest, and they may be dealing with the symptoms of a deeper problem of monetary management in which asset markets are disregarded.

Second, debt, or 'leverage', matters – be it private or public, personal or corporate, or in financial institutions. What has made this crisis so extensive and destructive is the sheer scale of the leverage achieved on the underlying assets, through financial innovation: the development of securitization markets and the proliferation of complex, exotic, financial instruments. Investment banks – stand-alone institutions like Lehman Brothers or Bear Stearns, or embedded within universal banks like RBS, Barclays and Credit Suisse, or within the banking arms of insurers, as with AIG – were stuffed full of such derivatives. They were rendered illiquid when confidence was lost and they became insolvent when large-scale asset impairment was exposed.

Much has been done to repair financial sector balance sheets, to identify and write down dodgy assets, and to write off bad loans – in part by transferring obligations to governments and also by offloading debts into shadow banking. But there is more involved than the balance sheets of financial institutions. The overhang of personal and public debt also remains very substantial and is growing. The Bank for International Settlements has shown that public and private debt (excluding financial institutions) as a share of global GDP rose from 160 per cent in 2001, to around 200 per cent at the onset of the crisis, to 215 per cent in 2013. In developed economies taken as a whole, debt levels were roughly double those of emerging markets before the crisis, and have continued to grow, with China catching up. Figure 1.1 shows that continuing increase on top of historically high levels.

The UK had one of the highest levels of debt to GDP before the crisis, at 240 per cent. Although household indebtedness did decline for a while, it is rising again and the overall debt figure remains high, at 275 per cent. The government obsession with public debt, now falling to a predicted 60 per cent of GDP by 2020, while household debt rises towards new heights of 170 per cent, according to the OBR, is particularly perverse. These figures do not reflect offsetting assets, such as appreciating house prices, but these are volatile and reversible, unlike the debt. A debt overhang, either business or household, has a dampening effect on spending and investment: what is called 'debt deflation'. If debt is owed to foreign investors, it opens up the prospect of a crisis of sovereign risk, as has happened in Southern Europe (or Latin America in the 1980s), or, if it remains with the banks (or shadow banks), of a fresh banking crisis. And as we move towards a more normal interest rate environment, debtors, both personal and commercial, dependent on low interest rates will struggle to remain solvent. Nor is there any easy escape. The classic remedies for debt overhangs – rapid inflation to wipe out the value of debt, or default and debt relief – are not available, at least at present. A continued period of very low inflation, or deflation, with low economic growth, will see an increased real burden of repaying debt.

A further feature of this particular crisis is that, more than with any other in history, it has involved globally integrated financial markets. Multinational companies have developed an appetite for sophisticated financial products supplied by their banks, which have in turn expanded to operate globally. A combination of technology, financial innovation and deregulation has made cross-border flows easier. Financial securities of growing complexity and variety have been traded in growing volumes in big financial centres like London, and markets have deepened, with risk quantified by credit agencies.

Since the crisis there has been some retreat by banks into national jurisdictions, and tighter regulation has been somewhat piecemeal and uncoordinated. Nonetheless, the fabric of financial market integration remains largely intact. What also remains is the way global financial markets continue to act as intermediaries, managing liquidity, as between countries that generate a surplus of savings (like Germany, China and OPEC Gulf States) and those that absorb the surpluses (like the UK and the USA). What isn't yet clear is whether the fundamental weaknesses of international governance – lack of policy coordination, with global institutions like the UN, World Trade Organization (WTO) and the International Monetary Fund (IMF)/World Bank being highly circumscribed – are storing up bigger problems for the future. One of the attempts to involve global institutions in a localized problem is the role played by the IMF, alongside European institutions, in the Greek problem. That stemmed from the recognition that a specific euro-zone problem might well have global implications. The apparent failure of the interventions, and Greece's default on IMF loans, has undoubtedly weakened the IMF's authority though the US has now agreed to more capital.

Finally, we have seen that the issues of global financial markets, macroeconomic management and the debt 'overhang' are inter-connected. Larry Summers, who developed the concept of 'secular stagnation', argues that there is a structural and global, not just a temporary and local, shortage of planned investment relative to savings. This is for a variety of reasons: businesses, collectively, may anticipate a period of slower growth – much slower in China, for example; governments, collectively worried about their own creditworthiness, may be reluctant to borrow to invest; pessimism may boost savings everywhere, as people anticipate harder times and falling prices. The savings surpluses generated in Germany in particular can no longer be easily absorbed, particularly as conditions in the eurozone do not allow for a revival of public or private investment. Interest rates, real and nominal, remain depressed, which feeds speculative credit bubbles, as with property. The Summers view is hotly disputed and it may prove to be wrong, but it is all too plausible. The evidence to support the idea that there is a glut of savings comes from negative yields on long-term government bonds – the fact that savers will pay, rather than be paid, for holding the debt of the French government, for example.

———

Although the storm was global in reach, and in causation, the impacts have been felt very unevenly. The emerging economies, led by China, Russia, India and Brazil, were hit initially by the sudden contraction in world trade, as trade credit dried up, but the damage was not remotely on the scale of the Asian financial crisis of a decade earlier, and quickly gave way to growth as rapid as before 2008. Since the main developed economies were going backwards in this post-crisis period, the global economic centre of gravity has shifted even more strongly to the emerging economies, especially in Asia. In the two decades before the crisis, developed economies grew by 2 per cent per annum, and emerging economies, taken as a whole, by 6 per cent. The differential initially widened in the wake of the crisis. On a purchasing power parity basis, emerging economies now account for half the world economy, and China, on recently adjusted data, is close to being the world's largest economy. India is perhaps the third. One consequence is that emerging markets provide well over half of incremental demand, which throughout the crisis continued to provide strength to commodity markets, especially oil (until a price slump in late 2014). Figures 1.2 and 1.3 illustrate the way in which emerging markets have increasingly driven global growth, and also the way in which, taking a long view, China and to a lesser degree India are resuming the economic dominance they enjoyed two centuries ago.

But that pattern is not guaranteed for the future. Russia and Brazil have seen negative growth. China is crucial now. When China sneezes, the world catches a cold. The phenomenal growth of the past – about 10 per cent per annum – cannot be sustained. China is clearly struggling to adjust to an economic structure less dependent on exports and investment, and more on domestic consumption, for growth – and for growth that is more environmentally sustainable. But the issues that emerging markets in general face – particularly adjusting to the high expectations of a growing population moving out of poverty, or switching from growth dependent on surplus labour to higher productivity – have relatively little to do with the lingering malaise affecting the main Western economies. Even a lower level of growth – say, 6 or 7 per cent per annum in China and India – is still much faster than in the developed world, and the rapid shift in the centre of gravity of the world economy might reasonably be expected to continue. I review in chapter five some of the conflicting views on the prospects of this very disparate group of countries. However, I broadly accept the argument that the scope for technological catch-up and the fierce ambition of hundreds of millions of people to escape poverty are sufficient to sustain this process for another generation.

Japan, by contrast, is still living with the after-effects of a banking crisis over two decades ago. Throughout this time there has been negligible growth, and the major preoccupation of macroeconomic policy has been to stop the country sliding into a downward spiral of deflation. Japan is often cited in the West as a horror story to avoid: a cautionary tale for governments that fail to manage balance-sheet deleveraging by quickly refinancing, and cleaning up, damaged banks. But the Japanese experience might also come to be seen quite differently, as a relative success story, demonstrating how to avert depression through an active monetary policy – very low interest rates and quantitative easing (QE) – and an expansionary fiscal policy, which has taken public sector debt to levels otherwise encountered only in Greece. (In Japan, however, the government debt is held by patriotic Japanese citizens and is therefore more stable.) It may be, however, that longer-term forces, like the demographic challenge of an ageing population, will overwhelm the expansionary efforts of policy-makers. The current Japanese prime minister, Shinzō Abe, is seeking to ratchet up expansionary policies even further with an ambitious new round of QE, but his government is still struggling to sustain a weak recovery (as discussed further in chapter three).

The two countries that were at the heart of the storm – the USA and the UK – best conform to the archetype of the highly leveraged asset bubble bursting, leading to financial collapse and recession. Both had prolonged periods in which domestic savings were insufficient to finance domestic investment, sucking in large volumes of cheap capital from overseas, fuelling asset inflation as this money expanded the base of the banking system, enabling a big growth in mortgage-lending. Both had highly developed, sophisticated, innovative, internationally integrated banking sectors, which saw extreme leverage and the large-scale use of complex derivatives based on questionable underlying (mortgage) assets. Both reacted to the crisis in much the same way, with aggressive, creative monetary policy designed to keep short-term interest rates as low as possible (negative in real terms) and to boost the supply of money through the banking system via QE (whereby the central bank bought up assets, pushing liquidity, or lending capacity, into the system). Both also, initially, used modest fiscal stimulus, which has since been reversed. Both intervened to save banks from collapse, and in some cases nationalized them in order to make them secure.

Seen in a broad historical context, their response to the financial crisis has been a success, particularly in the USA, where GDP fell by less than 5 per cent and had recovered to pre-crisis output levels three to four years after the crisis hit. By contrast, after the crash of 1929, GDP fell 30 per cent and took ten years to recover previous levels. With continued growth, US unemployment has now dropped back to under 6 per cent, less than a third of the level during the Great Depression. With seemingly solid growth of over 2 per cent per annum, lower inflation and modest fiscal and current account deficits, the USA appears to be a model of health. It also has, relative to countries like Japan, a youthful and expanding population – thanks in large part to (legal or illegal) immigrants – and a highly innovative economy. But it is in the USA that concerns over 'secular stagnation' – essentially a pessimism over future productivity growth – are being most forcefully expressed. I review this argument in chapter three, contrasting the US experience with Japan, where growth pessimism is far more deeply rooted.

The UK story in many ways follows that of the USA, though recovery has been slower. The country is now experiencing recovery, low unemployment (under 6 per cent) and low inflation (close to zero) all at the same time. But there is still a damaging legacy from the crisis in the form of structural budget deficits, banks still reluctant to lend to small businesses, and an overdependence on property inflation as a source of demand.

Analysis of the crisis period as a whole suggests that by the end of 2015 the UK's potential output was still over 10 per cent below the level expected on the pre-crisis trend. A recent study by Laurence Ball of Johns Hopkins of 23 high income counties suggests

AFTER THE STORM 59

that in aggregate the loss was 8.4 per cent. The UK suffered more damage than Italy and less only than Spain, Ireland, Hungary and Greece (the figure for the last three being around 30 per cent less). Probably the most important factor in inflicting damage was the sheer scale of the banking sector, with bank assets close to 500 per cent of GDP, as against just over 100 per cent in the USA. Consequently, the rapid deleveraging of the banks, resulting in a severe contraction of credit, has had exceptionally severe impacts. A further factor could be that price adjustment in the US housing market has been large and severe, and painful for those caught with negative equity, but appears to have been largely complete, whereas in the UK house prices are way in excess of what would be expected at this stage of the economic cycle and relative to fundamentals such as affordability.

There has been an economic and political debate as to whether the UK recovery has been unnecessarily retarded by fiscal consolidation, whether austerity has been 'too much, too fast'. In fact (as opposed to the rhetoric, and as opposed to the intention of policy), structural fiscal consolidation in the UK was less than in any other major economy, and significantly less than in the USA – around 1.5 per cent of GDP in 2012 and 2013, as opposed to 3 per cent in the USA. I was, of course, involved in government in arguments about the speed of consolidation and have publicly and privately defended the pragmatic approach adopted. I shall pursue these issues in more detail in chapters seven and eight.

One of the paradoxical consequences of the crisis is that the epicentre of the storm has moved away from the USA and the UK to the eurozone, which was only glancingly affected by the original banking crash, had not experienced a housing bubble (except in a few countries, notably Spain and Ireland), and, taken as a whole, was not a net importer of capital from the rest of the world. Indeed, when the crash occurred it was widely regarded in the eurozone, particularly in France, as an Anglo-Saxon problem. Continental economies were assumed to be significantly insulated, albeit with some damage to individual banks in Germany,

France and Belgium necessitating rescue operations and a short, sharp period of recession in 2009.

This complacency was rudely shattered when, in early 2010, there was a collapse of confidence in Greek government securities, leading to greatly increased bond yields (long-term interest rates) on Greek government debt, and significant, albeit lesser, deterioration in the position of Portugal, Spain and Italy. In the subsequent six years there has been a severe crisis, centring initially on doubts about Greece's ability to maintain its position in the eurozone, and contagion affecting other weak eurozone economies, most importantly Spain and most critically Cyprus. The future of the eurozone was brought into question and is still far from secure. In essence, the banking crisis may have had little directly to do with the eurozone, but it led to a flight from risk in general. Markets increasingly saw the eurozone as fragile and poorly constructed to deal with major adjustments among its member states. And the mechanisms used in the USA and the UK to combat recession and the threat of deflation – notably, the aggressive use of monetary policy – have proved very difficult to operate in the eurozone, where there is no consensus over the need for such policies. The German authorities, in particular, are sceptical.

There is a severe lack of demand in the eurozone, with a large excess of savings, especially in Germany, yet little acknowledgement that this is the problem. Slow growth is becoming entrenched, leading to the spectre of prolonged depression, especially in southern Europe, with very low inflation and low growth together preventing progress in reducing the overhang of debt. In *The Storm* these problems had barely become apparent, but I shall deal with them in more detail in chapter four – because the eurozone has the capacity to cause immense damage, way beyond the eurozone itself since, treated as a whole, it is the world's biggest single economy. And while the UK is not a member of the eurozone, there are powerful linkages to the UK. The latter's perceived success or failure will also be crucial to British perceptions of the European project in the coming referendum.

Seven years on from the beginning of the storm, the provisional conclusion has to be that the world's biggest economic disaster of the post-war era was managed remarkably well. Half the world economy, and around 90 per cent of the world's population, was barely touched by it. Successful, aggressive use of monetary policy minimized the damage in the USA, which has not suffered a repeat of the 1930s, and, to a lesser extent, in the UK. There has been a resurgence of the 'politics of identity' and of nationalism, mainly directed at immigrant minorities, but the threat of a return to economic nationalism and trade protectionism, as occurred between the wars, has not happened on any scale. There is, nonetheless, certainly a backlash against liberalizing initiatives like the proposed transatlantic and trans-Pacific trade and investment deals and the multilateral talks of the WTO. Moreover, there remain very serious economic problems in the eurozone and Japan, though the more apocalyptic forecasts for the eurozone have not materialized.

But is all this too complacent? Has the threat of a global slump really been seen off? At first sight, yes. A powerful case has been made, by Gerard Lyons and others, that the transformational potential of the wave of innovation set off by computing and information and communications technology is very large, especially allied to the catch-up potential of emerging economies. And certainly, in the USA, there is now sufficient confidence in recovery to see the beginning of a return to 'normal' monetary policy and higher interest rates. But policy-makers also agonize over the risk of premature tightening, as against the risk of delayed tightening and asset bubbles. And deflation is a serious continuing risk in Japan and the eurozone. Highly indebted households in the USA and the UK now face the threat of rising interest rates. China has experienced extraordinary growth for three decades, defying repeated predictions of disaster, but it is now experiencing a significant slowdown, and deflationary forces are being transmitted to commodities and the countries that rely on them. This mixture of cyclical and structural factors has fed the narrative of 'secular stagnation'.

So, is the global system any better placed than it was five years ago to manage structural imbalances between the major economies? The fundamental imbalances between Germany and the peripheral eurozone, resulting from both savings surpluses and higher levels of productivity and cost competitiveness in Germany, remain as a threat to the stability of the eurozone. There has been, on the other hand, exchange rate adjustment as between China and the USA, greatly reducing current account imbalances, and trade conflict has been defused somewhat. But there is no sense that big decisions – like further moves to raise interest rates in the USA – will be decided on any other than national criteria. It would be quixotic to imagine that there is a shared sense of global economic management. And even more challenging issues of global governance, like collective management of climate change, are so far only at the declaratory stage.

And has the financial system been stabilized to the point where 2008 cannot recur? Banks in the main market economies are now better capitalized and subject to stronger regulation. Serious, if uncoordinated attempts have been made to reduce the too-big-to-fail problem. But Gordon Brown is not the only observer to have argued that 'we are stumbling towards the next crash' with shadow banking – investment by lightly supervised, non-bank financial institutions – being a potential trigger point. Others worry about the financial health of Chinese banks and the dire consequences of a serious failure. Another source of anxiety is the 'repo' market, which involves US$1.6 trillion of trade per day in short-term loans. The extreme volatility seen in October 2014 is a signal of potential illiquidity in money markets in the face of a new shock. In short, the case can plausibly be made that a period of financial crisis lies ahead of us, as well as behind us. I turn to that issue in more detail now.

2

Banking: Regulate, Retreat and Regroup

It is now seven years since the storm: the banking crisis that shook the British economy to its foundations, the nationalization of leading banks and the subsequent serious recession. One of my more important tasks as a UK economic minister was dealing with the aftermath of the banking collapse: creating new vehicles for lending to small and medium-sized enterprises (SMEs) and promoting structural reform and more competition within the banking sector. At the beginning of the coalition I pressed for the maximum degree of involvement in bank reform and regulation and, as a result, secured a joint role in relation to the Vickers Commission, of which more below. Moreover, there was a broad acceptance across the coalition that the government must intervene to promote lending to small business, which had collapsed in the wake of the banking crisis. Gradually, differences emerged over the degree of radicalism that should be employed, and in particular the Treasury's unwillingness to lean heavily on RBS or to set net lending targets for the banks. These domestic issues I pursue in more detail in chapter ten.

The crisis was, however, a global one and affected over forty countries, including most major developed economies. And it followed an era in which banks had expanded their balance sheets, relative to the economies in which they operated, on a scale that was historically unprecedented. Since then, we have seen played out a radical process of deleveraging – downscaling operations and reducing lending – and government interventions designed to reduce systemic risk and to change the behaviour of banks and other financial institutions.

What is very striking is that two very different – indeed, opposite – interpretations can now be plausibly applied to the banking sector. One is that, like Gulliver, it is now tied down by innumerable complex national, EU and global regulations, stifling innovation and growth, and is a much diminished industry operating largely domestically rather than through cross-border transactions. This is the view most likely to be heard from the industry.

An alternative view, more persuasive to the Lilliputians, is that not much has changed and that the next financial crash is being incubated a few years down the track, albeit in a different form or with different players. The argument has several elements. Systematically dangerous behaviour remains, but has migrated to shadow banks – financial institutions (hedge funds, for example) that can act like banks but are less closely supervised – and to new countries, notably China. In their attempts to reduce risk, banks have offloaded products like corporate bonds, which are now held by asset managers that may become illiquid in a new panic. The 'bonus culture' in the main investment banking centres like London, which led to reckless trading in pursuit of short-term rewards, is only temporarily submerged and is resurfacing. The too-big-to-fail, universal Western banks remain intact, albeit under greater regulation, and are more dominant, rather than less. Worrying levels of mortgage-lending, linked to high multiples of borrowers' income, are restarting in the UK and are rampant elsewhere, particularly in Asia. Much bad debt remains unaddressed. There is a large and growing connection between bank and sovereign debt. The patchwork of inconsistent and uncoordinated regulation is an open invitation to regulatory arbitrage and manipulation of rules by banks. If some of these things are as worrying as they appear, the Lilliputians have bought time but they still live in a dangerous place.

A key question, moving forward, is how governments perceive

the balance of risks around their financial sectors, particularly international banking. This question is especially an issue for major countries like the UK, with a large banking sector relative to the economy.

———

I was often accused, before and after the crash, of 'banker-bashing'. But criticism of the conduct of the banking sector has become commonplace, and whenever it appeared that there was an end to the reputational damage a new scandal would emerge. In mid-2012, in the wake of news of the Libor scandal, involving price-fixing between the banks, *The Economist* ran the headline 'Banksters', which captured the mood of the time. The cross-party Parliamentary Commission on Banking Standards, chaired by Andrew Tyrie and including Archbishop Welby as well as other parliamentarians, chronicles the technical and moral failings of the sector with admirable clarity. The issue that caused the greatest difficulty in government was the annual bonus round and the apparent inability of leading bankers to understand that, at a time when many people were suffering hardship, there was a problem with the millions of pounds of bonuses being paid to individuals whose activities were ultimately underwritten by the taxpayer. Senior Conservatives were deeply embarrassed by the greed and insensitivity of people they probably knew socially and politically. I recall meetings with the Chancellor and the prime minister to resolve how to deal with RBS, which the government owned. Decisions to prevail on the CEO to rein in investment bank bonuses and to show restraint in his own personal demands were among the factors that he regarded as 'interference' and which led to his eventual ousting.

Criticism, and sometimes hatred, of moneylenders has, of course, an ancient history going back to Jesus and probably long before. At times of economic distress, anti-banker hostility resurfaces – especially, and visibly, when the problems originate in debt, much of it bank debt. Such crude stereotyping is foolish and unjustified. Some banks and many individual bankers behaved impeccably during the banking crisis. Generalized hostility is just as misplaced as is the exaggerated respect and deference given to the top bankers and 'masters of the universe' in the run-up to the crisis. We need a balanced assessment. An eloquent statement of the case against banker-bashing was recently set out by Mark Carney, Governor of the Bank of England, when he argued that 'a vibrant financial sector brings substantial benefits' and is 'both a global and national asset'. He also stated that some would 'react to this project with horror' if bank assets as a share of GDP more than doubled in coming decades, but would be less horrified if banks were made safe and no longer dependent on taxpayer bail-outs.

Critics, including me, are sceptical about whether large banking sectors can be made truly safe. But even if the safety issue can be resolved through effective regulation and supervision, there are good reasons to question the benefits of encouraging, or even allowing, the banking sector to expand so much. Research by the IMF and the Bank for International Settlements shows that, while a larger financial system helps economic growth in underdeveloped economies, as in Africa or South Asia, 'there comes a point – one that many advanced economies passed long ago – where more banking and more credit are associated with less innovation and efficiency and with lower growth.' Recent analysis by Luigi Zingales of the Chicago Booth School of Business reinforces the conclusion that a large financial sector is damaging because it destroys trust in the private enterprise system more widely.

I shall turn later in this book to the specific issues around banking in the UK. But the UK illustrates particularly well some of the benefits and costs of a large financial services sector, especially in banking. The benefits include a large amount of often lucrative employment, much of it only indirectly related to banking. The UK's professional and business services industry – accountants, lawyers, recruiters, advisers – has grown on the back of financial services. Of the 700,000 employees in the City, only 143,000 are bank employees, and 95,000 others are in insurance and fund management.

The evidence also suggests, however, that bank lending does not perform the role of economic lubricant very well. In the UK, the volume of home mortgages and lending on commercial property and financial businesses has tripled from 33 per cent of GDP in 1990 to around 100 per cent today. The share of lending to non-financial businesses has remained at 25 per cent of GDP over the same period. Manufacturing attracted a mere 1.5 per cent. There is a similar story in other economies, such as the Netherlands and Luxembourg, which also have big banking sectors. Bank lending is not supporting added value, but instability and debt. Professor Dirk Bezemer summarizes the research data: 'countries with larger financial sectors have less investment and innovation, more instability and lower growth rates.'

Lord Turner, formerly chair of the Financial Services Authority (FSA), argues that there are four key respects in which the financial sector generates potential problems, different from other industries: the generation of macroeconomic instability, booms and busts; exploitation of consumers because of asymmetry of information about complex products, hence the endless scandals around the mis-selling of pensions and personal protection insurance, the derivatives promoted to small businesses that didn't need or understand them, endowment mortgages, and much else; unproductive 'churn', with rewards to intermediaries but minimal wider economic value, in wholesale markets; and ethical risk created by the possibilities for vast rewards for greedy individuals unconnected with underlying performance and value, as with Libor rate-fixing. Turner's optimistic view is that these problems can be dealt with through well-designed regulation and supervision allied to good leadership within the industry.

The simple fact is that a very large global banking sector may not be good for Britain. On this point, I believe, Mr Carney is wrong. The current relative contraction of the sector may be healthy in the long run. That might seem a cavalier judgement.

Readers might recall, however, that thanks to Mrs Thatcher Britain's underground coal-mining industry was allowed to disappear. It had vast reserves, provided a lot of employment and held the potential for wealth creation, but the subsidy required – just like the implicit taxpayer subsidy to the banks – and the threat of periodic disruptions, more than offset the benefits. That is an extreme example, and I would not advocate such a drastic outcome for the banking industry. But it is useful to reflect that there are apparently valuable industries that bring serious problems in their wake.

Other industries have comparable challenges too. Having worked in the oil and gas industry (though not in financial services), I have been struck by the parallels. The upstream extractive end of the oil industry, for example, is often associated with economic instability, booms and busts, in host countries. Ethical problems arise from rent-seeking behaviour and corruption when there is a largely unaccountable windfall of riches to host-country governments, while there are minimal spillover benefits to the economies of the host countries. Indeed, I have often drawn the parallel between the role of the financial services sector in the City of London and the enclaves of oil production in Angola, or Gabon, or Nigeria. Good governance and regulation can ensure that natural resource enclaves can serve the wider economy (Botswana is a happier African example), but there is certainly no automatic benefit from the industry, and there are many risks and costs. I do not want to overstate the analogy – banking has a far greater capacity for creating systemic risk. But I turn now to how those risks and costs are being managed in the financial sector.

———

As described in *The Storm*, the 2008 banking crisis became so extreme in its impact because governments felt obliged to accept that they could not let 'systemically important financial institutions' fail. The taxpayer was ultimately responsible for the vast exposure to risk taken by financial institutions of all kinds, which included universal banks, specialist mortgage-lenders, stand-alone investment banks, and a global insurance company (AIG). The belief that the state will ultimately step in to protect the system from collapse provided an incentive to bankers to escalate risk-taking to a scale where their institutions were too-big-to-fail and therefore would always be rescued. Thus the banking sector enjoyed a large, implicit, taxpayer subsidy.

However caused, the full weight of the burden of carrying systemic risk only became clear with hindsight. In nineteenth-century banking crises, of which there were many, and up to and including the 1930s, insolvent banks were allowed to fail, just like other companies (though a set of rules laid out by the banker and journalist Walter Bagehot defined conditions under which temporary liquidity, at penalty rates, could be extended). The effect was, often, to magnify crises by creating widespread panic as investors tried to retrieve their savings. There were some massive crises, some more serious than the one we encountered in 2008, in terms of their impact on financial markets as well as the real economy. In the post-war era, the recognition of the need for a stable banking system led to the widespread adoption of deposit insurance schemes which carried the implicit threat that the institutions themselves, and investors other than depositors, were not protected.

The limitations of deposit insurance became brutally apparent in 2007 when Northern Rock got into difficulties after liquidity dried up in the wholesale markets on which the bank depended. Depositors didn't believe in the promise of depositor protection, or understand it (or perhaps they understood its limitations) and panicked. After a period of procrastination, the Bank of England decided that the 'moral hazard' of saving the bank by providing liquidity was less dangerous than allowing it to fail. That decision was in line with a long history of willingness, in times of crisis, to back deposit-taking institutions – for instance, in UK secondary banking in the early 1970s, and in the US savings and loans crisis of the 1980s – as provided for in the Bagehot principles. Part of the confusion around Northern Rock was caused by uncertainty over whether the bank was just illiquid or also insolvent; the bank had over-lent at the peak of the housing market, but it had quite a good default record. A similar confusion, or overlap, between liquidity and solvency issues affected a succession of financial institutions in the UK and the USA as the crisis unfolded.

What was certainly never envisaged was that the state would underwrite securities brokers and investment banks. After the 1929 financial crash in the United States, Congress passed the Glass–Steagall Act in 1934 to ensure that these activities were formally separated from commercial banks, in order to prevent any such cross-contamination of systemic risk. (Unlike the USA, the UK did not experience a banking crash after 1929 and so the issue never arose, and there was no comparable legislation.) But that Act was repealed a decade ago by the Clinton administration during the hubristic days of investment bank expansion when no one seriously believed that such institutions could fail. Then there was remarkable deference to the 'masters of the universe', who appeared capable, through financial alchemy, of turning mundane business into staggering amounts of wealth. Institutions that had hitherto relied on income from securities underwriting, raising capital for business and advisory work, moved heavily into trading, especially in bonds and currencies, and increasingly in the form of complex, exotic products. By 2010, 80 per cent of the biggest investment banks' income came from trading activity, providing ample scope for generous bonuses without making a tangible contribution to socially useful wealth-creation.

The threat to the future of Bear Stearns in early 2008 tested the US authorities' commitment to allowing such institutions to fail. Such was the perceived systemic risk of allowing Bear Stearns to go down that the authorities intervened with a rescue operation. Yet a few months later, when Lehman Brothers was threatened and lost its access to liquidity, the US regulators adopted a tougher approach and allowed it to collapse. They judged that it was insolvent because of losses and bad debt, and feared that a dangerous precedent would be established if it were rescued, encouraging institutions to take extreme risks in the knowledge that a bail-out would follow. In the event, the degree of systemic risk involved was considerable, as the leading banks, and many others acting as counter-parties to derivatives held by Lehman's, faced potentially large and unpredictable losses.

These derivatives included credit default swaps and options – effectively insurance contracts against the failure to honour liabilities – which had no effective collateral in the event of large-scale credit default by the banks. What was exposed very quickly was the scale of interconnectedness of financial markets. The shock waves reverberated through the system, leading after a short time to the rescue and semi-nationalization of RBS, at that stage the world's largest bank by assets; the near collapse of Barclays, which was rescued by Arab financial institutions; and the largest rescue of all, that of the insurer AIG, required because of the failure of credit default swaps in its trading arm. As one of the leading financial centres, London was a central part of this disaster, not just on account of the British-based banks but because Lehman's, AIG and other key institutions had major operations there.

It was now too late to redeem the purity of the principle of allowing institutions to fail. Governments since then have been grappling with the issue of how to ensure that this sequence of events does not happen again.

The regulatory response to this crisis has consisted of several overlapping elements. First, under internationally agreed rules, known as the Basel rules, banks and other financial institutions have tougher capital requirements, so that they have to have sufficient shareholders' capital (known as Tier 1 capital) at stake to offset their liabilities and absorb losses. The effect of such rules is to make banks more resilient, and therefore less likely to need help in the event of heavy losses, but also to be less inclined to risky activities that require a bigger capital buffer. As a consequence, the Basel Committee on Banking Supervision estimates that the world's top ten banks have increased their capital by over US$470 billion (as at June 2015). This is still work in progress – there is no agreement as yet on the capital needed for trading activities – but in the USA and the UK, especially, a lot has been done.

One unintended, and undesirable, side effect has been that economically important activities, like lending to SMEs that are judged particularly risky and attract high risk weightings, have been curbed. There has been a large fall in net lending, though weak demand has also contributed to the decline. In my capacity as business secretary, I challenged the rigidity with which the Bank of England, the UK regulators and the banks themselves were interpreting requirements that effectively penalized the one sector, that of SME lending, that had played virtually no part in the crisis. But rules were rules. In the event, constant pressure on the banks and attacks on their reputations did produce a genuine effort by some of them – notably Lloyds, and later Santander – to build up their SME lending, though RBS was conspicuously a back-marker. In due course the establishment of the British Business Bank provided a catalyst for new kinds of lending.

Capital rules are further complemented by leverage rules. But these same rules still allow banks to leverage their equity by a factor of thirty-three to one (fifty to one during the crisis), which permits very high levels of risky lending in some areas. There are also liquidity rules, which ensure that banks have substantial assets that are easily saleable in an emergency – particularly important when it isn't totally clear in an emergency whether there is a liquidity or a solvency issue. The resilience of banks under these new rules is established through laboratory experiments, so-called 'stress tests'. The UK's seven leading lenders are tested against plausible disaster scenarios – 'known unknowns' – such as a near repeat of 2008, or a severe slowdown in China and a sharp contraction in the eurozone. So far, the leading banks have satisfied the tests (with the exception of the Co-operative Bank in the wake of a near collapse).

A second, complementary step, applied in the UK, has been to separate retail deposits and conventional lending from riskier trading – the so-called 'casino' activities. Even leading bankers like John Reed of Citicorp have acknowledged that the culture of investment banking undermines traditional banking. The UK coalition government agreed to address this problem, and immediately on entering government the Chancellor and I set up the Vickers Commission to examine how this should best be done. It concluded that full separation would be too costly and disruptive, and recommended strict ring-fencing of the two sets of activity. My own instincts had been for full separation, but lack of agreement in the commission on the more radical option meant that nothing would have happened. I suspected that the more conservative, City-based voices on the commission, such as Bill Winters, prevailed over others of a more reforming bent, like Martin Wolf. And I am sure the Treasury discouraged ideas that would alienate leading bankers.

The ring-fencing proposal has completed its passage through parliament, which strengthened the ring fence by requiring full separation in the event of breaches of the rules. There has been a great deal of debate, and detailed rule-making, over what is inside and what outside the ring fence. But a vital structural reform has now been agreed, effectively separating the different kinds of banking, despite much foot-dragging and complaints from the banks. Britain is, as a consequence, in the lead internationally on structural reform. The European Commission promoted a basic approach similar to the UK model and the European Parliament has agreed to tighter supervision of unusual banks albeit without mandatory separation.

A third, somewhat different approach has been adopted in the USA, following the Dodd–Frank law of July 2010. This saw a comprehensive overhaul of banking legislation, reversing the liberalization of the Clinton era and reinstating the Glass–Steagall principles. It is of great complexity: 848 pages of law, backed up by 30,000 pages of rules. Within it is an attempt to restrict banks from trading using their own money or from investing in institutions like hedge funds which have extensive trading activities. The so-called Volcker Rule is controversial because of its extra-territorial application to non-US overseas capital markets, not to mention its unintelligibility (eleven pages of Dodd–Frank, which has since expanded to hundreds of pages of interpretation). But the underlying aim – to separate trading from 'real' banking, turning savers' deposits into productive loans – is similar to that of structural separation in the UK and the EU.

A further set of regulatory reforms is to force banks to prepare for orderly insolvency should they indeed fail, so that the taxpayer is not involved and there is a clear process for meeting legal obligations. So-called 'living wills' are being prepared under guidelines agreed by the G20 countries. So far, most have been rejected by US regulators as being too weak. Yet the issue of too-big-to-fail banks remains highly relevant, since the world's biggest banks, with a few exceptions such as RBS, are bigger than ever and continued to expand their assets after the crisis (Figure 2.1). Large banks continue to have balance sheets bigger than their host economy (Barclays and HSBC in the UK) or close to it (Deutsche Bank in Germany).

There have also been regulatory reforms to ensure that there is a market, and identifiable market values, for derivatives, so that big losses cannot be hidden in opaque, complex instruments. The mechanism for achieving this aim has been the creation of clearing houses for derivatives to be traded and valued.

Finally, there have been attempts to change bankers' behaviour by regulating the incentive structure for pay and bonuses. Prior to the crisis, bankers in investment banking operations had every incentive to take high risks and collect bonuses for trades, in the full knowledge that they had little personally at stake should their activities lead to large losses. Regulations have, in a variety of different ways, sought to limit bonus pay-outs that provide for short-term rewards without long-term responsibility.

Some sensible reforms have sought to lock in bonuses in the form of stock which cannot be redeemed for, say, five or seven years, creating an incentive to make sustainable long-term investments. A less sensible approach has been, as in the EU, to cap bonuses and replace the remuneration with salaries, which makes trading institutions less stable by locking them into fixed costs without reducing total remuneration.

There is, however, a wider ethical and economic argument for moving towards a non-bonus culture in banking, so as to disincentivize mis-selling and encourage a considered, long-term approach to lending. This already occurs in some banks, like Handelsbanken, and in mutually owned institutions. Bonus pots have generally shrunk in recent years, in London and New York, but it is more likely that this reflects depressed profits than anything deeper. Without effective regulation and cultural change, we can expect to see the glory days return before long.

A separate development related to bankers' behaviour has been called 'regulatory revenge'. Banks are fined for past misdeeds, from mis-selling to manipulation of the Libor rate, breaking sanctions, or non-compliance with money-laundering rules. By mid-2015, the top sixteen Western banks had paid fines of over US$300 billion – with more expected. Even HSBC, whose reputation had escaped from the financial crisis largely intact, has faced heavy fines over irregularities in its US operation and, more recently, in Switzerland. As a way of expressing public outrage, these fines have some symbolic value – and perhaps some real value if they hit shareholders who pursued unrealistically high rates of return, as well as the senior managers who committed the offences. But in reality the bankers who were individually responsible have largely moved on. Even in the less forgiving environment of the USA, there have been pitifully small numbers of bankers imprisoned for fraud and other illegal practices. Only Iceland, which jailed 26 bankers, has taken that route. Very few bankers have even been disqualified as directors. Although I sought to expedite the inquiry into RBS directors, the Scottish government, which has legal responsibility in this area, has been unable so far to find sufficient evidence to prosecute. The burden usually falls on the bank's customers.

The cumulative effect of this regulatory wave has undoubtedly been to make banks safer, but duller and less profitable. Before the financial crisis, the big, systemically important banks in the USA were earning 30 per cent returns on equity. This is currently down to around 10 per cent, with tougher regulation to come. The same banks have reduced their average leverage – that is, loans as a multiple of loss-absorbing equity – from twenty-three to fourteen. Along with these changes has come a severe correction which has taken the market value of the top global banks from several times their book value to a small fraction of it, albeit with big variations among the banks themselves. One of the implications of this change is that banks are having to change their business model, specializing as well as downsizing, and shedding many staff. The process of regulatory reform, and regulatory revenge, still has a long way to go and different jurisdictions are developing different approaches, which is a major problem in itself.

———

Mervyn King's observation that banks are global in life but national in death has resonated through the regulatory response of governments. National governments that have paid the heavy bill for failing banks have, not surprisingly, tried to shape the response to their own particular needs and political pressures.

There has been a lot of evidence of a retreat from international banking. Between 1990 and 2007 annual cross-border bank flows grew ten times, to US$5 trillion. In 2012 this sum had fallen to under US$2 trillion. The UK has seen the retreat of Icelandic and Irish banks. Leading European banks – RBS, Commerzbank, Crédit Agricole – have announced their withdrawal from overseas markets. Eastern European countries – Romania, Hungary, Croatia, Slovenia and the Baltic states – have been particularly exposed to the withdrawal of cross-border funding and banking networks.

Exposure by eurozone banks to the countries of the southern periphery halved, from US$2 trillion to under US$1 trillion, after 2008.

Various factors have reinforced this process. Politicians have deliberately leant on banks domiciled in their own countries, and rescued by their taxpayers, to support their domestic economies. Iceland notoriously discriminated against overseas creditors in favour of domestic depositors when its banks collapsed. A more far-reaching influence is that national systems of regulation may have the effect of curbing international banking. Rules on capital and liquidity requirements, for example, might have the effect of encouraging holdings of seemingly low-risk government debt, or they might treat overseas assets more harshly. The EU, the USA, Singapore and Hong Kong are all developing different rules on derivatives clearing houses, encouraging the development of separate infrastructures. Home-country 'living wills' may bring pressure on banks to develop overseas branches, rather than to rely on subsidiaries regulated by host countries, since the former allow money to be moved around more easily. And there is simultaneously pressure from host-country regulators in the opposite direction, encouraging banks to develop self-contained subsidiaries. Banks are being pulled in different directions by global and national regulators. The effect of nationalizing regulation has been to reinforce the link between bank risk and sovereign risk.

There is general acknowledgement in the international community that a coordinated approach is best. The G20 Financial Stability Board has set out a blueprint for cross-border cooperation to deal with the too-big-to-fail problem. In November 2014 there was agreement on a new, internationally agreed test, going beyond the previously agreed principles governing capital, liquidity and leverage. Under the new rules, a tier of bond-holders' as well as shareholders' capital will be at risk ('bailed in') before a bank can call on the government for help. But good technical work and good intentions are being bypassed, and six years after the 2008 crisis there were still strong disagreements over important technical details and exceptions. What has been agreed is a 'single point of entry', such that one crisis-hit national regulator would be allowed to do its work with the support of others. And there has been sufficient joint discipline to ensure that the world's top ten banks have increased their capital by more than US $470 billion, as noted above.

There are, however, two different sets of worries about the fragmented and inconsistent way in which regulation is evolving. One is the immediate concern about protectionism and nationalism leading to a costly, less efficient system. There is also potential for conflict between leading jurisdictions, as with the complaints about US extra-territoriality (the application of US law in other jurisdictions) and repeated clashes between the UK and the European Commission over attempts to impose common rules. The EU commissioner Michel Barnier became a bogeyman in London over his attempt to create strict EU rules applicable to the UK under the single market. I disagreed with the priority the prime minister and Chancellor gave to promoting City interests in their EU negotiations, but on specific issues, like the legal battle over the proposal to define the share of bonuses in pay, they were right to oppose badly thought-through EU legislation.

The attempt by the European Union to go further and create a banking union could be seen as a step forward in creating international rules, rather than fragmented national regulation. It is trying to do several things: to underpin economic and monetary union by common supervision of 5500 eurozone banks that could produce sovereign liabilities; to reduce systemic instability through an agreed single resolution mechanism for failing banks (but it has failed to get agreement on common deposit insurance to stop governments outbidding their neighbours in offering guarantees to depositors as in the 2008 panic); and to create non-discrimination rules for a single, competitive market in financial services. However, these interventions also create potential barriers for non-members of the eurozone.

The second danger is that a fragmented system of regulation simply creates opportunities for banks to exploit differences through 'regulatory arbitrage', seeking out the weak spots in regulation and concentrating highly profitable but risky activities there. Once banks have understood the new, highly complex regulatory regimes in the USA, the EU and elsewhere, their emphasis will shift from complaining about the cost to finding ways of exploiting ambiguities and differences in regulatory treatment. And the effect of requiring banks to hold much more capital – a threefold increase is mooted under the Basel 3 capital standards – will be to drive down the return on equity (which is currently below the cost of capital), enticing investors into higher-yielding and less regulated vehicles outside of banking. The Bank for International Settlements has already expressed concern that the stringent application of global rules in the USA is diverging from the EU, which was judged 'materially non-compliant' in 2014 in relation to rules it had agreed to but had not applied.

———

As for future dangers, there is a particular concern over shadow banks. This is a loose concept applied to around a quarter of the global financial sector, with assets of around US$50 trillion, which is in turn around two thirds the size of the global economy. (Other estimates place the category at around US$75 trillion in 2013, up from US$60 trillion in 2008 and US$26 trillion in 2002.) Shadow banks include hedge funds, special-purpose vehicles (often set up to circumvent regulation) and a wide variety of short- and long-term funds operating in money markets. But concepts and definitions constantly change.

Shadow banking covers activities that involve credit intermediation – that is, lending – outside the banking system. Problems could, in principle, arise if shadow banks create substantial leverage, by borrowing on a narrow base of equity. Investment funds do not do so, but hedge funds can and do. Problems are most likely to arise if there is a maturity mismatch, as with lending long and borrowing short, a process recognized and regulated in banks but not necessarily in shadow banks. Thus shadow banking may, because it is often driven by a wish to avoid and undermine regulatory reform, be a growing worry, though it is not inherently a major threat to systemic stability. Although a substantial number of hedge funds failed in the financial crisis, none required – or, apparently, sought – state rescue, and there appears to have been no major systemic risk involved. When they failed, their investors met their liabilities without dragging down other institutions.

But that is perhaps too sanguine and generous a view. Hedge funds were largely responsible for creating high-yielding collateralized debt obligations (CDOs). These were among the complex derivatives that proved to be illiquid and often incomprehensible during the financial crisis.

Under recent regulatory changes, introduced by the Financial Stability Board of leading regulators, there is to be more monitoring and surveillance of shadow banks. Specifically, hedge funds will be subject to greater disclosure in future, but there are only limited controls over their products and conduct. There is also controversy around EU and US proposals for curbing money-market funds – that is, short-term funds offering guarantees of redemption. This is another US$3 trillion industry, and one that was directly involved in the 2008 crisis when a prominent fund faced difficulties and US authorities had to intervene with support.

In the months and years to come, as memories of the crisis recede, there will be other market-based product innovations that will manufacture risk and add complexity. They will mutate and grow faster than regulators can keep up and in due course they may become systemically significant and, in some cases, unsafe. Novel trading platforms, like the 'dark pools' of security trading 'off-exchanges', and high-frequency trading, can incubate new systemic risk. A warning that the risks may come from currently improbable sources appeared in the case of a sole trader, Navinder Singh Sarao. He operated an automated trading programme for Chicago futures contracts from a suburban house in Hounslow and triggered a Dow Jones crash of 1,000 points in a day. And so, on to the next crisis.

Another way of looking at this set of problems is in terms of products, rather than institutions – in particular, derivatives. It has been estimated that the total value of global equities in March 2015 was around US$70 trillion, but the value of outstanding debt-based derivatives contracts is ten times that amount.

There is nothing inherently sinister or even problematic about derivatives, which date back to the beginning of organized commerce. Ancient Greece had futures markets for commodities, helping farmers to hedge – that is, to insure – against the risks of future price fluctuations. Modern financial markets have produced a vast range of products, to hedge mainly against the risk of future interest rate changes, but also fluctuations in exchange rates, commodities and other prices. Taken as a whole, this vast network of insurance is a public as well as a private good, enabling trade and investments to be transacted that would otherwise be considered too risky.

However, like opiates or guns, which in the right hands can kill pain or deter violence, much damage can be done by derivatives when they are in the wrong hands. The wrong hands are often assumed to be those of speculators who trade, not to reduce the risk of their own commercial activities, but to gamble against future movements in prices. Serious abuses can occur when particular speculators have sufficient weight in the market to make their gamble a self-fulfilling prophecy, or when speculation adversely affects the affordability of necessities of life. But taken as a whole, speculation should, in general, stabilize volatile markets, as Milton Friedman has shown.

Rather, the wrong hands have been those confecting on a large scale highly complex, artificial derivatives which are imperfectly understood by those who buy, sell or hold them. This matters when the derivative contracts are called in and there is a serious mismatch between the assets and the quality of the collateral held by the counter-party – when, in other words, the contract amount cannot be honoured. This is what happened during the credit crunch.

Are we now safer than before the credit crunch? Regulations in the UK, as in the USA and the rest of Europe, demand more transparency and better reporting, and have sought to create and regulate clearing houses. They have also sought to regulate more effectively the institutions that hold and trade in derivatives. But we simply do not know how clearing houses or regulatory structures would cope in a new emergency. To paraphrase Warren Buffett, we have seen a financial atom bomb explode, but not a hydrogen bomb.

Alternatively, the vulnerabilities could be in financial sectors normally considered safe. Insurance, for example, is not vulnerable to the liquidity problems of banks, which originate in their maturity structure – that is, borrowing short (deposits) and lending long (mortgages and commercial loans). In contrast, insurers tend to borrow long (life insurance policies and pension savings) and lend relatively short (investment in easily traded government bonds and shares). They may not face a 'run', like a bank, but bad investments and aggressive acquisitions can still lead to bad losses and collapse of value, threatening insolvency. It is worth recalling that the biggest bail-out in the financial crisis was of an insurer, which required US$182 billion of US government funding, twice the cost of bailing out RBS in the UK. AIG had a trillion-dollar balance sheet, like the big banks, although its problems were in areas where it had strayed from insurance narrowly defined.

Regulators are well aware of the potential vulnerabilities of the insurance sector and have sought to regulate more aggressively. The EU promoted Solvency 2, tightening capital and risk management requirements for European insurers. There was a strong reaction from the industry, concerning both the reach of the new regulations (the extra-territorial issue) and whether they would suffocate a move to more long-term investment. The more creative insurers see a market for long-term investment in infrastructure and housing, or in buying securitized SME loans which produce a higher return than government paper, thus matching their assets and liabilities and doing something economically useful. Indeed, the UK Treasury attached great importance to insurers plugging the gaps in PFI-funded infrastructure projects left by the banks and by the government's own reluctance to borrow to invest – though very little capital appears actually to have been mobilized for this purpose. It seems that the industry has largely won the argument against excessively conservative regulation, but the looser the regime the greater the risk of opening the door to the Fred Goodwins and Bob Diamonds of the insurance world. Indeed, there is already concern that segments of the insurance industry are meddling in dangerous financial innovations. A recent study showed that the US$575 billion global catastrophe insurance and reinsurance business was attracting complex arrangements to shift risk, using techniques not dissimilar to those used for credit default swaps and options in the subprime mortgage world.

So, there is a threat from new products in shadow banking and in sectors like insurance that were hitherto not thought to be a source of systemic risk, and from the sheer scale and complexity of derivatives markets. There are also emerging economies, not subject to the same post-crisis regulatory scrutiny as the USA and EU. Shadow banking is expanding rapidly there. China is the most obvious source of concern, since it has seen a massive expansion of commercial credit, much of it in the Chinese equivalent of shadow banking. Domestic credit has more than doubled to US$23 trillion, from US$9 trillion in 2008. There are strong similarities to Japan in the boom years before 1990, with inflated property values and extremely opaque bank accounting. Japan's crash and prolonged stagnation had relatively little impact on the rest of the world. A Chinese crash would have a much more profound impact, through interconnections with Asian financial markets and a link to London via trading in the renminbi (China's currency), as well as through the real economy effects of a Chinese slowdown.

Other commentators have pointed to threats not from the exotic and complex, or from the other side of the world, but from simple and familiar products. Gillian Tett, among others, has warned of the consequences of banks offloading hundreds of billions of corporate bonds on to asset managers like mutual funds – the offloading being to reduce risk, the asset managers seeking to achieve higher asset yields. The market for high-grade bonds has almost doubled since 2008, to US$5 trillion, and the asset managers who are acquiring them may or may not have the capacity to sell them in liquid markets should their own investors pull out. The most extreme example of this phenomenon is what is happening in the market for sovereign government bonds, large volumes of which have been trading at negative yields. Markets deem them to be totally safe, but it does not require much imagination to see how circumstances could change, leading to large, panicky sales of these assets.

Each and every one of these potential threats may prove not to be a problem, or to be manageable. But the broader point is that national governments and regulators are struggling to catch up. Coordination is weak, leaving numerous opportunities for greedy and reckless individuals and institutions to exploit. A retreat, almost certainly temporary, from global to national banking is merely disguising the problem. As long as international governance of financial markets remains so underdeveloped and weak, the threat of a returning storm – an even bigger one – remains, which is why the halting initiatives at G20 or European Union level are so important.

The fragmented and complex regulatory reforms of national governments represent a missed opportunity to look at more radical options. In some cases, as with the Vickers reforms in the UK, significant change has been implemented in the form of a compromise, with more far-reaching ideas like breaking up the universal banks being left to one side. In the immediate aftermath of the crisis there was a rare opportunity for governments, individually and collectively, to utilize the public's outrage and fear to override powerful producer interests in banking. There was for a while some serious public debate over such basic issues as why banks are allowed to create credit. This is also an issue pursued in a powerful new book by the former UK financial regulator, Adair Turner, who argues that financial crises follow inevitably from credit creation by banks. A renewed financial crisis would bring a fresh opportunity to look at such fundamental questions.

One of these would be to shift, using regulation and taxation, the basic business model of banking away from debt and towards equity. Martin Wolf has argued that the 3 per cent leverage ratio (that is, equity relative to debt) of the Basel rules is hopelessly inadequate, and argues for a 10 per cent minimum. He believes that in a crisis banks would not be able to realize capital in a hurry and therefore need to hold a lot more. This would, at a stroke, destroy the ambition of bankers to make very high returns on equity, with associated bonuses. He argues, furthermore, that banks cannot be seen in isolation from the rest of the economy. As long as a substantial part of bank lending is based on property lending, as it is in the UK, there is an unnecessarily high level of risk to the banks in inflexible debt contracts (mortgages), since the price of housing can fall as well as rise.

His approach merges into a more fundamental reform, which is to stop bank leverage altogether and, by implication, to stop banks creating money (that is, credit). The alternative is so-called 'narrow banking'. Bank lending would be 100 per cent backed by deposits. Banks would only lend the money deposited with them, not a multiple of deposits as now. A modern version of an old idea – it was advocated in the 1930s in the wake of the Great Depression – has been advanced by John Cochrane of the Chicago Booth School of Business. It separates lending, which would be financed by investors using their own money, from deposits, which would have 100 per cent liquidity and could be withdrawn on demand. Money would be created, not by banks, but by the central bank – that is, the state – in the form of 'fiat money', with the state attracting the windfall ('seigneurage').

That approach is so radical that policy-makers have shied away from it and it is not currently on the political agenda. To realize it could involve banks offloading vast stocks of loans into the market, with associated losses. And there would be major policing issues around different kinds of financial institutions and different kinds of debt. But another major banking crisis might well tip the balance towards narrow banking. It would be prudent to be prepared for such a crisis and to have a blueprint for narrow banking ready.

Then there are issues around how we create or protect the social functions of banking without the hazards. In the UK, for example, there is a serious market failure in the provision of capital for small, growing companies and social enterprises in the form of 'patient capital', which produces decent returns over a long time period. There is also very little local community banking. Banking in general is highly concentrated. By contrast, the USA has generated a very diverse set of markets in loans and equity, local and national, commercial and mutual (as in credit unions). The USA has seen a succession of crises, big and small, but there is real competition and diversity. That is also true of Germany, which has a strong network of community-based business banks (*Sparkassen*), as well as big complex global institutions like Deutsche Bank. For the UK in particular, a major challenge is to draw on the best of US and German experience. This is why I took the lead to establish a state-owned British Business Bank to act as a catalyst for SME lending in unconventional forms like peer-to-peer lending, to help the expansion of new challenger banks, and to promote new vehicles for equity finance. I discuss these developments in chapter ten, but one of the positive outcomes of the banking crisis is undoubtedly that a more varied ecology is beginning to appear.

The central issue faced in fostering this, more varied, ecology is how to encourage genuine innovation which reduces the costs of financial transactions for individuals and firms without creating destabilising systemic risk. Innovation is especially needed to facilitate high risk lending (as well as equity capital) for small and medium sized growth companies and startups. One danger of cruder forms of bank regulation is that they produce the stability of the economic graveyard.

A lot now hangs on the success of Fintech, the new technology platforms operating outside the banking system (and, therefore, part of shadow banking). Crowd funding is one example – and an early success of the British Business Bank was financing groups like Funding Circle and Zopa to expand rapidly. Globally the Fintech market (total investment) has grown from $12 billion in 2014 to $20 billion in 2015, expected to grow to $30 billion in 2016, and there are an estimated 10,000 lending platforms, 2,000 in China (the UK has around 20 of the top 100). Inevitably there is pressure to regulate the market (including from incumbents) to prevent abuse and systemically dangerous activity. Libertarian champions of distruptive technology are resisting. This could be a major regulatory battleground in years ahead.

On the wider global picture, it is important to acknowledge the real progress that has been made to understand and, where necessary, regulate the dangers – or at least the known dangers – in financial markets. But the biggest danger is when market players and policy-makers start to believe that they are safe.

3

Different Routes out of the Great Recession

At first sight, the world economy seven years after the storm looks to be in fair shape. The IMF's global estimates, made in October 2015, were of 3.1 per cent per annum growth in 2015, and 3.6 per cent predicted in 2016. These are figures represent a downgrade but are far from the sense of impending disaster that prevailed in the immediate aftermath of the financial crisis in 2008/9. To be sure, there were different routes out of recession. The USA has led the way in growth, in terms of both speed of recovery and continued recovery, while Japan and the eurozone have lagged behind. Emerging markets are slowing to a collective 4 per cent in 2015.

Does this mean that the great recession is now history? It may do, if the financial sector risks described in the previous chapter are managed. And it is possible to construct a plausibly optimistic scenario for future growth. In such a world, the eurozone has passed the nadir of its fortunes; in mid-2015 the IMF estimated a 25 per cent risk of recession, improving from 40 per cent a year earlier. In the next chapter I review the evidence for that cautious optimism. It also assumes that Japan, after almost a quarter of a century of stagnation following its banking crisis, is finally returning to normality and steady growth. It takes as given the continuation of the US success story: steady recovery, pulled by aggressive and unorthodox monetary policies designed to ensure that the great recession did not become a second Great Depression. And it assumes that emerging economies continue to grow strongly. China is slowing down to rates of growth that are still very respectable (6.8 per cent in 2015 and 6.3 per cent in 2016), and Indian growth accelerates (to 7.3 per cent in both years).

————————

The recovery story, however, looks at the trading accounts of countries, not their balance sheets, which are decidedly less healthy. The G7 countries are emerging from the great recession with a legacy of levels of debt, owed by governments, financial institutions and in some cases (as in the USA and the UK) households, which were last seen only after major wars. That poses a threat in some cases, especially in Europe and Japan, of debt deflation, where the overhang of debt and debt reduction leads to a reluctance by governments, individuals and companies to spend and invest. This in turn could lead to weak demand and a downward spiral of falling prices and further weakening of demand.

In this chapter I contrast two experiences in particular. Japan has not, until now, escaped from the stagnation induced by the after-effects of a banking crisis and accumulated debt. The USA, in contrast, was at the heart of a classic boom and bust credit cycle based around surging property prices and reckless banking, but it seems to have managed to exit the crisis in fair order. While the economy has grown, so has debt.

In the USA, corporate, financial and household debt rose from 50 per cent of GDP after the Second World War to around 300 per cent in 2007. In the UK it rose from 200 per cent to 500 per cent. But recovery has not improved this story of over-extended balance sheets. In the USA debt ratios, both private and public, have deteriorated further, as we saw in chapter one.

In order to head off debt deflation, activist central banks have resorted to very low interest rates allied to unorthodox expansionary monetary policies. These in turn run the risk of creating asset bubbles and new cycles of credit boom and bust. Governments have found themselves caught between the risks of stagnation and of credit-induced crises.

An aggressive monetary policy response to the crisis emerged in the USA. Milton Friedman had argued that the Great Depression had been caused primarily by a collapse of the money supply, specifically of broad money or credit. As it happens, it was a student of the Great Depression, Ben Bernanke, who shared Friedman's analysis, who took the helm at the Federal Reserve in 2006 and was shortly afterwards confronted with the financial crisis. Bernanke's response was first to prevent the banking system from collapsing, which would have resulted in massive credit contraction, and second to use monetary policy aggressively to sustain credit and aggregate demand.

The latter policy took the form of slashing short-term interest rates from 5.25 per cent in June 2007 to zero in the wake of September 2008. The next step was to try to drive down long-term interest rates by buying up government bonds, which pushes the price of bonds up and the yield down – so-called quantitative easing, or QE. The effect of these very low interest rates has been to discourage saving and to encourage consumer spending and business investment, thus counteracting the slump. QE has had the effect of pumping liquidity into banks and other financial institutions which hold, and then sell, the bonds. QE was also used for other assets, including mortgages and corporate bonds, in order to inject liquidity into those sectors. (The Governor of the Bank of England was, by contrast, reluctant to use the central bank's balance sheet in this more expansive way.) But the wider significance of QE has been that it has enabled monetary policy to progress beyond the 'zero bound', which means that central banks are unable to stimulate the economy via short-term interest rates once they have fallen to zero. Under conditions of deflation, as in the 1930s, the problem gets worse, because real interest rates are positive as a consequence of negative inflation. Were the crisis to have deepened further, Friedman would have advocated the printing of money: the so-called 'helicopter drop' of money to get people to spend. That has proved unnecessary, at least so far.

In evaluating the experience of ultra-loose monetary policy, it is important to acknowledge that experience has been very different. QE was extensively deployed in the USA (as in the UK) and the policy debate has now shifted to tapering or reversing it. In the eurozone it was tried later, and on a smaller scale, and the question is whether that was enough. Japan also has little to show, so far, for attempts at monetary stimulus, and would be the lead candidate for monetizing its budget deficits (in effect, printing money). Japan has already made far more use of monetary easing than has the US Federal Reserve.

Critics of the aggressive monetary response make several, somewhat contradictory, points. One is that the policy has not been very effective. Vasco Cúrdia and Andrea Ferrero argue that QE added a mere 0.13 per cent to US GDP growth in late 2010. Sceptics argue that indebted companies and individuals would not borrow even if more credit was available. At the other extreme, Ben Bernanke himself cites studies suggesting that QE boosted US GDP by as much as 3 per cent – and such is the extent of recovery in the USA (and the UK), and the fall in unemployment, that his account, however self-justifying, rings true.

But that leads to the second, quite different, criticism, that QE is potentially highly inflationary, with inflation currently visible mainly in asset markets, including housing in the UK and stock markets in the USA. Such asset inflation also, arguably, exacerbates wealth inequality, and asset-rich households have undoubtedly done well from QE. The critics say that, despite a long period of discussion and preparation, the US Federal Reserve has yet to exit the period of extraordinary monetary policy, so we cannot yet know what the long-term consequences are. The transition has been eased by 'forward guidance', setting out two years ahead the conditions under which monetary policy will be tightened. The exit from QE (tapering) must involve selling bonds and other assets without causing asset markets to crash again or choking off recovery. The mere expectation of the beginning of this process caused a major and somewhat panicky market reaction in September 2014.

At the time of writing, the Federal Reserve had after numerous hints and nudges made the first, very limited (0.25 per cent), move to raise interest rates since 2006. Their nervousness may well have been heightened by the experience of Sweden, which led, in 2012, the return to 'normal' monetary policy and higher interest rates. Sweden crashed back into recession, though it has since recovered. There is also concern that continued moves to higher interest rates in the USA will trigger growing capital flows from emerging markets, precipitating crisis conditions in some of those countries. Such capital flows could drive up the dollar to an extent that US exporters would face competitiveness issues and there would be a revival of protectionism in the USA. Congress is already twitchy about 'currency manipulation' after a 20 per cent rise in the dollar over a year.

Taken as a whole, the evidence is clear that expansionary monetary policy, led by the USA, was necessary. There remain, however, problems of managing the exit, and of managing demand during the exit and after. There are also critics, this time with a broadly Keynesian approach, who believe that fiscal policy, the use of deficit finance, should have played (and should play) a bigger role. In fact, Keynes attached considerable importance to monetary policy and saw low or negative interest rates as necessary to combat a slump. But he also believed that monetary policy was insufficient, and that governments should run temporary deficits in order to sustain demand. With unemployed resources available, output could expand without creating inflation and, by adding to tax reserves and subtracting from unemployment benefit, offset damage to the public finances. A modern version of Keynesian ideas is that the structural (debt) issues cannot be ducked, but that expansionary fiscal policy can help sustain demand while deleveraging is happening and dragging down demand.

In the early stages of the recent crisis, the Keynesian approach played a modest role. There was agreement between the main governments in the wake of the 2008 collapse to provide a coordinated fiscal stimulus of 1 per cent of GDP on top of monetary stimulus. The Obama administration committed itself to continuation of the policy, with a stimulus of 2–3 per cent of GDP in both 2009 and 2010, through a large public works programme, though the fiscal stimulus was then reversed. In practice, it is difficult for the US government to pursue a consistent fiscal policy because so many tax and spending decisions rest with Congress, which has been hostile to the Obama administration for much of its life.

Nevertheless, President Obama's advisers, who have a broadly Keynesian bent, have been influential in international forums like the IMF and the Organisation for Economic Co-operation and Development (OECD) in arguing against the more fiscally conservative voices in Europe. This Keynesian approach has surfaced at important times in recent years. The work of the IMF and World Bank published in autumn 2012 suggested that fiscal multipliers may have been underestimated and may be large especially when monetary policy has run out of road and exchange rates are fixed. Towards the end of 2014 the IMF, along with the OECD, was recommending fiscal expansion in the UK and the eurozone for the first time since the crisis.

There has been growing acceptance, too, that under conditions of very low long-term interest rates it makes sense for governments to borrow to invest in infrastructure projects which boost long-term growth and can reduce debt ratios. Thus, Keynesian public works projects may have an important role, acting not just as a short-term stimulus but as a long-term contributor to growth. That line of argument has, however, been resisted by orthodox finance ministries, including the UK Treasury. As I will argue later, that represented one of my main areas of disagreement within the coalition government and with the Conservatives, since.

———

Japan is often cited as the precedent Western economies should avoid: a financial crisis, caused by extreme over-leverage in a credit boom in the 1980s, evolving into a prolonged battle against deflation, coupled with economic stagnation and rising public debt. Richard Koo's analysis of 'balance sheet recession' is based on Japanese experience, but has potentially wider application to Western economies. He has argued that, if deep depression and deflation are to be avoided, low interest rates alone cannot do the trick. The government has to run a large fiscal deficit. Japanese governments have to a remarkable degree absorbed that lesson and avoided a slump (as opposed to stagnation). There has been more aggressive use of monetary easing than elsewhere, and extreme recourse to fiscal deficits. As a consequence, gross public debt has ballooned from 60 to 250 per cent of GDP, though net debt is probably around 130 per cent. Japan was able to get away with such policies in a way Western economies could not, because the Japanese public sector deficit has not been financed by foreigners (who hold only 8 per cent of Japanese government debt) but, at one remove, by Japanese savers. Domestic savers accepted very poor returns from banks and savings institutions, which in turn were persuaded to accept large amounts of low-yielding government bonds.

In retrospect, this policy, in tandem with other measures like the recapitalization of banks, worked well, at least for a while. Japan seemed to have recovered after a decade of stagnation following its financial crisis twenty-five years ago, and was growing again at around 2 per cent per annum after 2002, while unemployment remained low. But a price has been paid. Debt service, even with interest rates at 2 per cent, grew steadily and has been crowding out more and more public spending, including useful public investment. Debt service interest accounts for 25 per cent of the budget. Banks have also lent less to business while acquiring more government bonds. The return to recession after the global crisis in 2008/9 added to the problems. Japan is also grappling simultaneously with the long-term consequences for growth and with the cost of an ageing population and a contracting workforce. The population is set to decline steadily from 127 million to 87 million by 2060, 40 per cent of whom will be over sixty-five. The trap into which Japan has fallen is that, because growth is so slow and is weighed down by demographic pressures, the economy is expanding less rapidly than the multiplication of debt, even at low interest rates. Accordingly, the ratio of public debt to GDP has risen inexorably.

As a consequence of these long-term and short-term factors, the Japanese economy has stagnated. A new, reformist government under Shinzō Abe has endeavoured, since April 2013, to inject a new monetary and fiscal stimulus into the economy, working in parallel with a central bank. The main aim has been to stop Japan being caught in a cycle of price deflation and depressed output. One aim of the monetary expansion is to drive down the yen. It devalued by 25 per cent against the dollar over this period, so pushing up import prices and raising domestic inflation. But inflation remains well below the target level of 2 per cent. The second of the 'three arrows', as Abe describes the policy, is a fiscal stimulus of 2 per cent of GDP, though its effect was blunted by an increase in consumption taxes. The strategy is one of using expansionary fiscal policy to go for growth, hoping that the rate of growth will then exceed the growth of debt. The third 'arrow' is the implementation of long-promised structural reforms, including liberalization of markets which will hopefully raise the underlying growth rate.

So far, the programme has been largely unsuccessful. Japan remains the world capital of 'secular stagnation'. Growth remains very low, with around one per cent growth in 2015 estimated. The policies headed off deflation because a big devaluation increased living costs via imported inflation. But because wages were stagnating, real incomes were cut and people reduced their spending – the opposite of what the policy was designed to achieve. Despite very low official unemployment, wages remain stubbornly depressed. Moreover, Japan is no longer an export-based economy, much industrial production having relocated overseas, so there has been little boost from exports. Businesses won't invest and continue to sit on large cash piles. In Japan environmental policy is exhausted. Continued stagnation, or worse, will see more QE under which the Central Bank already holds 30 per cent of public debt. And beyond that lies outright money printing: monetising of government debt.

The main test of the success of the policy response to the financial crisis comes from the USA, which is by far the largest economy in the developed world and is now roughly equal to that of China. The USA is important in itself, but also because of its impact on the rest of the world. It is important, too, because it has been best in the class in policy terms, with a timely fiscal stimulus, expansionary monetary policy, a radical approach to bank debt restructuring and a liberal, business-friendly environment encouraging start-ups and investment. It has so far recovered more quickly and more strongly than other major economies. It contracted less than its peers during the crisis and recovered quicker. Output is up 10 per cent on the pre-crisis peak. Unemployment has fallen below 6 per cent (the post-war average) and is falling. Economic growth has averaged 2.5 per cent per annum over the last three years, and most forecasts are positive – over 3 per cent growth in 2015 forecast by the IMF.

So, the US recovery is, on the surface, impressive – comparable to that of next-door Canada, which avoided the banking crisis. But it has become dependent on extraordinary monetary policies. These produced rock-bottom short-term interest rates (along with low market rates, in the form of bond yields of just over 2 per cent, barely higher than inflation), augmented by money creation through QE. The Federal Reserve's waves of asset purchases, mainly government bonds, have amounted to US$4.4 trillion, which now rest on the Fed's balance sheet.

The problem of achieving an exit from this passage of economic policy is far from trivial. The Federal Reserve has explicitly 'tapered', or phased out, new asset purchases, but even this has caused tremors in international financial markets, particularly in emerging markets which had benefited from the inducement to buy riskier assets provided by QE. The process of selling back the vast stock of assets into the market will be extremely difficult to manage without precipitating a collapse in equities and bonds, the latter potentially raising long-term interest rates, and thereby knocking the recovery on the head.

A more immediate issue has been when to increase short term interest rates in anticipation of the fact that the USA is now at, or close to, full employment and could soon see a return to domestic inflation through stronger wage growth. Market expectations of a rate rise led to a considerable strengthening of the dollar against the yen, the euro and most emerging market currencies (except the Chinese).

In October 2014, the Federal Reserve gave the clearest indication yet that interest rates would soon rise and that the US recovery was now strong enough to absorb the impact. Months passed and nothing changed. The calculation being made was that, on the one hand, while the risk of inflation remained low – core inflation has been firmly under 2 per cent – the risk of continued low interest rates incubating another period of financial instability was real. A miscalculation leading to a serious loss of confidence and a return to recession could have very negative and enduring consequences.

In the event, the Fed took the plunge and increased interest rates by 0.25 per cent in December 2015. The issue now is how fast interest rates will rise in the future. The Fed predicts one per cent increases for three years to 3.25 per cent in 2018 but markets expect slower increases. Further tightening could also come from repurchase of the US$4.5 trillion of assets sitting on the balance sheet of the Federal Reserve, the legacy of QE, or, if recession returns, more QE is possible. Indeed there are profound disagreements among economists as to whether the need is for monetary tightening or the opposite.

In the latter camp Summers and others argue that the USA and the Western world in general, perhaps even the whole global economy, suffers from 'secular stagnation'. The secular stagnation argument is a mixture of short-term pessimism about the difficulty of achieving a sustainable recovery with a large debt overhang, and the risks of triggering fresh financial instability, together with longer-term worries about productivity and labour force growth. The continuation of very low long-term interest rates – close to zero in real terms – is both a consequence of policy (large-scale bond purchases) and a market signal of expected low growth (and low inflation).

The USA has a much more positive story about productivity and demographic trends than either Europe or Japan. But even there, Robert Gordon and others have pointed to slowing productivity as the stimulus from the maturing IT sector diminishes. Although US technological prowess remains dazzling, and the productivity gains from cloud computing devices and smartphone apps are not yet properly captured in the statistics, there is uncomfortable evidence from the National Science Foundation and others that corporate America is investing less in R&D, especially in research. The Congressional Budget Office has estimated that long-term potential growth has slowed from 3 per cent pre-crash to 2 per cent per annum, caused in part by slowing productivity growth but also by demographic trends as baby-boomers retire, immigration is more severely restricted, and fertility rates fall. There is also an alarming decline in labour force participation (unlike the UK). The long-term structural issues and the problems of macroeconomic management are connected because weak growth leads to underinvestment, particularly in skills and innovation, weakening future growth potential.

Summers argues, furthermore, that 'normality', by which he means pre-crash levels of growth, will not return. He points to the lack of any evidence of growth recapturing the lost production from the crisis period, with output remaining stubbornly below the long-term trend. The choking off of credit and the loss of skills, he argues, have depressed potential permanently. In addition, there is a continued weakness in private investment (as also in the UK), which is not only significant for the USA in sapping productivity growth, but bad for the world because the continued glut of savings, even at very low interest rates, cannot be absorbed. Research by Deloitte suggests the largest non-financial companies in the world are sitting on US$3.5 trillion of cash, double the level of 2005. Half of these cash piles are in US companies, with Japan having 13 per cent, and Germany, France and the UK together 18 per cent. In the USA there is a mergers and acquisitions boom taking place utilizing this cash, but investment is stagnating just as it is elsewhere. The optimists' response is to say that there is merely a time lag; the problem will sort itself out. Those who see a deeper problem want more public investment to fill the gap, exploiting low interest rates. I am sure that is the correct response.

The main streams of economic thinking can all draw some encouragement and support from trends in the post-crisis period. The Austrian preoccupation with debt and its impact on financial stability was vindicated by the crisis itself, and by the continued problems of banks, companies, households and governments that suffer from a large, untreated overhang of debt. The reluctance of Japan to engage with the bank debt problem at an earlier stage explains its lingering troubles, and the converse accounts for the relative success of the USA.

The monetarist emphasis on aggressive monetary policy has clearly worked to prevent a slump of inter-war proportions, particularly in the USA, but we have yet to see a successful exit, and the asset bubble problem remains a major threat. Japan has also demonstrated the limits of unconventional monetary policy, and may have to try extreme forms of monetary stimulus, such as printing money.

Conventional Keynesian economics played a marginal but useful role in macroeconomic management after the crisis. The value of public investment and public works may, however, now be coming into its own, not as a necessary stimulus for recovery but to support long-term growth when private investment is weak and capital is cheap. And a synthesis of these approaches may be one of the legacies of the crisis, alongside the emergence of 'macroprudential' policy to deal with asset bubbles.

What is clear is that the negative legacies of the crisis are still very much with us. Japan's imaginative use of expansionary policies appears to be too little too late to escape the trap of low growth and rising debt. Even the USA, the most vibrant and successful Western economy, is showing signs of running out of steam, with slower growth, weakness in investment and innovation, and the 'bubble' effects of a prolonged period of low interest rates.

Moreover, the issue is not merely economic. Low productivity growth has led to stagnating or falling incomes for the 'middle class', and an increase in those in or on the edge of poverty alongside an increase in rewards to the wealthiest. The politics of resentment is feeding off perceived economic failure and inequality. Yet in terms of recovery, the US is well ahead of both Japan and the eurozone (with the UK somewhere in the middle) and it is at a different stage of the cycle of interest rates and monetary policy. I turn now to the eurozone where economic and political problems are more acute and imminent.

4

The Eurozone: Existential Threat

The storm was experienced in its greatest intensity at the end of 2008. But it took almost three years from the first squalls felt in the Newcastle bank, Northern Rock, until the full scale of the damage became apparent in the Greek islands and the resorts of southern Spain. There were, of course, harbingers of disaster to come in early May 2010, when the Greek problem started to manifest itself in a loss of confidence in Greek government debt, and a surge in long-term bond yields.

The main centres of the storm, London and New York, are now enjoying a recovery. But European countries, which regarded the financial crisis as a product of Anglo-Saxon capitalism and therefore only incidental to themselves, are now seen to be the main casualties. Seven years after the onset of the crisis, US GDP had recovered to 9 per cent above pre-crisis levels, but the eurozone as a whole was still below and there has been near stagnation since 2011. Unemployment, which is how the crisis is being experienced in human terms, has, fractionaly, improved from 12 per cent at its peak in 2013 to 10.7 per cent at the end of 2015 but is over double that level in Greece and Spain and 40 per cent or more among young people in Spain and Italy. The inflation target is 2 per cent but inflation has been close to zero for three years and close to outright deflation. Looking forward, the IMF is moderately encouraging and estimates growth of 1.5 per cent in 2015, with 1.7 per cent in 2016, with stronger recovery in Spain and Ireland. This growth is partly attributable to the temporary windfall of cheap oil, and its continuation depends heavily on demand stimulants from the European Central Bank. At the time of writing, the seemingly endless Greek melodrama continues without long-term resolution and the possibility remains of a Greek exit, with unpredictable knock-on effects on confidence in the future of the eurozone.

There is clearly still much social distress and political anger as a result of the economic pain being experienced, mainly in southern Europe. Yet taken as a whole, the eurozone has a current account surplus with the rest of the world. Its overall public debt in relation to GDP is smaller than that of the USA and the UK, let alone Japan. Its problems are almost entirely internal to the eurozone itself, and relate to the management of imbalances within it and to maintaining internal aggregate demand. It is as if the storm, having almost passed continental Europe by, caught in its wake the weaknesses of a half-completed dwelling and seriously damaged it. The dwelling has for the moment been made just about habitable through quick repairs, but the fundamental question is whether to press on and make it secure or to demolish it. The first step in answering the question is to understand the original design.

———————

The eurozone is both an economic and political project. The politics stems from a deep belief in the concept of Europe: closer union, falling short of immersion in a single state (though, for many, that is indeed the end point). The idea of creating a new kind of closely integrated union of states is easily disparaged by sceptics unable to see past the traditional world of nation states, or by nationalists threatened by such a vision. But looking back over the awfulness of twentieth-century European history makes it easy to understand the ambition for integration.

As for the economics, the eurozone can be seen as the next step in the creation of a genuine common market. The single market rests on freedom of trade in goods and services, and free movement of capital and workers. Europe is still a long way from realizing the full potential of the single market, and one of the obstacles has been a combination of risks and costs associated with multiple currencies. Monetary union potentially eliminates those risks and costs, albeit at the expense of removing one mechanism of adjustment to deal with divergences in economic performance within the union (the other mechanisms being adjustment through real wages and productivity levels).

The issue of whether the advantages of a monetary union outweigh the disadvantages is a well-established problem in economics. The concept of an optimum currency area defines the conditions under which a currency union is likely to be beneficial and successful. These include high levels of trade integration, synchronous cycles of economic activity, ease of movement of labour within countries and between them, and strong mechanisms of fiscal support (transfers) to help regions that need to adjust. Critics of the eurozone project point to the extent to which these conditions are unfulfilled; defenders of it argue that necessity will accelerate meeting the conditions. Among the conditions, the most difficult at present is lack of agreement on how, in the absence of automatic transfers, strong economies should support weak ones, such as Greece, and what should be the conditions attached to that support

It was well understood from the outset, when the eurozone was launched in 1999, that different parts of the eurozone would need to adjust to divergences caused by different rates of productivity growth and/or wages, without the use of differential interest rates and variations in nominal exchange rates. In addition, there would be asymmetric shocks not shared across the union, including German reunification, natural resource windfalls and housing bubbles. Federal states like the USA, Canada and Germany have shown that it is possible to use fiscal transfers and overall economic flexibility to manage economic union between greatly different regions. On the other hand, Europe contains bad examples of how, even within unitary states and with big transfer pay-outs, major regional disparities persist – notably between northern and southern Italy. And the eurozone is not a federation, except perhaps in embryo. These arguments, of course, exclude the UK, where eurozone membership has not been a live issue for a decade or more, since Gordon Brown set five tests for UK entry which have never been close to being met. Even some of us who were sympathetic to membership were also mindful of the difficulties of adjustment and argued that there had to be a competitive exchange rate at entry.

The eurozone envisaged three main mechanisms to facilitate adjustment in the absence of flexible exchange rates. The first was to be the influence of differential interest rates in bond markets, as weaker, underperforming sovereign states paid penalty rates on their euro-denominated borrowing. The second was to be fiscal disciplines, for budget deficits and government debt, mandated through the so-called Maastricht targets. The third was micro-economic, 'supply side' reforms envisaged in the Lisbon agreement, designed to make markets work better. These included labour market flexibility, pensions reform to reflect ageing populations, and the removal of barriers to competition. In the event these mechanisms did not work at all well. Why not? And what should happen now?

————

The corrective mechanisms envisaged for the eurozone failed to stop a decade-long process of widening disparities. German labour costs per worker rose by around 12 per cent from 1999 to 2013, while Greek, Spanish, Italian and Portuguese costs rose by 20–30 per cent. Quite small differences in inflation rates – 3 per cent in Ireland, Greece and Portugal, as against 1 per cent in Germany – became cumulatively large over a decade (Figure 4.1). Germany acquired a current account surplus of 6 per cent of GDP, mostly with the rest of the eurozone (now 8.5 per cent of GDP). The current account surplus is a measure of two things: one is an excess of savings over domestic investment, leading to an outflow of capital; the other, a corollary of the first, is a surplus on trade in goods and services, also reflecting cost competitiveness.

The signalling device of long-term interest rates didn't work as theory indicated it should. For the first decade of the eurozone, bond markets failed to signal any discomfort at the divergences opening up. Indeed, periphery countries enjoyed a decade of exceptionally low interest rates. In November 2009 the yield of a Greek ten-year bond was only 2 per cent higher than that enjoyed by the German government, which, given the known fragility of Greek public finances, was remarkable in itself and further encouraged cheap borrowing. The ratio of public debt to GDP had been bobbing around 100 per cent and rose with further borrowing, as also happened in Portugal, albeit at a lower level. In Italy and Spain, imbalances widened further as private sector business was able to obtain cheap eurozone capital. In November 2009, loan costs for business borrowers were no higher in those countries than in Germany. There was a predictable credit boom, feeding especially the Spanish, as well as the Irish, construction sectors. The finance for this low-cost borrowing came from German and Dutch savers, investing via private banks. Those who are wise after the event have deplored the 'feckless' behaviour of private and government borrowers on the EU periphery, but the market adjustment mechanisms also failed to operate and there was little protest from Germany, where a large current account surplus provided a boost to export industries.

Indeed, one of the least productive and most damaging consequences of the eurozone crisis has been the blame game. Lazy, spendthrift, corrupt Greeks; chaotic, irresponsible Italians; hard-working, frugal, honest Germans – or jackbooted oppressors, according to taste. There have been design faults in the eurozone and policy failures in each of the main actors. But national stereotyping allied to moralistic policy prescription is bad history and worse economics. It is possible to believe, as I do, that there is much to learn from Germany about systems of training, local banking, the promotion of innovation and manufacturing excellence, without buying into the idea that there is something clever or even sensible in piling up trade and budget surpluses. Yet Germany has been remarkably successful in portraying its abnormal macroeconomic behaviour as a role model, and its admirers included Conservative colleagues in the coalition for whom Angela Merkel and Wolfgang Schäuble were inspirational figures.

Many of the policy failures now subject to much finger-pointing are not particular to the eurozone. After all, the UK and the USA, as well as Spain and Ireland, allowed a housing bubble to build up on the back of easy credit, and savings imported from Germany and elsewhere. Italy, Ireland and Portugal have public debt exposure (net debt to GDP) that makes them among the worst in class in the eurozone, but their performance is better than the Japanese. The country most damaged by the aftermath of the storm was Latvia, which was not at the time a member of the eurozone. But what assorted imbalances in the eurozone have led to is an existential crisis, a questioning of whether the eurozone is inherently capable of dealing with imbalances and accumulated debt obligations once they reach unsustainable levels. Greece, with the most extreme debt exposure, is potentially testing the system to destruction.

The eurozone crisis, and the concomitant threat to the existence of the monetary union, has essentially evolved in three stages. First, the eurozone was hit by the global banking crisis. In 2009 the eurozone economy contracted by around 6 per cent. The European Central Bank (ECB) followed the USA and the UK in slashing rates – from 4.25 per cent down to 1 per cent. Property bubbles burst in Ireland and Spain. There was recession and rising unemployment in Spain, but at that stage Spain was not judged to be a sovereign or banking risk. Ireland was, however. A measure of its loss of confidence was that spreads over German bonds shot up to around 250 basis points. There was a very deep economic slump which saw Irish GDP fall almost 15 per cent in the year after the crash. The major national banks collapsed with the housing bubble bursting and had to be rescued by the state. Yet with emergency funding from the eurozone and the UK, Ireland was treated as a special case, as a victim of the wider banking crisis and not as a symptom of failure to adjust within the monetary union.

The eurozone crisis began in earnest when markets lost confidence in Greece at the end of 2009. It became clear that what had begun as a global banking crisis had widened into a flight from risk, including the risk of sovereign states defaulting on their debt. At that time Greece had government net borrowing of 15 per cent of GDP on top of inherited public debt well in excess of 100 per cent GDP.

Greece was the weakest link in the euro and as investors pulled out, the spreads on Greek debt over German bonds widened to – at the end of 2011 – an astronomical level of almost 40 per cent, from 2 per cent in November 2009. In the years that have followed the onset of the crisis, Greece has stayed within the euro, with the help of rescue financing from the eurozone's own euro fund (the European Financial Stability Facility) and from the IMF, but it suffered GDP contraction of over 20 per cent. It also signed up to 3,000 reform benchmarks, ranging from radical privatization and overhaul of corrupt tax administration to the dismissal of tens of thousands of government officials and action against monopolies. These reforms were implemented with varying degrees of sincerity and a remarkable turnaround in public finances and trade occurred. But the election of the Syriza government in January 2015 signalled a refusal to continue with the reforms and austerity without substantial changes to ease the pain. It is now clear with hindsight that the original 2010 Greek bail-out of 110 billion euros was badly flawed in that while it was reasonably linked to measures requiring Greek adjustment, it did nothing to address the problem of Greek debt. European taxpayers and the IMF were, in effect, bailing out private creditors, rather than Greece itself. Whatever its other foibles, the

Syriza government was right on this central point and the IMF has now belatedly agreed that debt relief is necessary.

In the wake of the Greek crisis, lack of confidence spread throughout the eurozone periphery, led by Portugal, where the interest spread over German bonds rose to almost 15 per cent at the end of 2011, followed by Italy and Spain, where the differential rose to around 5 per cent. Each country had a different set of issues, but the pattern was broadly similar: foreign investors pulling out of sovereign bonds, led by banks from elsewhere in the eurozone; attempts to restore confidence by budget tightening, with emergency ECB lending; economic contraction caused by austerity policies and the tightening of credit to business as banks lost capital; and lingering fears that the eurozone itself might fracture. When Prime Minister Tsipras capitulated to creditor demands in 2015, splitting his party but securing support for continued Greek eurozone membership calm was restored to markets. But it is an unstable set-up, underpinned by policies that rely on the periphery countries to shoulder the costs of adjustment and that do nothing to sustain demand in the eurozone as a whole. That is almost certainly unwise and may prove unsustainable.

The trigger point of the eurozone crisis was the loss of confidence of overseas, often German, private investors, whose capital flows had financed the periphery over the previous decade. The arrangement had been mutually beneficial, for the periphery had been able to obtain finance at low interest rates for investment or for personal or government spending. Germany was able to recover from the painful period of reunification on the back of an export boom to those countries (and, of course, to the world at large) with the help of a euro exchange rate that was lower and therefore more competitive than would have otherwise been the case. To reiterate a complex story, Germany exported savings and goods to the periphery, providing a return to German savers and jobs in export industries, and the periphery enjoyed the benefit of increased foreign savings to invest and imports to consume. Once investors in the panicky environment of the banking crisis concluded that this cosy arrangement might not be sustainable, a rapid forced adjustment took place.

In an ideal world, the adjustment could, and should, have been balanced with reciprocal obligations. The periphery would have tightened policy to import less and save more domestically, while Germany, along with Holland and other surplus economies, would have tried to rebalance and relax their economies to import more from the periphery and consume more domestically. With monetary policy set centrally and exchange rates fixed, the clear conclusion is that the periphery should have tightened its budgets, while Germany should have done the opposite. In the event, a mixture of dogma and short-term self-interest ensured that the former happened but not the latter. Indeed, Germany's current account surplus grew during the crisis to almost 7 per cent of GDP, at US$290 billion the biggest imbalance in the world economy. And since, as a result of austerity, the periphery countries now also run small surpluses, the matching deficits are in the recovering US and UK, and major emerging markets like Brazil and Turkey.

Austerity in the periphery has occurred through three mechanisms. The sharp increase in long-term interest rates raised the cost of borrowing generally, for business and households as well as governments. Second, governments were required to cut spending and investment, and increase taxation, and private lending flows were replaced by rescue funding from the ECB which attracted conditionality, requiring fiscal tightening. The third mechanism was that recession, induced by the two preceding factors, curbed wage costs and helped to restore loss of competitiveness. Wage costs fell from 2009 to 2014 by 15 per cent and 8 per cent, respectively, in Greece and Portugal, compared with Germany where they rose by around 11 per cent. Italy, in contrast, saw an increase in labour costs. The combined effect of these measures was to contract output. A recent study for the

European Commission estimates the cumulative losses of GDP between 2011 and 2013 as 18 per cent in Greece, 10 per cent in Spain, 9 per cent in France, and 8 per cent in Germany, as the reduction in demand spread across the eurozone.

The combination of higher interest rates on official debt and deflationary, recession-inducing policies led to another damaging consequence: a debt trap. Countries with a large stock of official government debt – 150 per cent of GDP in Greece at the onset of the crisis, and over 100 per cent in Portugal, Italy and Ireland – face the growing problem of servicing the rising costs of that debt. But at the same time, contraction of the economy reduces the resources generated, and specifically government revenue, to service the debt. Thus governments are sucked into a vicious circle of rising debt service, economic contraction and rising debt. The European Commission estimated that the Greek public debt ratio had risen by the end of 2014 to 180 per cent, Portugal's to 135 per cent, Ireland's to 145 per cent, and Italy's to around 140 per cent. (Spain, by contrast, has a debt ratio of around 75 per cent, below the eurozone average, though the shakiness of its banks means that there is still a threat.) These numbers contrast with the 60 per cent figure set in the Maastricht Treaty as representing a safe level. For these countries in particular, if debt servicing appears to the bond markets to be unsustainable, then interest rates will rise, via the mechanism of bond yields, making the debt problem even more unmanageable. Put another way, when debt exceeds 100 per cent of GDP, then there is a need for solid growth to prevent the situation deteriorating even with a balanced budget, because interest payments still need to be met. If interest rates are 3 per cent, then growth needs to be at least 3 per cent.

Another factor is aggravating the sovereign debt problem: deflation. Weak demand has contributed to very low inflation throughout the eurozone. The otherwise welcome fall in oil prices has, in mid-2015, turned inflation negative. It is possible, and is feared, that a deflationary cycle could arise, with consumer expectations of falling prices leading to the postponement of spending and hence of business investment. The absence of inflation also closes off one of the mechanisms by which outstanding sovereign debt has historically been written off. Debt has to be repaid and serviced out of real resources, not eroded by 'funny money'.

One further complication adds to the problems of periphery countries: the instability of their domestic banks. The banks have been weakened by the withdrawal of funding from parent banks and other investors. Recession has added to their bad debts, especially where there has been a major property crash, as in Spain. Other banks are weakened by large holdings of government debt which is no longer seen as secure – 25 per cent of Greek bank assets, 15 per cent in Italy, 12 per cent in Spain. All of these factors add to the deflationary impact of credit contraction. And they raise doubts as to whether banks are stable and, if not, are in need of rescue by already weakened sovereign states or even European-level bail-out funds. The Spanish crisis has centred on this problem because of the scale of bad property debt in some banks, rather than fiscal incontinence, which is the perceived problem in Greece, Portugal and, to a degree, Italy. The collapse of Cypriot banks in 2013 underlined just how fragile some banking systems actually are. Stress tests in the autumn of 2014 suggested that eurozone banks are now stronger. But this is at the expense of dramatically negative implications for small business and business growth, as banks have cut credit.

All of these negative factors continue to bear on the crisis-hit countries on the periphery. But in several cases there are positive signs. Ireland now has one of the strongest growth rates in the Western world, based in large part on exports outside the eurozone. Spain is estimated to have grown by 3 per cent in 2015, though large-scale unemployment at 24 per cent, and especially youth employment at 50 per cent, have helped fuel one of the strongest anti-austerity movements in the form of Podemos. Podemos did very well, coming second in votes in Spanish elections in 2015; but not well enough to oust the centre-right government. Greece, however, remains the main litmus test for austerity polices.

————

Designers of political and economic projects, like architects and aircraft designers, should know that their structures are as strong as their weakest link. The rather absent-minded decision to admit Greece to the eurozone, seemingly based on a sentimental duty to the country that gave birth to democracy, has created a seriously weak link in the chain of economic integration. With hindsight, there are many pundits pointing out what a bad idea it was, though that was less obvious at the time. It is said that the Greeks cheated and massaged the numbers in order to gain admission – but then, someone should have checked! For over five years Greece has dominated the headlines and seemingly epitomized the uncertain future of the eurozone – and this a country accounting for under 2 per cent of eurozone GDP.

The onset of the Greek crisis was described above: the loss of confidence in Greek debt which took long-term market interest rates (ten-year bond yields) to over 10 per cent in 2010, coinciding rather fatefully with Britain's general election and the formation of the coalition government. The crisis reached a climax at the end of 2011 when bond yields reached almost 50 per cent and fear of a Greek exit from the eurozone triggered contagion in financial markets based on the belief that other southern European countries could also be forced to exit.

By mid-2014 the Greek crisis seemed to have gone away. Bond yields had fallen to around 5 per cent and financial contagion no longer affected the rest of southern Europe. Greece had painfully adjusted, to the extent of producing a surplus on its current account, thanks to rising exports of goods and services and dramatically falling imports, as well as a surplus (before interest payments) of 2 per cent of GDP on its budget. It cut the so-called structural deficit by 20 per cent of GDP between 2009 and 2014. No other country either inside or outside the eurozone had achieved fiscal adjustment on that scale. The various conditions attached to the 2010 IMF and ECB emergency loans were being patchily implemented. For example, in terms of international metrics of the ease of doing business, Greece, like Italy, Spain and Portugal, greatly improved between 2010 and 2015. So the Greeks had every reason to believe that they were genuinely doing what was required, but were suffering for it. Moreover, the loans of over 250 billion euros supplied by the eurozone and the IMF had gone overwhelmingly to service Greece's external debt. Only 10 per cent of that sum went to finance Greek government spending. Public debt had reached 175 per cent of GDP, the increase almost entirely composed of obligations arising from the emergency loans.

It is not surprising that Greek democracy rebelled against the pain of austerity which led to mass unemployment, touching almost 30 per cent overall and 50 per cent among the 15- to 24-year-old age group, with a fall of GDP of 25 per cent (Figure 4.2). The new Syriza-led government demanded relaxation of the conditions attached to its bail-out package and less austerity, and threatened to default on its loan obligation if it did not receive further help and relaxed conditionality. The creditors' conditions required further contraction, of around 1 per cent of GDP, which Greece was resisting. The ECB in turn threatened to withhold undisbursed bail-out funds of 7.2 billion euros, needed by the end of June 2015, and 30–50 billion euros in July and August, which would make it impossible for Greece to meet its domestic and foreign obligations. Months of negotiation led nowhere. In July, Greece effectively defaulted on its debt payouts to the IMF and the ECB (in the IMF's case, following a handful of precedents, mainly rogue African states). The ECB responded by cutting its line of liquidity to Greek banks, which were forced to close their doors to limit a run on deposits. An irresistible force confronted an immovable object. But after a show of defiance and obtaining the support of a referendum opposing the creditors' terms, the Syriza government capitulated in order to secure a new bail-out package in return for more 'reform'.

This latest crisis appears to have been contained, for better or worse – but kicking the can down the road has been an unsuccessful strategy for dealing with Greece, and the problems will very likely return. Five years of agonizing about Greece has led to several conclusions. First, a Greek exit from the eurozone, followed by the reintroduction of a national currency and devaluation, would be a bad option for Europe because it would reopen the issue of whether the eurozone is an irrevocable currency union. Beneath the bravado of those publicly contemplating a Greek exit, there is a deep anxiety about southern European contagion and about the destination of a Greece plunging into the unknown, and, from Americans and others outside the eurozone, the fear that Greece could help create a 'Lehman's moment' as a result of other potential weaknesses in the financial system. Others, however, argue that this risk could be managed and that, paradoxically, a Greek exit might actually strengthen the political unity and policy disciplines of the eurozone, if one limb were amputated *pour encourager les autres*. The hard-line position of Germany is shared by some governments on the periphery that would have difficulty explaining to their electorates why they are allowing more leniency to Greece than to their own countries.

Secondly, a Greek exit would be very bad for Greece, which is why the Syriza government has made it plain that it does not want to leave. The transition to a new currency would be bound to inflict a further round of hardship. A devalued currency would squeeze living standards, though in time it would boost tourism. Banks might well collapse in the panic. Debt obligations, in foreign currency, would remain – unless Greece were to default, which would stop access to new credit except at considerable cost. In the absence of a 'sugar daddy', the country's future would be bleak. (Russia, the country most likely to fulfil such a role, has serious financial problems of its own.) The July crisis did, however, crystallize a possible exit strategy, whereby Greece would default on its official debt (160 billion euros owed to EU governments alone, besides the debt to the IMF) but would seek in time to restore its capacity for market borrowing by servicing private debt. In the event the option was not pursued.

Thirdly, debt default is not the same as a Greek exit. Greece cannot pay its debts but it does want to stay in the eurozone. Many countries before have been unable to service their sovereign debts and have either defaulted or been granted relief. Post-war Germany and the UK both benefited from debt relief by the USA. Some governments, seen as important to Western interests, were given very generous debt relief, as in the case of Indonesia after Sukarno. A system of debt relief, ranging from rescheduling of principal repayments to write-offs to concessional interest rates, was institutionalized for official creditors (the Paris Club) and commercial creditors (the London Club). These negotiations played an important part of resolving the Latin American debt crisis, in reviving African economies, and in helping some economies in Eastern Europe. Poland, for example, was able to prepare itself for entry to the EU after enjoying a programme of debt relief. Within federal states, debt default by state governments, like Louisiana and Mississippi, was a feature of nineteenth-century US economic history, and more recently US cities such as Detroit have been in effect bankrupt. Bankruptcy, including the wiping out of debt, is common in the corporate sector and is often seen by entrepreneurs as a rite of passage. There has already been an acceptance that Greece cannot service its commercial creditors in full, leading to the so-called 'haircut'. The reason why the option of further debt relief is not politically easy is partly the reluctance of creditors (EU member states, Germany in particular, acting on behalf of both their banks and their taxpayers, and the IMF), but also the resistance of other debtors in the eurozone who fear that their own creditworthiness would be called into question.

It is possible that Greece could default on its debt obligations but continue to use the euro buttressed by capital controls, as occurred in Cyprus, along with a form of parallel currency – but this is uncharted territory. Moreover, the creditor countries in the eurozone have sought to disabuse Greece of the idea that continued membership could be an option – though there would be nothing to stop Greece continuing to use the euro, as some European non-members, such as Montenegro, already do.

It is clear that in a rational world, in which there was trust between partners, the Greek problem could be solved by a combination of less austerity, debt relief and genuine Greek government commitment to long-term structural reform, making Greece a modern economy. Large scale, ECB support for Greek banks to stop capital flight is also needed to permit the lifting of capital controls. But the rationality and trust needed have all but disappeared.

———————

As the eurozone crisis moves into its seventh year, the differences in outlook and policy between Germany and the surplus countries on the one hand, and the periphery countries on the other, remain very substantial. On the basic macroeconomics, Germany does not accept that it should stimulate demand in its own economy in order to help the periphery export its way out of trouble. Moreover, Germany insists not only that it will not be bullied into fiscal indiscipline, but that all eurozone members should observe the requirement to keep their budgets balanced, or in surplus, by law and subject to sanctions (the so-called 'stability and growth union' arising from the December 2011 summit). The effect of this fiscal conservatism has been that cyclically adjusted deficits in the eurozone as a whole have shrunk to less than 1 per cent, though there is a question mark over how much of this is cyclical and how much structural. Since Germany itself continues to maintain budget balance – indeeed, the law requires it – other member states have had to carry out drastic deficit reduction.

Also, Germany has been acting behind the scenes to restrain the ECB president from extending his attempts at greater monetary expansion along the lines of QE in the USA and the UK. There is little scope for further interest rate cuts since the main intervention rate and the deposit rate for commercial banks at the ECB have reached their lower bounds, at 0.15 per cent and -0.1 per cent, respectively. The ECB has also attempted a form of monetary easing, known as Outright Monetary Transactions, essentially offering lender of last resort facilities to investors worried about countries leaving the eurozone. It has embarked upon asset purchase schemes and this has helped to prevent an ever deeper depression. The mere announcement by Mario Draghi of the ECB of monetary loosening in July 2012 – doing 'whatever it takes' – had the effect of driving down bond yields in periphery economies like Spain and Italy from high-risk levels to around 2 per cent, lower than the UK, where they stayed.

From June 2014, Mr Draghi announced further expansionary steps, cutting deposit rates to below zero along with a programme of buying assets, mainly government securities. But Germany has been a serious restraining influence, even in the face of risk of genuine deflation. Germany has its own historical experience of the opposite problem of hyperinflation, but this is a case of generals fighting the last war – in this case, an economic war eighty years ago. Some credit should be given to the Germans for allowing Draghi to launch a fresh round of anti-deflationary QE in January 2015, with 1.1 trillion more euros of bond buying. But the total QE, around 3 trillion euros, is modest (the UK's QE programme is several times greater relative to the stock of government debt). Moreover, the responsibility for losses from the bond purchases is not mutualized but falls to national central banks. And it is not obvious how QE will stimulate Europe much more since bond yields are already very low and bank lending impared. The real stimulus has been the psychological boost provided by the commitment to keep buying bonds until there is no further risk of deflation. More radical – and necessary – options like 'helicopter' money or money printing to support public investment are taboo.

A second source of resistance from Germany has been an unwillingness to accept a write-off, or substantial reduction, of sovereign debt, though some Greek private debt to German banks has been subject to a 'haircut'. Debt relief is seen as rewarding fecklessness – one of several ways in which moralistic judgement has replaced practical economic sense. Yet, historically, debt relief or default has usually led to faster growth and better credit worthiness.

Thirdly, Germany will not countenance additional financial mechanisms beyond the 5 per cent of eurozone GDP committed to the European Stability Mechanism, operating via the ECB. The issue of eurobonds by the ECB is the obvious way in which a federal body could mobilize capital from the markets to help finance the budgets of member governments, or specific projects, but the Germans have repudiated the idea of sharing the liability involved. There is also the 1 per cent of GDP committed to the European Commission budget, but this is not specific to the eurozone and the UK has strenuously opposed its enlargement. By contrast, the US federal government – not conspicuously lavish by international standards – offsets around 15 per cent of economic fluctuations of individual states and Canada over 25 per cent. Before the eurozone was launched, the MacDougall Report envisaged a 20 per cent offset mechanism, far in excess of current levels. Again, German concerns over fiscal frugality loom large. More encouragingly research has shown that if there are also integrated private capital and savings markets, 80 per cent of consumption losses can be offset in the US, Canada and within Germany as against 40 per cent in the eurozone, and there is general support for integrated capital markets.

Fourthly, it is proving very difficult, in the context of discussions on banking union, to cut the link between weak sovereign states and their weak banks, in order to prevent doubts about the solvency of one affecting the other. Governments continue to back-stop their banks. Progress on a banking union is blocked by German consensus over common deposit insurance. Again, Germany fears that it will be landed, through joint liability, with financial responsibility for bailing out other countries' banks.

On each of these issues the German position is emotionally and politically understandable. They fear that were Germany simply to accommodate the deficits of the periphery through expansionary policies, there would be no leverage to achieve structural reforms. The German view of successful economic and monetary union is one in which all members follow strict fiscal disciplines and monetary policy is firmly anti-inflationary, with members adjusting through 'competitiveness' measures alone: improved productivity and wage restraint.

Unfortunately evidence from the IMF suggests that such structural reforms in the eurozone have little impact on productivity and growth and labour market reforms are productivity reducing. There are some other legitimate German concerns: that their own capacity to absorb direct financial obligations and contingent liabilities is limited, and that too much commitment to sovereign or banking bail-outs in the eurozone could impair their own credit standing. The consequence of a decade of lending to peripheral Europe via the banking system has left Germany's own banks badly exposed to overseas bad debts. Wolfgang Münchau believes the German banking system may already be insolvent if transparent accounting were to be applied.

That excuses some of the lack of ambition and a wish to play for time to recapitalize banks. But the German approach to monetary and fiscal policy in the current context is damaging and counterproductive, making eurozone adjustment even harder and debts even more difficult to service. It is also – and this may prove crucial – contributing to stagnation in Germany itself. Since Germany accounts for 27 per cent of European GDP, German stagnation or recession would create a negative feedback loop into the rest of the eurozone. And the German obsession with obtaining growth only through trade has led to an extraordinary, extreme, current account surplus of 8.56 per cent of GDP in 2015.

A consequence of the German policy position is that periphery country governments are expecting to preside over a long period of debt deflation, low or even negative growth and living standards – that is to say, austerity. Yet the fear of the eurozone breaking up has prompted Germany in particular to concede just enough to enable the periphery countries to continue to service debt, providing a welcome respite but nothing more. What is lacking is a strategy for escaping stagnation through bigger support mechanisms and macroeconomic stimulus, which would allow the periphery countries to expand and adjust while managing their weak banks and fiscal legacy issues. The 300 billion-euro Juncker investment programme of 2015 for infrastructure projects was an attempt to provide a stimulus through public investment, but the reluctance of the UK and Germany, among others, to allow 'new money' means that in practice there is no meaningful stimulus.

———

There is a German saying: 'better an end with a shock than a shock without end'. That, in crude terms, is the way the debate has become polarized. It is presented as a choice between a eurozone break-up, with all the associated costs and uncertainties, and endless economic agony. But this is very much a counsel of despair and the major intellectual and political challenge for European decision-makers is to find a way between the two extremes. It is necessary to review these extremes before considering other constructive possibilities.

I have implicitly made the case already that continuing endless agony in the periphery is not a durable option. The electorates of southern Europe have so far been remarkably stoical, especially given that just over a generation ago there was prolonged authoritarian rule in Greece, Portugal and Spain (and, of course, in Eastern Europe, under a different ideology). Continued democratic forbearance requires that there should be light at the end of the tunnel, that responsibility will have its reward. The Greek revolt under the Syriza government, and the consequent referendum, was essentially a demand that the reward, in the form of growth, should come sooner be and more tangible.

It is becoming increasingly difficult to see how, under current policies, that hope can be sustained. The disappearance of private capital inflows and limited ECB flows means that periphery countries are forced to run current account surpluses to service debt to the rest of the eurozone. To achieve this, in the absence of any demand pull from Germany and other surplus countries drawing in imports from weaker economies, requires that those countries' industries have to become more competitive. That can only happen if wage costs fall relative to Germany. But since Germany enjoys minimal inflation, that means that wages have to fall substantially elsewhere. That will only happen under conditions of deflation and mass unemployment. But deflation in turn adds to the real cost of debt, thus creating a downward spiral.

Europe has been here before with the so-called 'Transfer Problem', under which Germany was required to service onerous reparations after the First World War without the ability to export its way to a trade surplus. Keynes regarded the Transfer Problem as one of the underlying causes of subsequent German hyperinflation and political extremism. There have been modern variants of the Transfer Problem in the big surpluses of OPEC countries and in the wake of the Latin American debt crisis of 1981/2, but these were managed by a combination of large new financial flows from surplus countries, substantial export growth by deficit countries, and debt relief, none of which are currently on offer in the eurozone. That is why the option of exit has at least superficial attractions.

———

It is perhaps surprising that, until the re-emergence of the Greek crisis, there had not been more consideration of an exit, given the extremely challenging circumstances in which southern European countries and, from the opposite standpoint, Germany, found themselves. After all, the Lisbon Treaty does provide for departure, mainly to reassure the UK that the euro was, *in extremis*, reversible. Before the crisis fully hit Greece in December 2009, a Greek academic and lawyer, Phoebus Athanassiou, had already reviewed the possibilities, in the process identifying severe legal problems ranging from the creation of a new currency and repatriating reserves from the ECB. Two years earlier, Barry Eichengreen had reviewed the economics of break-up and highlighted the negatives. The one tangible advantage – freedom to devalue – could be quickly eroded in real terms by inflation in the new currency. Euro-denominated debt would remain, unless there were a formal default, and would become more onerous to service in the local currency, and there would be extensive litigation over individual contracts with foreign creditors. The extensive planning that went into creating the euro – reprogramming of computers, modification of vending and payment machines, printing and distributing of new notes – would have to be reversed, probably in disorderly conditions.

Those are merely the technical problems, which would be small compared with the bigger risk of contagion to other vulnerable economies leading to a disorderly break-up, and of a speculative panic exposing other vulnerabilities in the global financial system. For these reasons, exiting is a deeply unattractive option. What has, however, changed as a result of the Greek crisis is a greater willingness by some of the stronger economies, notably Germany, to use the threat of a Greek exit as a way of binding the remaining members into a tighter set of disciplines.

Anglo-Saxon critics of the eurozone have repeatedly underestimated the degree of commitment to it, the willingness of periphery countries to accept painful austerity and of the seemingly inflexible Germans to make compromises. More thoughtful Germans understand that a break-up of the eurozone would leave Germany with a much stronger currency inimical to exporting, temporarily devastated export markets, and banks badly damaged by large-scale defaults, as well as the write-off of large amounts of loans to other governments.

An increasingly compelling response is to say that the inevitable way forward is full political union so that the eurozone becomes effectively like the USA or Canada, with a large-scale federal funding mechanism (in the form of eurobonds) or large transfer payments (as occurred between West and East Germany at reunification) and a banking union, severing the link between banking risk and sovereign risk. But although there are Euro-federalists within the European Commission and the European Parliament who are urging such a model, there are few takers in national capitals. It may be, however, that a continuing crisis forces member states down this road. Foreign policy challenges, as with Russia and the Middle East, make an increasingly compelling case for a strong and unified EU.

In the absence of an immediate move in that direction, it is nonetheless possible to see how more flexible and cooperative arrangements could be made to work. Martin Wolf argues that if the radical option of close union is politically infeasible, progress could be made to establish a combination of an 'adjustment union' – genuinely symmetrical commitments between deficit and surplus countries – and an 'insurance union', with collective insurance against shocks affecting particular countries or groups of countries – a larger version of existing bail-out funds, run on insurance lines.

However sensible they may be, neither of these approaches is being pursued. It is difficult to imagine the German government embracing public sector deficit financing – although it could and should. It is, however, possible to see how the ECB could expand its current tentative foray into monetary expansion along US/UK/ Japanese lines. Currently, nominal GDP growth is close to zero and this could be expanded in order to give more time for dealing with the structural imbalances and debt burden. This would not be straightforward, since the ECB is legally constrained. But a stronger programme of QE, perhaps targeted at non-government assets in the periphery (helping, for example, to extend credit to businesses), is essential until the eurozone pulls out of the slump. And while it is always tempting to take refuge in technical fixes, there is no escaping the necessity for closer political integration to make them work.

It would also be necessary to have a greater degree of coop-eration to restructure failing banks. Whatever the German government currently says, a degree of federalizing and forbear-ance of member states' debts may well be necessary, as has already partly happened for Greece. With the president of the ECB now pressing for, and partially securing, more expansionary monetary policies, there is at least some scope for a consideration of growth-enhancing initiatives. Some of these involve the 'outs', like the UK, as well as the 'ins'.

Britain is not a member of the eurozone and has no prospect of joining in the near future. It has therefore not been a party to the policy debates within the eurozone. My Conservative colleagues in the coalition were, from my observation, somewhat ambiva-lent in their reactions to the crisis. Some revelled in *Schadenfreude*, barely concealing their glee that their predictions of doom and disaster appeared to have been vindicated. More typically, there was genuine fear that the UK would be dragged down by deep recession in major export markets. Forty per cent of UK exports go to the eurozone. There is also the risk of further damage to UK banks with big exposure to the eurozone, in terms of both balance sheets and funding costs (a quarter of UK international bank claims are in the eurozone). When the eurozone problems were at their most acute, in 2012 and again in 2015, Whitehall hummed with committees carrying out scenario planning and disaster preparation should the worst happen, requiring emer-gency help for British tourists stranded in Greece or lines of credit for exporters. Whatever the triumphalist instincts of my former Tory colleagues, it is fair to say that the Chancellor, in particular, recognized that while it was necessary to plan for disaster, it was in Britain's interests that the eurozone should succeed. We recog-nized that British carping from the sidelines would be unhelpful and unwelcome, and that we had a limited role beyond wishing to safeguard the single market and providing targeted help to Ireland because of our close economic ties.

Fifteen years ago it was possible that the UK could have been a member of the eurozone. Some of us argued that, on balance, it would be economically beneficial, subject to entering at the right exchange rate (substantially lower than was prevailing at that time) and to political endorsement in a referendum. The Labour government kept open the possibility of entry, subject to conditions, and extensive euro preparations were undertaken. I was part of the cross-party team assembled by Gordon Brown to oversee these. But in the event, the conditions were never right.

With hindsight, it is tempting to say, as is the conventional view, that Britain had a narrow escape from disaster. But actually it is not possible to judge whether membership would have been a success or not. It is possible that, as with Germany, holding down the exchange rate would have allowed for a more export-based, balanced form of growth than we actually experienced. Or it could have been that the property bubble and the surge of reckless banking would have occurred unchecked, as it did in Ireland and Spain. In the event, Britain experienced a bigger, deeper shock than most of the eurozone, but with the help of monetary flexibility, including a floating exchange rate, it now enjoys the prospect of an earlier exit from crisis conditions. Counterfactual history does not give clear-cut answers.

Looking forward, there is understandably little appetite for reviewing the issue of British membership at a time when the eurozone is in a state of upheaval and may conceivably not survive. I would not want to revive the issue of membership, but equally it would be foolish to use the word 'never'. There are a couple of reasons why a closer alignment with the eurozone, and possibly even membership, may return to the agenda in years to come. One is that the eurozone might succeed in overcoming its present difficulties, while the UK remains trapped in a dreary boom–bust cycle and remains seriously structurally imbalanced.

The grass may come to seem greener on the other side of the continental fence, as it did back in the 1970s.

A more plausible factor is that issues around reform of the single market, where the UK has a clear agenda for further liberalization and deregulation, may shift to the eurozone, which would become a *de facto* and possibly even *de jure* single market. At present, the UK is one of ten 'outs' as against eighteen 'ins' and is able to give strong leadership to like-minded countries. But since most of the 'outs' will become 'ins' if the eurozone stabilizes and succeeds, the UK would then be seriously isolated and less able to influence the direction of the single market. The idea that Britain can permanently inhabit a comfortable halfway house, seeking to preserve and reform the single market, particularly in areas like banking, while remaining outside the decision-making of the eurozone, are illusiory.

The foundations of the halfway house are, moreover, already cracking. The UKIP tendency in the Conservative party, and among the public, is creating a demand for concessions which the twenty-seven other member countries may be unable or unwilling to accept. At the end of 2015 negotiations for British reforms to the EU as a prelude to referendum looked as if they would produce some helpful, but non-binding, declaratory language protecting the 'outs' and some restrictions on benefits for EU migrants (but not on EU migration). It is unlikely that concessions, when finally secured, will match the demands of critics. Nor is there any guarantee that the promised referendum can be timed to avoid another convulsion in the eurozone or, for that matter, some unforeseen issue in the UK itself. That is all part of the uncertainty that will weigh on voters and investors over the next year or two. It is a reasonable working assumption that a cross-party and cross-industry consensus in favour of continued membership will prevail, but as we have seen in Scotland, referendums generate their own emotional and political dynamic. Losers prove reluctant to accept a close result and dissatisfactions re-emerge in a new form.

One way of resolving the dilemma is for Britain simply to leave the European Union and seek some looser association, as yet ill-defined. That is a possible outcome of the referendum, and this is not the place to rehearse all the arguments for and against. Suffice it to say that in international relations as in domestic life, divorce is rarely clean and amicable. Britain would remain vulnerable to upheavals on the continent. A generation spent integrating British laws and institutions and adapting businesses to a European future would have been wasted and another generation would be needed to redefine those roles. For a country not at ease with itself and facing possible internal break-up, that is not a very cheery prospect.

But I wish to focus on the problems now in front of us, rather than those over the horizon. The more immediate question is how the eurozone countries find their way out of a downward spiral of negative growth, deflation and growing debt burdens, through more expansionary demand management and greater solidarity between the core and the peripheral states. It is tempting for the UK to say that this is purely a eurozone problem. But it isn't. The UK has much to lose if the current tentative recovery is knocked on the head – as it was in 2011 – by weakness in the eurozone.

There was an explicit recognition of mutual self-interest when the UK agreed to co-finance the support package for Ireland and participation in the Greek rescue by the IMF. What would be both self-interested and enlightened would be for the UK to use its influence, such as it is, with the German government to press for measures of solidarity and stimulus within the eurozone, alongside the structural reforms – deepening the single market, opening up to freer trade, deregulation – that Britain has long urged. In other words, to get off the sidelines. While the British Conservatives and the German government have the same fiscal instincts, they differ radically on monetary policy. The UK is in a good position to champion any expansion of Mario Draghi's stimulus package, underlining our wider interest in ensuring that the eurozone succeeds rather than fragments and fails.

There is also a common interest in a more effective and unified foreign policy response in relation to Russia and the Middle East, as the USA disengages from Europe. The large scale migration of refugees from Syria to Germany and Sweden in particular, and Chancellor Merkel's forthright and courageous commitment to accommodate them has brought foreign policy – and migration – to the centre of the stage. It has even put weak economic growth, the eurozone and Greek exit into the background for the moment. The short term consequences have largely been negative for hopes of a cooperative approach to the succession of problems facing the Economic Union. Chancellor Merkel's position is politically weaker with even less room for manoeuver on economic policy. Bitter divisions have opened up with more nationalistic governments of Eastern Europe over freedom of movement. Many governments are looking over their shoulders at populist opposition exploiting discontent over economic stagnation, unemployment, immigrants and, increasingly, the European project itself.

The issue of British membership has come at an unwelcome time, alongside other headaches. A choice between disorderly disintegration and closer integration may not be welcome for those who are toying with the idea of British exit from the EU, or for those who believe that the current semi-detached arrangements can be sustained indefinitely. But unless the 'ins' and 'outs' of the eurozone collaborate and hang together, they will surely hang separately.

5

China and the New Economic Centre of Gravity

One of the main themes of *The Storm* was that the emerging economies, notably China, were increasingly driving the world economy. Because of their growth in per capita incomes, global poverty has tumbled. The share of the developing world's population living on less than the internationally defined level of poverty fell from 30 per cent in 2000 to under 10 per cent in 2014. Chinese surplus savings also helped to fuel the expansion of Western economies prior to the crisis. Furthermore, the rapid growth of those countries sucked in raw materials and now is a key determinant of world prices of fuel and food. After a couple of decades in which the developed economies grew by roughly 2 per cent per annum and the emerging markets by 6 per cent, a point has been reached where the collective GDP (on a purchasing power parity basis) of the emerging economies has overtaken that of the developed economies for the first time since Britain started to industrialize over two hundred years ago. Issues of economic measurement are important here. On traditional measures of GDP, at current exchange rates, the emerging economies are less significant. And developed economies, like ours, remain major players. Roger Bootle, for example, recently predicted that the UK could become the fourth biggest economy in the world, whereas on a purchasing power parity basis it will almost certainly be somewhere in the teens.

———

Beyond the day-to-day problems of government and differences of policy within the coalition, there was a shared understanding that we needed to help shape the British economy to respond to this new world. I had many disagreements with David Cameron and George Osborne, but I cannot fault their clarity of thinking and commitment when it came to promoting trade and investment opportunities, and political dialogue, with China, India and other emerging economies, either unilaterally or as part of the European Union.

Within a few weeks of the government being formed, David Cameron had organized a visit and trade mission to India, designed to develop a 'strategic partnership'. I was encouraged to build on the momentum through regular visits with trade missions and strengthening long-term relationships with leading Indian companies like Tata – with, I think, some success. The process of engagement was smoothly transferred to the new Indian government under Narendra Modi. There was a similar commitment to China under President Hu Jintao and Prime Minister Wen Jiabao, and their successors, President Xi Jinping and Prime Minister Li Keqiang. An important part of my job was to encourage Chinese investors and to establish good relations with government and party officials at provincial as well as national level.

The welcoming and self-confident approach of our government, even to the extent of promoting Chinese investment in sensitive areas like nuclear power and telecommunications, was, I believe, entirely correct, but it raised eyebrows in more suspicious circles in Washington and the European Commission. George Osborne in particular championed closer financial and business relations with China and took the initiative to support the new Chinese-led Asian Infrastructure Investment Bank, much to the annoyance of the US government which was bent on containing Chinese influence.

While China and India were the main focus of attention, I visited Turkey, Brazil, Nigeria, South Africa, Korea, Japan, Indonesia, Vietnam and Singapore as targets of UK PLC, usually with delegates of British companies of all sizes in tow. This was just part of a wider ministerial effort. It is perhaps not sufficiently understood outside of government how much time and effort is deployed in this way, not just by trade and foreign affairs ministers, in activities that produce little short-term domestic political gain.

Several questions are prompted by this effort. Is it really necessary? Does it work? There is a free-market viewpoint that derides trade and investment promotion as the product of a mercantilist mindset. It would leave business to discover through market signals where best to sell and to operate. The counter-view, which is now firmly embedded in government – and is, I think, correct – is that there are serious market failures facing especially SMEs trying to trade or develop business collaborations overseas. These include lack of information and understanding of rules, lack of trust, lack of access to networks, and exposure to politically capricious procurement decisions. It is the job of our government to help overcome these through UK Trade and Investment (UKTI) and local embassies, competitive export credit guarantee products, which I improved in 2011, and ministerial engagement with overseas governments. Suffice it to say, this is also the model employed by other major developed countries. One of the frankly embarrassing aspects of UK trade promotion is discovering that British exporters lag way behind Germany, and also France and Italy, in market penetration in countries like India with which the UK has historic ties, let alone Brazil or China. British inward and outward investment is much more successful.

Building ties with emerging markets presents problems, however, that are distinct from business in the US or the eurozone. There are often sharp differences in business culture. State capitalism is the best way of describing the standard model in China, India, Brazil, Russia, Indonesia and elsewhere, though in each case there are many entrepreneurial private sector enterprises operating fully independently of the state, especially in India and Brazil. State capitalism has considerable strengths in providing long-term certainty and stability around strategy and ownership, but it is often associated with cronyism, corruption and bureaucratic inefficiency. The experiences of GSK in China, of Western oil companies in Russia, of contractors dealing with Petrobras and anything to do with military contracts – all, as I saw at first hand, involve a messy mixture of business and politics.

Then there are conflicts of objectives. Although coalition ministers generally worked well in this aspect of government, some had a different agenda. While the rest of government was promoting two-way business and academic visits and the export industry of overseas students, the Home Office saw China and India primarily in terms of hundreds of millions of potential illegal immigrants and asylum-seekers. The issue was how to keep them all out. Relations with India were constantly undermined by hostile immigration rhetoric from Home Office ministers and tighter visa restrictions on students coming to study in the UK. My department was able to fight off the more draconian proposals of the Home Office, but damage was done relative to the more accommodating rules of the USA, Canada and Australia. Relations with China were constantly bedevilled by difficulties in obtaining UK visas, stories that businessmen intending to do business in the UK were being turned back at Heathrow, and constant unfavourable comparisons with the more visitor-friendly regimes of France and Germany. George Osborne was generally an ally in these scraps, but neither he nor David Cameron was ever willing to face down the Home Secretary. I developed a grudging respect for her obdurate defence of her ministerial silo, even though I could see that serious damage was being done to the wider economic objectives of government.

Government split along different lines on other issues. Having spent several years quite successfully promoting trade with Russia, our most rapidly growing export market amongst the emerging economies, and developing good relations with the top Kremlin economic technocrats, I questioned the wisdom of colleagues who thought that Britain should take the lead in punishing Russia through economic sanctions, rather than move at the more cautious pace of the Germans, French and Italians. I found myself in a similar role in relation to Iran, where Britain has been almost uniquely fastidious in observing the letter as well as the spirit of sanctions. I lined up against more liberal colleagues in believing that it was counterproductive publicly to lecture the Chinese about human rights and the Dalai Lama. My experience had been that the top Chinese were responsive to challenging conversations in private, but would react badly to what they perceived as public insults.

On one level, I was playing my departmental role. But I was also reflecting a personal view that if the UK is to have a successful economic and commercial role in relation to the main emerging powers, it has to be single-minded and long-term in building relationships. It has to operate within alliances, especially the EU, rather than unilaterally, and it has to maximize the advantages of being open to trade and investment and prevent cack-handed policies from undermining them. In the world that is emerging, the UK is, along with France and Italy, an economic power of middle rank and will in due course be overtaken in economic importance by the likes of Indonesia, Mexico and Nigeria. The days of relationships conducted *de haut en bas* have gone. Nonetheless, it is important to respond to sceptics who question whether the world will continue to evolve in this way.

———

It is now possible to envisage two radically different scenarios. The first is that the trends of the last two decades continue and strengthen as the remarkable advance of China and, to a lesser extent, India are emulated on a sustained basis in Africa – currently the most rapidly growing continent – and elsewhere. In this world, developed countries continue to limp along, weighed down by the legacy of the financial crisis – damaged banks, deleveraging and debt – and then by the growing burdens of supporting an ageing population.

Reflecting this trend, between 2007 and 2014 the Chinese economy expanded by 75 per cent, emerging Asia as a whole grew by 65 per cent, and developed countries by only 6 per cent. The last two years have seen a less extreme divergence, but the IMF's forecasts for the next few years envisage a return to the trend of recent history, with developed countries growing at just over 2 per cent and the emerging economies at around 6 per cent. The IMF predicts that emerging markets (an increasingly odd term in this context) will account for 60 per cent of world output of goods and services by 2020. They will have already contributed three quarters of world growth from 2012 to 2017, as opposed to one third in the period 1982 to 1987. The gap in living standards remains large – a factor of five, on average – but is narrowing fast.

This was the world I described in *The Storm*. Indeed, it was the essence of the New Frontiers scenario I developed with my colleagues in Shell in the early 1990s. And it no longer appears surprising but rather an extrapolation of the past, sustained by powerful momentum derived from technological diffusion and the widespread adoption of growth-supporting policies. One powerful factor in this convergence is that of purchasing power, as well as 'real' growth achieved through productivity growth. Prices and exchange rates tend to rise more quickly in emerging economies where, initially, the prices of goods and services are often very cheap compared with developed economies. This process of price equalization, through appreciating real exchange rates, has the effect of increasing the purchasing power, and the economic size, of poor economies, thus creating convergence.

Yet there is a counter-view, based partly on healthy scepticism about extrapolating long-term trends, partly on a belief that the law of diminishing returns may be eroding the potential for emerging market growth, and partly on worries about the sustainability of continued rapid growth in China with knock-on effects on commodity exporters. This scepticism has been reinforced by some recent developments.

There has been a dramatic reduction in recent growth in some of the main emerging markets: China from an extraordinary (official) 14 per cent in 2007 to around 7 per cent and slowing in the period 2013–5; Brazil from 6 per cent to minus 3.5 per cent in 2015 – the worst recession since the 1930s. As a whole, Latin America has seen a serious slowdown from 5 per cent per annum growth in the 2003–10 period to a decline, of 0.3 per cent, in 2015. Russia has also seen serious contraction. Data from the World Bank's International Comparison Programme does indeed suggest that convergence in per capita terms has fallen from a differential in per capita growth between developed and emerging markets of 4.5 per cent in 2000–09 to under 2 per cent in the 2013–15 period (around 1 per cent if China is excluded). The overall slowdown, observable over a period of around five years, has been used to construct a long-term argument that the process of catch-up is running out of steam.

There are some short-term factors at work. The global financial crisis did not leave the emerging markets unscathed, though they rode it remarkably strongly. Many emerging economies, including Brazil, Russia and Malaysia, benefited initially from the boom in commodity prices now being reversed especially for metals and oil. Some countries, notably China, Malaysia, Turkey, Thailand, Taiwan and Korea, saw a massive expansion in credit, which is proving difficult to curtail while maintaining growth.

Some countries, such as China, Russia, Korea and Taiwan, have seen large-scale capital outflows in 2014 and 2015 prompted by a strengthening dollar, which may also be a symptom of growing problems in their economies. Emerging market companies have acquired $9 trillion in dollar borrowing with private debt of GDP rising to over 100 per cent from 70 per cent pre-2008. US money tightening is leading to reverse flows and potentially a credit crunch and corporate defaults.

But the bigger argument is that we may have reached an 'inflection point', with a process of deceleration taking place. Several factors are said to be involved. The adoption of new technology, including the spread of mobile telephony and apps, the use of superfast computers, and the uptake of new generations of hybrid or GM seeds in farming, could decline over time as the easiest applications are exhausted. The penetration of most of the innovations of the IT revolution is however still low and the catch-up potential is enormous.

A second factor is demographic. The apparently inexhaustible supply of young, cheap labour from the countryside dries up as urbanization proceeds and the population ages. Growth becomes less dependent on the quantity of labour and more dependent on skills and mechanisms for allocating investment efficiently. Demographic factors are already a constraint on Chinese growth, as the one-child policy works through into a reduced labour supply. China seems to have reached a turning point – recognized in development economics through the work of the Nobel laureate Arthur Lewis – where the supply of surplus labour will dry up. But this is much less of a concern in the Indian subcontinent and in Africa.

The effect of these two factors is sometimes described as the 'middle-income trap'. Unlike the poorest countries, those supposedly caught in the middle-income trap no longer have a reservoir of cheap labour for growth and increasingly rely on productivity improvements, but they lack the technological sophistication and knowledge base to achieve rapid innovation. However, while there are examples of countries that do seem to have fallen into a middle-income trap, like Argentina and Venezuela, there are rather more examples of very dynamic middle-income countries, including Korea, Taiwan, Malaysia, Singapore, Colombia and Chile. Some evidence suggests that economies in the middle of the income range have achieved growth in per capita income (as opposed to GDP per se) more impressively than others. Studies by Barry Eichengreen and his associates identify growth hiccups and a gradual slowing of productivity as economies approach maturity, but little evidence that middle-income countries face some kind of trap as they run out of labour and catch-up opportunities.

Another reason advanced for believing that the going will get harder is that the emerging markets emerged in highly favourable international conditions, where the rich world was positive and optimistic about globalization. China in particular has generally been seen as a business opportunity, rather than as a threat to jobs and wages. The use of technology and management skills to develop complex global supply chains brought real benefits in living standards to rich and poor alike – or seemed to – and also meant that winners and losers were disguised in a myriad of cross-border relationships.

The aftermath of the storm is generally an angrier, more sullen, less secure public in the rich world, more sceptical of the benefits of globalization, prone to populist, xenophobic politics, and less indulgent towards countries seen as competitors free-riding on international disciplines. But as I shall explore further in the next chapter, the international order has held together remarkably well through this crisis, unlike in the 1930s. Despite the worst economic crisis for eighty years, there has been little fundamental questioning of the model of deep and growing international economic integration through capital flows and corporate supply chains. There is a lot of anger, but resentments have been channelled against migrants from neighbouring countries – Mexico and Central America in the USA, Eastern Europe and the Islamic peripheries in Western Europe – rather than against trade or foreign investors, except when they are believed to dodge taxes.

Some emerging economies have developed serious imbalances in the course of their rapid growth. China has a specific problem of adjusting to a different kind of growth model, based less on investment and exports and more on domestic consumption. But it is happening, and the technocrats who have run China for thirty-five years show no sign of slackening political will (though the current anti-corruption purge is certainly affecting decision-making). Some major emerging markets may well have tried to grow faster than their underlying potential, resulting in large current account and fiscal deficits, which are issues in Brazil, Turkey,

South Africa and Indonesia. Oil and metal exporters are having to adjust to much reduced export and government revenue and the problems of servicing dollar based debt used to finance expanded production. The hubris around emerging market growth has also disguised the demanding preconditions for successful development. They require political and financial stability, law and order, including some form of recognized property rights, basic infrastructure, both physical and human capital, and access to external markets and resources.

Moreover, economic mismanagement can disrupt growth for long periods. These constraining factors make it unlikely that many countries will achieve 10 per cent growth, following in the footsteps of Korea and then China. But taken as a whole, there is no reason to doubt continued convergence. In particular, China with real incomes at barely a fifth of US levels, and India at a tenth (and growing at an accelerated tempo: 7.3 per cent in 2015), have plenty of scope left for reaping the advantages of economic backwardness.

China is in a different league from the other emerging markets. Indeed, it is soon to be the world's largest economy, if it isn't already. The IMF's five-year forecast for the 2012–17 period shows even a slowing China providing one third of the world's growth; only the USA with 14 per cent and India with 9.5 per cent come close. It therefore matters enormously whether China's current slowdown, to a mere 7 per cent growth, represents an orderly adjustment or the first stage of a messy, costly, prolonged 'hard landing'. Statistics are unreliable. Harry Wu has estimated that the 1978–2012 trend growth was nearer to 7.2 per cent that the official 9.8 per cent. The current official 7 per cent may be around 5 per cent in reality.

China's prodigious export growth is less disputed. In 1999, Chinese exports were worth less than one third of those of the USA; a decade later China was the world's largest exporter by far. Trade was, moreover, highly unbalanced. China piled up large surpluses and, from the turn of the century, current account surpluses rose vertiginously from 1 per cent of GDP to 10 per cent in 2007. The trade imbalance triggered a strong reaction in the USA, where legislators complained of currency manipulation. China curbed any offsetting rise in the currency by buying large volumes of foreign currency, mainly dollars, acquiring over US$3,000 billion of foreign reserves. As described in *The Storm*, China's savings 'glut', provided the cheap capital that helped to fuel the unsustainable expansion of credit in the USA, the UK and elsewhere.

When the financial crisis hit, China could no longer rely on foreign demand and growth was instead driven by domestic demand. This took the form of investment, much of it in infrastructure: bullet trains, airports, roads and vast amounts of new housing. Reportedly, China poured more concrete in the period 2010 to 2013 than did the US in the entire 20th century. This investment boom, which took investment from an already extraordinary 42 per cent of GDP in 2007 to 48 per cent three years later, sucked in a large increase in imports, mainly raw materials. Prices of exports relative to imports also fell, an example of a country turning the terms of trade against itself. The current account surplus corrected itself remarkably quickly; it fell from 10 per cent of GDP in 2007 to just over 2 per cent in 2011, but had risen again to 4 per cent in 2015. As part of this adjustment, the authorities allowed the exchange rate to appreciate in real terms, by just under 25 per cent after 2007. The IMF, in mid-2015, judged that the Chinese currency, the renminbi, was no longer undervalued. (It is possible however that by capital outflows and the need to loosen money policy could now result in a big devaluation with associated problems following a small devaluation in April 2015).

The period of currency appreciation followed two decades of stability after the decade initiating Deng Xiaoping's reforms when the currency fell to a quarter of its earlier value in real terms. Real exchange rate appreciation was achieved partly through the nominal exchange rate, but mainly through rising labour costs. In recent years, labour costs have been rising by over 10 per cent per annum in the coastal provinces. Firms responded by raising productivity, increasing flexibility in supply chains, and switching from exports to domestic customers. This adjustment was painful for manufacturing but demonstrated the formidable capacity of Chinese business to adapt and of the authorities to deliver rapid change. The Chinese government was also smart enough to understand the need for China to play a more constructive role in the world economy rather than relying on mere mercantilism. The contrast with Germany is very striking. Germany is expected to have a current account surplus in 2015 of over 8 per cent of GDP, continuing a pattern established over a long period, with its leadership showing none of the understanding of the Chinese as to why such imbalances might be a problem for the rest of the world.

This seemingly successful external adjustment, however, has had internal consequences. A current account surplus is the mirror image of a capital account deficit – that is, savings exceeds investment, leading to capital outflows. China adjusted to this not by reducing savings but by increasing investment. Since the turn of the century, private consumption has fallen from 45 per cent of GDP to 35 per cent, and investment has risen from around 33 per cent of GDP to 46 per cent. Investment grew by 25 per cent per annum in the period 2005–12. By contrast, the investment to GDP ratio peaked at just under 40 per cent in Korea and Japan, and is around that level in India (Figure 5.1). In most developed countries it is closer to 20 per cent. There are, however, suggestions that these figures are less dramatic than they appear. The investment figures fail to allow for inflation and in particular for the rising cost of land and property acquired in the process of investment. Once this is allowed for, the investment ratio may be in the less stratospheric range of 38–40 per cent.

The investment boom was financed largely by credit, much of it advanced without careful appraisal. Loans rose 30 per cent per annum in 2009 alone, and total credit in the economy increased by 60 per cent in the period 2009–14, rising as a share of GDP from 130 to 220 per cent. Some of this investment has produced productive assets. But a lot has been wasted, particularly in property speculation – 45 per cent of credit growth has been in real estate – and much has been channelled through non-traditional, badly regulated, financial institutions – shadow banks – leading to fears of major defaults cascading through Chinese banking.

The challenge to Chinese economic managers and political leadership consists of several interconnected elements. The first is to reverse the decline of consumption as a percentage of GDP by boosting both public consumption, such as healthcare, and private household spending. There has been an estimated decline in private consumption since the turn of the century from 45 to 35 per cent of GDP, as noted above. If successful adjustment is to be completed, the consumption ratio will need to rise to at least 50 per cent. Yet, the Chinese have, arguably, been the most frugal people in modern history. By contrast, the 50 per cent ratio is roughly the post-war low for Japan and Korea – both thrifty countries, nonetheless – and the USA has never gone that low in modern history, even in wartime.

The second step, in parallel so as to maintain demand, is to reduce the scale of investment. That has the effect, however, of creating a lot of excess capacity in capital goods industries and sectors such as steel, leading to falling profits and some large plants becoming insolvent (if rigorous accounting standards are applied). The logic of such adjustment is large-scale closures, redundancies and restructuring – a serious challenge to Chinese economic managers and the Communist Party. There is a structure, known as the State-Owned Assets Supervision and Administration Commission (SASAC), that directly oversees and structures the top 120 or so state-owned companies. But large-scale downsizing or closures of numerous enterprises, with major redundancies, is a new problem. One coal company alone (Longmans) has laid off 100,000 workers.

Thirdly, the explosion of debt will have to be serviced by firms and banks, which becomes increasingly difficult as the economy slows, reducing earnings growth. That in turn becomes even more difficult as prices fall, with firms selling off goods cheaply in conditions of excess capacity. The export of cheap steel has already caused serious problems, and resentment in Europe and South East Asia. But the real problems are in China where falls in producer prices squeeze profits and make companies insolvent. The bad debt will in turn have to be identified and written off, which will affect the stability of financial institutions.

Some Western commentators have talked up the potential for a major crisis, comparable to that of Japan, when a period of over-investment, much of it unproductive ('roads to nowhere'), plays out as an inflated asset bubble. In Japan, lending to finance poor investments caused a banking crisis which has led to stagnation for over two decades. But the position in China is radically different. The stock of capital in China, as opposed to flows of new investment, is still low. One estimate is that China has 8 per cent of the capital stock per person of the USA, and 17 per cent of that of South Korea. A historical study suggests that China still has only a quarter of the capital stock of the USA in 1930, when it was at a roughly comparable stage of development. While some investment has no doubt been misallocated, much of it has been in badly needed infrastructure, transport or housing. Not all of this investment produces a tangible financial return, which is why some loans will go bad, but it may contribute to growth in the longer run. Moreover, research suggests that 'total factor productivity' in China is still growing impressively, contributing over 40 per cent of growth in the decade after 2000.

Moreover, after state enterprises drove China's earlier growth, there is now a corps of private companies with the potential to become serious international players: Huawei in telecommunications; Alibaba in e-commerce; Xiaomi, makers of smartphones; Tencent in social media; Baidu, the search engine company. These points all suggest that, while there will be a painful adjustment in some sectors and a day of reckoning amid some dodgy loans, China does not suffer from a classic crisis of overinvestment of the kind that led to Japanese stagnation and the Western banking crisis. There is still plenty of scope for new investment to meet unsatisfied demand.

The problems facing the Chinese authorities are more subtle. If capital is to be used more efficiently, that will require more transparent, market-based transactions and real domestic competition. This means financial liberalization, as well as local government and state enterprise reform. The new team of President Xi acknowledges this, at least in theory. One area of particular discomfort is the many state-owned enterprises that appear much less efficient than private companies, but which are often highly profitable on account of access to cheap credit or land, which in turn can be traced back to political connections and corruption in local and provincial government. The complexity of the social, business and political networks makes them difficult to unravel without destroying party control or the model of state capitalism that has served China so well to date. The administration of President Xi has made it clear that the party will not lose control. He has embarked on a far-reaching anti-corruption drive, affecting tens of thousands of officials and businessmen, often with political undertones. The danger is that fear of offending key party officials are resulting in a paralysis of decision-making and the stifling of reform.

There are particular challenges for the financial sector, where much of the bad debt is hidden. China has highly regulated banks which offer depositors poor returns and expand orthodox low-risk credit more sedately than the rapid expansion of business investment demands. This raises the question of who has been financing the extraordinary expansion in credit to the corporate sector, much of it state-owned, over the last five years, from just under 30 trillion to 90 trillion renminbi. This expansion has lifted aggregate debt of all kinds from 147 per cent of GDP at the end of 2008 to 250 per cent at the end of 2014. (By comparison, overall debt dependency is a little less than the UK at 277 per cent and the USA at 260 per cent.) Most of the increase, and half of all the outstanding debt, is financed through lightly regulated shadow banking – which in China refers mainly to high-risk investments by non-bank institutions in sectors such as property development: for example, the issuance of municipal bonds. The loans are generally poorly documented and promise investors returns higher than seem plausible in a slowing economy. These are also often short-term loans, lasting months rather than years. These are the classic ingredients of a credit bubble and a future crash were investors to panic and seek to withdraw credit.

The dilemmas facing the authorities were well illustrated by the sharp fall, of over 30 per cent, in the Shanghai stock exchange in the summer of 2015. The equity market had doubled over the previous year and the boom was officially encouraged as a way of getting state companies to switch debt for equity, and also enriching millions of middle-class investors. When the market fell, this was treated as an affront to the authorities and a signal of loss of party control. Heavy intervention followed, including a ban on short-selling. Given a choice between markets and control, the government opted for control.

Pessimists, like Ruchir Sharma, author of *Breakout Nations*, argue that because of the explosion of credit, China is bound to repeat the experience of credit crises in other countries, like Japan, leading to a prolonged and severe slowdown. I have already dismissed some of the comparisons with Japan. What is currently fuelling the pessimists' arguments is some evidence that the Chinese authorities are struggling to stop price deflation (consumer price inflation is around 2 per cent per annum and falling). The excess capacity is resulting in aggressive price-cutting, aggravating the problem of low profitability, causing consumers to delay spending and adding to the real cost of debt. Moreover, monetary stimulus appears not to be working. The pessimists argue that it is impossible simultaneously to manage down debt and to carry through complex liberalizing reforms of local government and state enterprises while maintaining party control.

The optimists, myself included, believe that the authorities are well aware of the risks and are currently allowing controlled corporate defaults. China, and the Chinese banks, also have very large savings; there is little or no reliance on foreign creditors and vast foreign exchange reserves. The level of government debt, at around 40 per cent of GDP, is sufficiently low that the state could absorb substantial bad debts from the shadow banks without risking either European-style sovereign debt problems or Japanese levels of public debt.

Economic history, captured in Hyman Minsky's theory of financial boom and bust, is on the side of the pessimists. But the optimists point to China's remarkable ability over thirty-five years to use the dynamic of capitalism to achieve growth, while using the control mechanism of a communist state to avert capitalist crises. The clarity with which the current leadership sees and articulates its policy choices, and the sheer competence of post-Mao economic decision-making, are good reasons for believing that this crisis will be managed and that, beyond it, rapid growth of 6 per cent or so per annum can be sustained.

What will gradually erode Chinese growth performance is demographics. The population is ageing fast and the total population will peak at 1.4 billion shortly after 2020 and then decline, to be overtaken by India. Demographic ageing has its upside. For the first time in Chinese history, life is no longer nasty, brutish and short, but will extend into a healthy old age. Life expectancy has more than doubled since the communist revolution, reaching seventy-five today. And the one-child policy prescribed by Mao and largely maintained by his successors has made it easier for growth to be translated into rising living standards, rather than swallowed up by growing numbers.

The downside of China's unique demographic transition is that the labour force is falling. Future growth depends on higher productivity across the board, with a stronger service sector and less reliance on crude industrial products. Also, there is a rapidly growing number of elderly people requiring care, in a society where services are pretty threadbare. These may not be insuperable problems. China's internal passport system can be further liberalized, enabling peasants to move more freely to areas of labour shortages. There are also growing reports of labour shortages and wages rising in rural areas. There is a clear understanding of the need for reforms to make China more flexible and productive. And it is possible that as society becomes richer, and children are seen as a source of enjoyment rather than as a burden to society, the one-child policy will be further relaxed and the birth rate will rise.

All these factors taken together point to serious challenges and the potential for shocks in the short run. But the chances of China running out of steam and succumbing to the kind of growth crises seen in Japan and the eurozone are low. My judgement, I stress, is not that of a China expert: but beyond occasional visits as a Shell executive and then as minister, it is based on interrogation of those who are experts, who have done business in China, or who now run the country.

———

The only other emerging economy that contributes substantially to global growth is India. The IMF's projections for 2012–17 have India contributing 9.5 per cent of global growth – short of the 14 per cent of the USA and the prodigious 34 per cent of China, but well ahead of Brazil, Russia and Indonesia at around 2.5 per cent each, and Turkey, Mexico and South Korea ranging from 1.3 to 1.8 per cent. India makes a difference. It is contributing substantially to the changing centre of gravity in the world economy. In the latter half of the decade 2000–10 there was GDP growth of around 10 per cent, and even the prospect of catching up, in size if not in per capita income, with China. Certainly, the Indian population will catch up with that of China within a decade.

I argued, in a comparative study twenty years ago, that, taking a very long-term view, India was also more shockproof – made of wrought iron as against China's cast iron – with a democratic, decentralized and less statist system, better able to absorb major crises. Indeed, having closely studied and reported on Indian economy policy for much of the last quarter of the twentieth century, I became convinced that the lumbering Indian elephant would catch up with the more temperamental Chinese tiger. That has not happened, however.

Indeed, experience of the last few years has reinforced a generally less sanguine view of India's potential. Growth fell to just over 4 per cent in 2013, though mainstream estimates are for 7.3 per cent in 2015, rising again in 2016. Furthermore, until lower oil prices provided relief, there was double-digit consumer inflation, which has much to do with an economy running up against straining infrastructure and domestic food supply, as well as a weak currency. There was, until the recent election, largely a standstill in economic reform, and the liberalizing energy of the 1990s seemed to have been dissipated.

Yet there is still much to be positive about. Even in periods of very weak or unstable government there has been, until very recently, a steady quickening of growth (Figure 5.1). This has ranged from the stagnation of living standards in colonial times, to the feeble 'Hindu rate of growth' of around 3.5 per cent (or 1.5 per cent in per capita terms) in the two or three decades after independence, to the 5 per cent or so as the 'green revolution' boosted agriculture and modest reforms were attempted, then accelerating to 9 or 10 per cent after the Manmohan Singh reforms of the early 1990s, before the recent setbacks. Much of this steady improvement has been based on growth-based initiatives at state level, or driven by dynamic entrepreneurs bypassing government altogether. India, unlike China, does not depend for leadership on one party controlling it from the centre. More than China, India has a strong indigenous business class, with some world-class companies used to operating in a framework of law and an ethos of enterprise and markets, albeit plagued by some serious corruption. Indian companies are prominent in the global knowledge economy. There is also now a vast middle class with expectations of rising living standards, increasingly articulate, well educated and, again unlike in China, with unrestricted access to information and opportunities for free expression. In the last decade, ownership of telephones has risen from 9 per cent of households to almost two thirds. There is rapidly rising literacy and female education, with a labour force growing at 1.7 per cent per annum. India has a demographic dividend over China, but also has the challenge of ensuring that the young population is educated, trained and employed.

The reforms needed to maintain greater budget discipline, improve infrastructure and remove obstacles to growth are well understood in India. There is already a high rate of investment, of around 38 per cent of GDP, and because living standards are lower than in China there is greater scope for catch-up. The issue is whether the economy will bump along with around 5–6 per cent growth, as now, or whether it will move up to a range of 8–9 per cent, which would in all probability be greater than China. The difference matters, since it affects the probability of tens of millions of Indians escaping absolute poverty and of India becoming, as China has, a major driver of the world economy. Sustained growth of 10 per cent seems highly implausible because physical infrastructure, such as roads, ports, telecommunications and power supplies, is often wretchedly inadequate. But some acceleration is certainly feasible.

The underlying strengths of India as a major emerging economy were boosted by the election of a new government led by Narendra Modi of the Bharatiya Janata Party (BJP). The election itself – decisive, legitimate and peaceful – spoke to one of India's greatest assets: a resilient, democratic political system. The new government is committed to a growth agenda, speeding up paralysed decision-making on infrastructure and policy reform, and has enthusiastic support from most of the business community.

Legislation has already been enacted to free up some inward investment and there is an attempt to make decision-making quicker and more transparent, an example being the auction-ing of mining leases. So far, however, business is watching rather than investing. And one should be under no illusions – the BJP is a nationalistic party that feeds off anti-Muslim prejudice and has its share of corrupt politicians and gangsters. But it has added confidence and political stability to an economy with formida-ble growth potential. It has also been lucky. The collapse of oil prices in late 2014 has simultaneously halved inflation, from 10 per cent in 2013 to 5 per cent in the early months of 2015, helped to reduce the oil subsidy bill in the national budget, and eased the balance of payments.

———

The continuing shift in the centre of gravity of the world econ-omy towards the emerging economies matters, most obviously, for the people in the countries concerned. Economic growth has halved absolute poverty from 1990, when almost 2 billion fell into that category, to 1.2 billion now (out of a much larger global population). On a rather spartan measure of US$2 per day, the proportion of the world population in absolute poverty has fallen from 70 per cent in 1980 to just over 40 per cent. China accounts for much of this progress. Since China's reforms com-menced in 1980, the poverty rate has been cut from 85 per cent to 10 per cent – that is, 680 million people, equivalent to the entire population of South America. Growth outside China, notably in India and Africa, has also lifted 280 million out of absolute poverty since 2000 alone. There are enormous methodological problems in making such estimates and making comparisons between countries and over time. Poverty, moreover, isn't just a matter of crude economic aggregates, but also involves income distribution. More equal countries cut poverty further and faster, as do policies that emphasize health, literacy and female empow-erment. But a continuation of present trends would achieve the aim of virtually eliminating absolute poverty on this, admittedly modest, measure within the next few years.

For those inclined to see a glass half-empty rather than half-full, a growing problem is that the vast majority of those who have climbed out of poverty have not climbed very far and are highly vulnerable to being sucked back down. Disaster can result from a slowdown in growth or a bad harvest or a family bereavement. Progress is real but precarious and a serious slowdown in the main emerging markets could be disastrous, not least for the governability of countries with large, poor populations with rising expectations. Also, many of the benefits of growth have gone to the 'haves'. In China, India and Indonesia, inequality has widened. In India, surveys of public opinion, as well as actual elections, show an acute and growing sense that inequality is a problem, along with the corruption of the rich and powerful and the neglect of basic health and education. The Chinese Communist Party, which does not have access to the Indian democratic escape valves, is also acutely aware of the risks.

But if, as I expect, the process of catch-up and convergence continues, there will be challenges of a different kind. What happens if the world's largest accumulation of capital, in the form of personal savings in China and India, starts to slosh around in Western economies on a big scale? The decade before the financial crisis saw the beginnings of a historic reversal of capital flows, after a couple of centuries in which, by and large, capital flowed in the opposite direction. At present, large-scale flows of capital are limited by capital controls, though these are somewhat leaky and there is a lot of illicit money that finds its way into receptive financial institutions and markets, such as property in London. There has also been a vast flow of Chinese foreign currency reserves, totalling an estimated US$4 trillion, into US Treasury bonds and other foreign currency assets. This in turn has created a set of reciprocal obligations, which has been described as a 'hostage' or 'bonding' arrangement, providing a form of political and economic equilibrium between the superpowers. Neither can afford default. These flows of capital from savings-rich emerging economies have been a big feature of the last decade, but they may herald much larger flows in future.

Indeed, they are relatively small compared to the potential flows from opening up the Chinese capital account by removing capital controls altogether and letting capital flow freely in and out. Chinese annual savings are of the order of US$5 trillion, compared with US$3 trillion for the USA, and have risen from barely US$1 trillion a decade ago. In practice, the conservatism, and patriotism, of small savers is likely to mean that they will continue to invest in poor-yielding Chinese post office accounts rather than in financially more attractive options overseas. But as savers become richer and more sophisticated, they will widen their search for yield. Companies, and some members of the rich elite, already deploy some of their savings in overseas investments, as do Indian multinationals on a larger scale. The Bank of England has estimated that the Chinese stock of external assets and liabilities could rise in the next two decades from under 5 per cent of world GDP to 35 per cent, meaning that Chinese savers and companies would own a much higher proportion of the world economy than do their US equivalents today. The IMF has made a similar estimate.

In this new world, there are severe risks of generating financial crises because Chinese financial institutions are not particularly developed and could export instability around the world, as well as exposing a fragile Chinese system to even greater risk of collapse. To set against that, greater freedom of capital movements could force political reform in China. It would also enable Chinese savers, companies and the state to earn better returns as China becomes more of a Western-style 'rentier' economy. The Chinese authorities, being well aware of the risks, have set out a phased programme, starting with allowing greater freedom to Chinese enterprises to invest overseas, then relaxing trade-related credit, then allowing more inward investment, both fixed and portfolio, into China. However, even that fairly modest objective is difficult to reconcile with the nationalist rhetoric and the intimidation meted out to some prominent foreign companies.

The transition is in practice likely to be stage-managed rather than chaotic, just like China's skilfully managed entry into world trade. The consequences for the rest of the world of an opening of the capital floodgates will be immense, should it happen.

One likely accompaniment of capital liberalization is the emergence of the Chinese currency – renminbi (RMB) – as a global currency. At present there are around US$4 trillion in currency trades per day, the vast majority for trading in securities and a tiny fraction for trade. The dollar is on one side of 85 per cent of all currency trades, the euro around 40 per cent, the yen 20 per cent, and sterling around 10 per cent, with a variety of smaller currencies making up the rest. The Chinese currency scarcely figures at all, except, and then only in part, in the settlement of trade transactions with China, mainly to allow renminbi to be used for importing into China. Yet there is an ambition to develop its role, and London has been chosen as the main market for RMB trades to grow. My former colleague George Osborne was an enthusiastic, well-publicized, promoter of that project. The IMF has also now given the RMB the status of third biggest currency in its reserve currency basket.

It is still some way from here to China having a fully fledged international currency, let alone supplanting the dollar as a reserve currency. To achieve that status, with foreign governments and individuals holding the currency as a store of value, China would require a fully convertible currency, with no restrictions on capital flows, stability in its macroeconomic policy and respect for commercial law and property. There are some obvious attractions in aiming for reserve currency status, not least that of being able to borrow cheaply in one's own currency. But it would be a China enormously changed from today.

———

A more immediate issue, which has been evident for some years, is that emerging markets, China especially, are now sufficiently important in the world economy that their growth drives the price of scarce raw materials. Already the long historic trend of declining commodity prices has been broken. In real terms, commodity prices have fallen relentlessly since the end of the First World War, to 20 per cent of the 1914 level, albeit with some deep troughs, as in the 1930s, and occasional peaks, as during the Korean War and the OPEC oil price hikes, along the way. Highly elastic supplies and substitutions of raw materials ensured that the 'commodity terms of trade' (against manufactured goods) continued to deteriorate, so much so that it became virtually axiomatic for developing economies to diversify from raw materials into manufacturing, preferably for export. This century, the trend appears to have been broken, benefiting raw materials exporters like Australia, Brazil and much of Africa, at least until the sharp market correction since peak prices in 2011, and especially in 2014 and 2015.

More specifically, commodity prices were not dragged down by the financial crisis and its aftermath, as they were in the interwar period. The dollar index for commodities rose by over 50 per cent in the three years after mid-2008. Oil prices doubled. Western economies like the UK suffered a squeeze in real incomes as a result of adverse terms of trade on top of the recessionary impact of the financial crisis. More broadly, developed countries became price-takers, no longer benefiting from a secular decline in these prices and creating serious complications for inflation management. China was at the heart of this phenomenon. China accounts for half of the entire world's consumption of iron ore, over 40 per cent of coal, lead and zinc, and over 30 per cent of aluminium, copper and nickel. These are, however, notoriously cyclical commodities and as China slows a little and large-scale mining investment has come on stream, prices have collapsed. Indeed, the dollar price of metals adjusted for US inflation had halved from the 2011 peak. Some analysts claim to detect a 40 year commodity 'supercycle' of which recent trends are the first for years of a downward leg.

The most dramatic turnaround has been the fall in oil prices from over US\$115 per barrel (Brent crude) in June 2014 to under US\$40 at the end of 2015. Oil prices had risen strongly over the previous decade and a half, from a trough of under US\$20 per barrel at the turn of the century to US\$140 at the pre-crisis peak. China has around 10 per cent of world consumption, but accounted for 45 per cent of the growth in demand in the decade 2003–2013. China is now the world's largest oil importer, at around 7 million barrels per day, overtaking the USA which now consumes less and produces more of its own. This is even more true of the emerging markets as a whole. The four BRIC countries – Brazil, Russia, India and China – were consuming 3.7 million barrels of oil per day more after the financial crisis (in 2012) than they were before (in 2008), exceeding by far the fall in demand in the crisis-hit Western economies (a fall of 1.5 million barrels per day).

In *The Storm*, I argued against a 'peak-oil' view that the inexorable rise in demand for commodities, especially oil and gas, would collide with fixed supply to drive up prices for a long time ahead. All previous experience, not least from the oil shocks of 1974 and 1979/80, is that higher prices stimulate investment, leading to increased supply as well as moderation of demand as technology leads to economy of use. This is precisely what has happened again. Supply has been increasing rapidly from Brazil, Canada, Angola and, above all, the USA. Shale oil fields have been adding an extra 1 million barrels per day annually, and now produce close to 3 million barrels per day. Despite the turmoil in the country, Libya has restored much of its production, as has Iraq. Moreover, if the relaxation of sanctions on Iran continues, then that country's large capacity will come back into play. Roughly 3.5 million barrels per day of capacity, previously sterilized by conflict, is potentially available. OPEC's production target of 30 million barrels per day faces a serious threat, as Iran and Iraq in particular throw off restraint. Were this to happen, the influence of the major oil producers, notably Saudi Arabia, would shrink with their ability to control the price.

That is the context in which Saudi Arabia and its smaller Gulf allies decided in 2014 to change tack and to stop exercising production restraint. They would have had to cut production by 1 million barrels per day to stabilize the price. Instead, they allowed the price of oil to drop in order to drive out higher-cost competitors, particularly US shale oil. The price of crude fell from US$115 per barrel in mid-2014 to US$45 in January 2015. With its oil in the ground and low-cost production, Saudi Arabia calculated that it can ride out a period of low oil prices, of around US$50–60. This approach is not without pain, since Saudi Arabia needs a crude price of US$90–100 to balance its budget, and there will be some difficult belt-tightening. The calculation it is making is that its aggressive approach will drive out new investors in US shale oil, who require around US$85 per barrel to be profitable, and perhaps US$60 to stay in business, as well as other high-cost competitors, such as Canadian and Venezuelan oil sands and deep-water exploration in the Arctic, the North Sea and Brazil.

By contrast, Saudi oil costs barely US$10 per barrel to produce, so it can survive and earn a substantial profit and finance a comfortable lifestyle even in a world where low oil prices continue for an extended period. In the process, the price fall is inflicting collateral damage on Saudi's strategic enemies, notably Iran, which requires prices around US$130 to balance its budget, as well as Russia. The expectation is that, as global demand recovers, helped by lower prices, by an estimated 7.5 million barrels per day over the next five to six years, there will be a better balance of supply and demand, with less risk of structural oversupply. Saudi dominance would continue as 'swing producer' through its control over spare capacity. The weakness in the Saudi position, however, is that while it may succeed in displacing US shale oil companies in the short run, those are also the most adaptable and flexible producers and are likely to re-emerge quickly once demand strengthens again.

While the oil price collapse has to be understood in terms of the fine margins that exist between supply and demand, and the interests of the dominant producers, the fall in prices has major economic consequences. A price of US$50 per barrel, if sustained, means a shift of roughly 2 per cent of world output from oil producer countries to oil consumers. Since consumers are more likely than producers to spend any windfall, the overall impact is a boost to world demand, somewhat akin to a global cut in indirect taxes. The impact is major, but not perhaps as dramatic as in the 1970s when economies were generally more dependent on oil (it is now almost entirely a transport fuel, no longer used for power generation on any scale) and its use was often profligate.

The biggest beneficiaries of the oil price fall have been the main net oil importers, including the eurozone, Japan, China and India, as well as important emerging markets like Turkey, Korea and Indonesia. A stimulus to these economies provides a powerful boost to the world economy. One complication, however, is that in the eurozone and Japan, and perhaps even in China, falling oil prices aggravate the risk of deflation, leading to the postponement of spending and a growth of debt burdens in real terms. Another potential negative is that the sudden collapse has aggravated the risk of a potential financial shock as oil companies go bust, creating problems for their bankers. Also, some oil exporters are especially vulnerable to a period of weak prices – Venezuela, Nigeria, Iran and Indonesia, for example – and may be forced into debt default or other drastic policy options.

The most obvious flashpoint is Russia, which is additionally struggling with the impact of economic sanctions consequent upon its intervention in Ukraine. Its current budget assumes oil at US$100 per barrel. The central bank predicted that, with oil prices even as high as US$60 per barrel, GDP would fall by 4 per cent in 2015. Interest rates were increased in mid-December 2014, to 17 per cent, in order to stop capital flight and a precipitate fall in the rouble. (It is sobering to recall that after interest rates were raised to 13 per cent in 2009, in order to arrest an earlier crisis of confidence, GDP fell by 8 per cent.) Even before the worries over oil prices, Russia saw a massive net outflow of capital, of US$232 billion over the period 2010–13. Russia has missed opportunities to diversify away from energy and still relies on oil and gas for 20 per cent of GDP, two thirds of its exports and half of its government revenue.

Russia's troubles matter for the rest of the world in a variety of ways. The most obvious would be if there were a repetition of the financial crisis of 1998 when Russia defaulted on its external debt. At first sight this looks unlikely. Russia has seemingly healthy foreign reserves of around US$400 billion, just under half of which are in somewhat illiquid wealth funds, though almost one third of those reserves has already been used trying to stabilize the rouble and refinance banks. Looking forward, the key pressure is overseas debt service by Russian state corporations and energy companies. An estimated US$130 billion is needed to repay debt in the forthcoming year alone. Sanctions against Russia will create obstacles to debt refinancing. And as the rouble falls in value, the burden of external debt service grows.

It would be foolish to try to predict how this particular set of developments will play out – how Russia in particular will respond to the external economic pressures of weak oil prices and sanctions, and how oil prices will fluctuate in response to changes in the margins of supply and demand.

The big picture, as sketched out in *The Storm*, remains largely unchanged. First, energy and commodity demand growth is dominated by the big emerging economies, led by China. Secondly, contrary to the pessimism of the 'peak-oil' theorists, supplies of oil and gas are proving very elastic. Whatever the short-term impact of the 2014 oil price crash, US non-conventional production will almost certainly grow in importance because of its flexibility and capacity to expand quickly with modest investment. And thirdly, as a consequence of the above, the global shift to the emerging economies is most unlikely to be stopped by energy supply bottlenecks and escalating prices. A more profound problem, shared by consumers and producers alike, will be the climatic consequence of growing emissions.

The shift in the centre of gravity of the world economy has gone further and faster than when I wrote *The Storm*. The awkward adjustment being attempted in China and the sharp slow down in commodity exporters like Brasil and Russia, will act as a brake on this process. But they are unlikely to change the underlying story of a world economy in which the USA and the EU become progressively less important. On one level, this is simply the arithmetical consequence of billions of people in poor countries progressing out of poverty, a benign development that we must support and applaud. It may well also involve continued absolute improvements in living standards and quality of life. And the values of the West, exercised through 'soft power', of individual liberties, democracy, diversity and openness to new ideas, may well prevail as a result of the success of countries that espouse them, such as India and Brazil, or might gradually assimilate them, like China.

In this chapter, I have also described some of the less convenient and comfortable ways in which this economic shift affects us. The main market growth is occurring in less familiar emerging markets, which have adopted international rules only recently, if at all. Competition and collaboration is with companies that have not originated in, and do not necessarily share, Western corporate governance. Cross-border competition through trade is ever more intense, involving economies that retain a comparative advantage based on low wages, but that also have capital-intensive industries and knowledge-based activities. The growing international mobility of capital means that capital markets and corporate ownership are increasingly being dominated by institutions acting on behalf of the savers of emerging economies. International commodity markets are increasingly being dominated by emerging market demand and suppliers, with the important exception of US gas.

What is even less comfortable is the ability of these increasingly important emerging powers to translate economic size into military spending, and its projection for defensive and offensive purposes. China spends roughly one sixth of what the USA spends on defence, but on current trends will equal it by around 2025. Nor do we know whether the structures of international cooperation, governing trade, international finance and standards, which are mostly fashioned around the ideals and interests of the Western world, will survive – though China and India seem eager to develop rather than to destroy them. Much depends on how national politics responds to the demands of a globalized world with shifting sources of power.

As I described earlier, the government of which I was part devoted a lot of time and effort to engaging positively with the emerging powers. The broad policy conclusions are clear for countries like the UK that are seeking to adapt to such a world but that have only limited capacity to influence it: continuing to maximize opportunities for trade and investment, including some labour and student flows; building relationships that survive temporary fads and spats; and being constructive in widening and deepening international rules and governance.

6

Globalization and its Enemies

The main themes of this book and its predecessor, *The Storm*, derive from the interconnectedness of an open, global economy. That globalized world has been a catalyst for the post-war expansion of better living standards and has given emerging economies scope to develop. The financial crisis represented the biggest challenge to this process of globalization. I argued in *The Storm* that there were serious risks of repeating inter-war history when the pre-1914 system of globalization was destroyed by nationalism and destructive politics, based on identity and territory. Extreme pessimism has been confounded, so far. The global system has not collapsed. But the gradual encroachment of the national politics of identity makes it harder to defend an open economy.

There remains a contradiction: a global system of exchange and interconnectedness depends on shared rules and norms, but the people who make those rules and norms are not global but national politicians. Except in a few extreme outposts of isolation like North Korea, the success of national politicians depends in significant measure on their ability to deliver prosperity, or the prospect of it, and that in turn depends, in varying degrees, on the country's participation in an interconnected international economic system. But if that system fails to deliver and becomes associated in the public mind with failure, pain, insecurity and unfairness, then it can unravel, as it has done before. Where the pain and sense of unfairness are acute, Greece being a current example, there is unsurprisingly a revolt against the system that is seen as causing those things.

———

As part of the coalition Cabinet, I was in a position to influence as well as to observe these conflicting pressures at work. There were strains and tensions within the coalition. But for the most part we agreed that government must remain outward-looking, despite the temptation to look inward at a time of fiscal austerity and economic and social stress. The coalition became the first UK government to deliver the United Nations 0.7 per cent of GDP target for overseas aid, despite relentless criticism from right-wing newspapers and Conservative backbenchers – an achievement that the critics of austerity usually fail to mention. Conservative colleagues were genuinely enthused by such projects as the UN campaign to eradicate female genital mutilation and the Millennium Development goals, and by the UK's being the first and most generous contributor to a variety of humanitarian disaster-relief schemes. I led for the government on a variety of international initiatives – to create a register of corporate ownership, to secure an international arms trade treaty, to strengthen the rules around overseas corruption and transparency in natural resource revenue payments – but in each case there was broad cross-party support.

Furthermore, issues like the foreign ownership of domestic companies, which are highly contentious in most parts of the world, aroused minimal controversy. Indeed, like its predecessors, the government made a virtue out of the fact that the UK is an open economy, welcoming inward investment. We were able to point to the record of the overseas car makers – Tata (Jaguar, Land Rover), Nissan, Toyota, BMW, Ford – as examples of long-term commitment to investment in the UK, and I was able to persuade the bosses of General Motors in Detroit to invest in the UK, at Ellesmere Port and Luton, rather than in Germany, on the basis of the UK's excellent working relations between overseas investors, government and manufacturing trade unions.

By contrast, some commentators, like Alex Brummer in the *Daily Mail*, have deplored the lack of concern over British ownership, and particularly the disappearance of high-growth, high-tech companies devoured by American predators. He has a serious point about the lack of funding for so-called 'gazelle' companies, which I sought to address through the British Business Bank. But nationality per se is not the issue. Indeed, Britain benefits from a disproportionate share of business start-ups being undertaken by foreigners. One takeover that was seriously contentious was the proposed hostile Pfizer takeover of AstraZeneca. But that was not an issue of corporate patriotism. (AstraZeneca is Anglo-Swedish, with a French CEO; Pfizer, though American, has a large UK footprint even after recent closures, and a Scottish CEO.) It could have become a seriously decisive issue because the prime minister and Chancellor broadly welcomed the bid, while I, with the Lib Dems and Labour, was much more negative because of the potential impact on UK R&D. In the event, Pfizer went away when they realized there was serious opposition. The other contentious takeover was News Corp's bid for BSkyB, but once again that was not an issue of nationalism.

Where Britain's openness became seriously uncomfortable for the coalition was in relation to immigration. The Conservatives had committed themselves in their 2010 manifesto to cutting net immigration to under 100,000, from just over 200,000 in 2010. This ranked with the Lib Dem tuition fees pledge as one of the grand follies of the preceding election and it hung like a millstone around the coalition's neck. It could never be realized because key elements in the metric, including British emigration, returning UK expatriates and movement within the EU, were variables beyond government control. The target was hopelessly missed, leading to a net figure of over 300,000. In an increasingly desperate attempt to meet the pledge, damaging restrictions were placed on highly skilled non-EU migrants and overseas students, who are not immigrants but who are included in the numbers because their stay is for over one year. My own relations with the prime minister and the Home Secretary were badly soured by repeated clashes over policy and statistical reports showing that the net migration target was receding. They and I were conscious that I was repeatedly tweaking a very raw nerve, the dishonesty of the claim that 'Britain is open for Business'. To my amazement, the Conservatives have lashed themselves to the same uncomfortable mast post-2015.

Immigration apart, the other sign that globalization was no longer seen as an unalloyed blessing came in the form of a highly effective social media campaign against the Transatlantic Trade and Investment Partnership (TTIP). Groups like 38 Degrees, allied to iconic figures like Jamie Oliver, as well as the TUC and a variety of charities, all challenged the conventional view about the benefits of freer trade, especially where it involves removing barriers created by different technical standards, such as the testing regime for car safety specifications. Across Europe, a million people signed a petition against TTIP and in the UK opinion polls have been negative. Until recently there had been a remarkably broad and deep consensus around these issues. The white paper on globalization prepared by Clare Short when she was development secretary was arguably the apotheosis of the self-confident belief that removing barriers was good, not just for Britain but for the rest of the world, including the poorest.

Some of the campaigning on TTIP has been exaggerated, yet the significance of the anti-TTIP movement has been that for the first time in post-war Britain there has been an articulate, well-supported campaign, allied to others in Europe (notably in Germany and Austria), challenging the established liberal assumptions about the merits of more trade and cross-border investment, especially the latter. The anti-globalization movement, which surfaced in the late 1990s with the Seattle riots, has become mainstream. When European parliaments and the European Parliament itself are asked to approve TTIP and other bilateral agreements in years to come, there may well be greater resistance than has been experienced hitherto.

Seen on a wider, global basis, the financial crisis had the immediate effect of drastically disrupting trade and capital flows. But prompt action to support demand through aggressive monetary and, briefly, fiscal policy, and intervention to stabilize banks, prevented the collapse of world trade and international investment.

Protectionism has been the dog that didn't bark – or at least not very loudly. Certainly there has been nothing comparable to the 1930 Smoot–Hawley Act which raised tariffs to record levels on thousands of items imported into the USA, with consequent retaliation elsewhere. But analysts have counted between 700 and 1,500 protectionist measures from October 2008 to October 2013, mainly anti-dumping and similar measures, rather than tariffs and quotas. The post-war and pre-crisis (and also pre-1913) pattern of global trade growing roughly twice as fast as GDP has not yet resumed. Over the four years 2012–15, trade grew less rapidly than global GDP (Figure 6.1). A sharp contraction in Chinese export growth as its economy rebalances has been one major factor, along with the contraction of imports by commodity exporters.

There has been a much more striking retreat from integration through capital flows. As a share of GDP of the G20, capital inflows fell from 17 per cent to 4 per cent from 2007 to 2013, but recovered to 6 per cent in 2014. Direct foreign investment fell from 4 per cent of world GDP in 2007 to 2 per cent in 2014. Much of the overall contraction was from a welcome decline in short-term 'hot money' fuelling asset price bubbles. Banks also withdrew from cross-border lending in order to strengthen their balance sheets. The decline in direct investment genuinely represents a process of corporate disengagement. But if we look at the stock of foreign investment, rather than the flows, companies are still operating at levels of overseas activity that are historically quite unprecedented.

One measure of overall integration is the DHL Global Connectedness Index, which measures both depth (how much of the economy is internationalized through trade and investment) and width (with how many different countries). Overall, Holland is first, the UK sixth, Germany ninth, the USA twentieth and China seventy-fourth, out of 140. Since the crisis, connections have become shallower and narrower as the focus has been on regional rather than global liberalization.

———

Broadly speaking, globalization has remained resilient in the face of a traumatic shock. Why? One possible explanation is that the rules of the WTO and the European Union are much stronger and more respected than comparable pre-war arrangements. Macroeconomic policy has also generally been more economically literate, or at least subject to much more peer-group interaction between central bank governors and finance ministries. And by and large, despite anger at bankers and austerity measures, the political ideology underpinning capitalism and globalization has remained intact.

Yet there is a growing gap between the globalization of economics and the national parochialism of politics. This matters because politicians have the power either to facilitate or to obstruct economic integration. While no coherent ideology of opposition to globalization has emerged, along the lines of Marxism-Leninism or National Socialism in the early twentieth century, there are plenty of populist movements feeding off people's dissatisfaction. Mostly they are directed at migrants, who are the most visible and easily demonized manifestations of globalization.

I wrote twenty years ago about the politics of identity: how, especially in the aftermath of the Cold War and the discrediting of communism as an ideology, the traditional divide between 'left' and 'right' had become less extreme and less meaningful. Instead, a different kind of dialectic has emerged between those whose appeal is inclusive and outward-looking and those who are preoccupied with identity, be it national, ethnic, linguistic or religious. In the UK there have been intense and divisive arguments around Scotland, Europe and immigration, all of which pose questions of identity.

Almost all European countries boast populist parties of what is often called the 'far right', but which are far removed from the free-market, libertarian ideology that embraces international integration and is relaxed about the loss of traditional identities. Indeed, some of these parties regard themselves as on the left, as is the case with the SNP and Sinn Fein. In many cases, their focus is on immigration in general, as with UKIP, the Danish People's Party, the Swiss People's Party, Sweden's Democratic Party and the Austrian Freedom Party. In some cases, however, the hostility is more focused, as with the anti-Islamic appeal of the French National Front, the Dutch Freedom Party, Pegida in Germany and Norway's Progress Party. Several of these parties are also hostile to the European integration project and accompanying loss of national identity, such as the Finns Party, UKIP, and Alternative für Deutschland. Some have secessionist agendas which put their sense of nationhood in opposition to multinational states: the SNP in Scotland, Sinn Fein in Northern Ireland, Corsican nationalists, Catalan and Basque parties in Spain, all of which see themselves as being on the 'left'; and the Italian Northern League and Belgian Vlaams Blok. Some feed off old prejudices against minorities, such as Hungarians in Slovakia, Jews in Hungary, Gypsies in Romania, other Yugoslavs in Croatia. Some are alarmingly close to inter-war fascism, like the Greek Golden Dawn.

As yet, none of these are more than fringe parties, though some have major influence in coalitions, in the European Parliament and in devolved governments. We have already seen in the UK that nationalist parties can have a profound effect on politics. The SNP's crushing defeat of Labour and the Lib Dems in Scotland, and the reaction to it among English voters, was arguably the single most important factor delivering the 2015 election to the Conservatives. UKIP obtained a derisory parliamentary return by contrast, but it is now the main challenger in many Labour and Conservative seats in England, has a large presence in the European Parliament and can reasonably claim to have shifted the Conservative position substantially on the EU and immigration.

The politics of identity is far from being just a European phenomenon. The USA has been preoccupied, at least among Republicans, with 'culture wars' and religion, and now with immigration. Canadian politics has long been dominated by the politics of language. The world's largest democracy, India, is riven by the politics of identity, centring variously on religion, language, caste and region, and its currently dominant party appeals overtly to religious identity. Where democracy has been allowed to emerge in the Arab world, as well as in Turkey and Iran, politics is about religion versus secular values, or religion versus religion. And in the most sophisticated democracy in the region, Israel, the politics of identity is all-pervasive.

In the world's most successful economies, in East Asia, the main beneficiaries of an open, global system, the politics of identity has grown in intensity in the form of nationalism. South Korea and China have seen the re-emergence of strong national consciousness, often feeding off the grievances left by the Second World War in relation to Japan, which itself has leading politicians revisiting its imperial history. Those looking for alarming historical parallels can find them in the Europe of 1913, when an assertive and ambitious new power (Germany) jostled for influence with mature and declining imperial powers (France, Turkey and Austria), with a somewhat equivocal and relatively declining superpower (Britain) waiting across the sea. It is improbable that successful Asian countries will risk their hard-won prosperity for conflict over a few tiny islands – but then, the politics of identity was never rational.

The politics of identity has emerged, or re-emerged, most virulently and dangerously in the former Soviet Union. This is not the place to get into the rights and wrongs of the dispute over Ukraine and Crimea, or the earlier interventions in the Caucasus. Suffice it to say that issues of national pride, of linguistic and religious identity and of physical territory have taken precedence over the peaceful absorption of Russia into the world economy as a trade partner and successful energy exporter. Moreover, the personalization of Russian politics in the form of President Putin rather misses the point that plausible alternatives, like the opposition figurehead Alexei Navalny, seem to be no less nationalistic. Conflict has led to economic interdependence being set aside, with the West invoking sanctions and Russia trying to use its somewhat overrated weapon of gas supplies to the EU. Even if Russia turns its back on the global economy, however, it does not necessarily mean the end of globalization, which has had to accommodate a variety of other deviant states, like Iran, or failed states.

Indeed, the politics of identity has not yet led to any significant breach in the structures of integration that have been built up. In Europe in particular, despite the seriousness of the economic crisis and the triumphalist predictions of Eurosceptics, the eurozone remains intact and there is a lengthening queue of applicants to join the EU. Years of anti-immigrant protests have not yet led to any significant breach of the EU *acquis* protecting the free movement of labour, and net migration continues to rise overall. Breakaway movements challenging the traditional nation state, like the British SNP, the Catalans or Sinn Fein, are usually at pains to stress their adherence to the wider European project, as well as wanting to attract international investment and trade opportunities. Even among countries displaying signs of assertive nationalism, such as Russia, membership of the WTO and kindred bodies like the OECD remains a valued objective.

The problem is a more subtle one, obscured by fashionable but silly parallels between Putin and Kaiser Wilhelm or Hitler, or comparing the Chinese government with the Empire of the Sun. To be sure, there are countries of relative growth and relative decline, but the perceived need in earlier times for territory and possession of raw materials is increasingly marginal to the digitally connected world of modern economies, the complex interconnectedness of modern supply chains and finance. The genuinely tricky issue is that globalization requires rules and standards – international public goods – which require patient negotiation, goodwill and a common framework of analysis and shared self-interest. Progress is difficult to make when there is heightened emotion around identity and when there are suspicions in national capitals that globalization is too much of a zero-sum game. Geopolitics comes into play when the enforcement of the rules rests on the power that can be exercised by a major state, particularly the USA. The USA's influence, exercised by the 'soft power' of example and by the long arm of extra-territorial law, far exceeds its relatively declining economic importance. Its role in reforming the corrupt global football body, FIFA, is an example. For those whose pessimism about the future of global governance is grounded in military parallels, the best analogies are not with the invading conventional armies of 1914 or 1939 but with guerrilla warfare gradually sapping the energies of multilateral bodies and undermining their rules.

Twenty years ago I wrote about the central weakness of the globalization process being a 'regulatory deficit'. I was not appealing for more red tape, but for more agreed rules and standards to minimize disputes and protect public goods, such as the environment. Since then a vast amount has been done, globally and regionally, to fill the deficit that grows as market- and technology-driven interconnectedness grows. Ever since the financial crisis and a more assertive politics of identity, there have been meaningful agreements on banking and on trade, and even an international arms trade treaty. But there are serious frustrations, too.

Trade and Migration

The tension between further liberalization and protectionism is finely balanced. I described earlier the spread of trade-restricting measures and a slowdown in trade growth relative to global

GDP. But the disciplines of the WTO's dispute settlement process were sufficient to force the USA to back down from protectionist government procurement measures in its 2009 stimulus bill. Russia has followed China and Vietnam into the WTO. A China–ASEAN free-trade area has been agreed. The EU has completed and implemented a free-trade agreement with Korea, has agreed another with Canada, and is negotiating fitfully with Japan and India. The coalition government championed these agreements enthusiastically (I was dispatched to all four of those countries in support), and the WTO Agreement and the WTO on trade facilitation (essentially, removing red tape at frontiers), was modest, but expectations have now been raised of progress on other fronts. China, the EU and the US have now come to an agreement also to cut tariffs affecting the IT sector. In that more optimistic climate, attempts are being made to negotiate a 'plurilateral' agreement on services in the WTO, including the EU, the USA, Canada, Japan and potentially China. An agreement already exists for government procurement, though without China its value is limited.

Another approach, as with the US–EU (TTIP) and US–Asia Pacific (TTP) partnership agreements, is to bypass the WTO. These negotiations are very far from complete and, if they were to be realized, there would be some concern that the rules of international trade were being fragmented, leading to discrimination and to the diversion rather than the creation of trade. In particular the TTP excludes China. While there is a powerful case for the purity of multilateralism, in present conditions any big liberalizing move forward would send a powerful positive signal,

Nonetheless, resistance to further liberalization is especially strong in the USA and centres on the impact on jobs and wages, particularly where it involves trade with low-wage economies. One of the oldest arguments in economics is about whether the real world corresponds to the logic of the simple model developed by Eli Heckscher and Bertil Ohlin, to the effect that free trade between capital-rich and labour-abundant countries will tend to equalize wages – by implication, at the expense of workers in the developed economy. Three decades ago I worked with US and other economists on the empirical evidence related to trade with low-wage economies, in products like textiles and clothing, shoes and toys. Broadly speaking, the data suggested that the impact on Western jobs and wages was small, compared with the impact of technological change. But since then the growth of manufactured imports from China has led to a much more negative view of the impact on real wages and job opportunities for relatively unskilled workers. Moreover, such trade has been blamed, especially in the 1980s, for widening income inequalities, as earning opportunities opened up for the well educated and highly skilled but contracted at the bottom. Larry Summers, the former US Treasury Secretary, has been a strong proponent of these arguments. However, others dispute the evidence and argue that the pressure on unskilled workers' pay and jobs, and rising inequalities, originate elsewhere and cannot be pinned on trade. It must be said that I never heard protectionist arguments advanced in the UK on these grounds, though they were common in the late 1970s. The pressures I experienced for the government to seek anti-dumping measures on imports into the EU were rare and highly specific, concerning such things as ceramics or Chinese 'rebar' steel, and had no wider ideological justification.

To the surprise of many who once criticized the EU as an inward-looking trading bloc, it has managed to deepen and widen its integration while remaining a champion of the WTO. The EU is, however, now being challenged over one of its most basic freedoms: migration within the single market. The populist, 'identity' parties like UKIP in the UK have built up support by campaigning against migration from the poorer countries of the EU, leading to UK demands for restrictions on freedom of movement. In the event, the Conservatives wisely concentrated on the issue of benefit entitlement for EU migrants, rather than freedom of movement and to work. The irony was that the most bitterly disputed issues within the coalition related to non-EU migrants, but it was EU migrants whose swelling numbers were the source of public disquiet and made the Conservatives' net migration target unreachable. For other EU countries, the main issue is economic migrants from outside the EU. Large-scale attempted illegal immigration across the Mediterranean has fuelled hostility, even while highlighting the desperate humanitarian issues involved. Chancellor Merkel's enlightened decision to welcome Syrian refugees had produced a severe backlash in Eastern Europe. Immigration has become a dirty word almost everywhere.

Economic research suggests, nonetheless, that gains from freer migration far outweigh the benefits of removing the remaining trade barriers. Full global labour mobility may be a distant prospect, but economic simulations suggest that it would more than double global output by letting workers specialize where they are more productive. Another study suggests that a rise of only 3 per cent in the rich world labour force through migration would yield more benefits than would the removal of all remaining trade barriers. A lot depends on the specifics of particular countries. An OECD study shows that there is a big variation, for example, in the share of the foreign-born population with degrees, with Canada at 52 per cent, the UK at 47 per cent, and Australia at 39 per cent topping the list. The USA is close to the average of 30 per cent, with Germany at the bottom at 19 per cent, along with France at 24 per cent.

There is, however, little political appetite for realizing these benefits other than through managed migration of specialized and skilled labour. A popular view in rich countries is that migrants from poor countries gain at the expense of local workers. Overall, however, there are relatively few studies in the USA or the UK that suggest a negative impact on native wages, though groups within the labour force may be hit. One study of Western Europe argues that migrant workers actually *raise* native workers' pay by encouraging them to pursue more complex, higher-paid, 'upgrades'. The overall conclusion is that while a rapid burst of migration, especially during a slump, may indeed reduce wages, managed migration, slow enough to allow markets to adjust, could benefit both natives and migrants. These positive impacts are over and above more specific benefits such as the impact on government budgets, where increased tax revenues from working-age migrants tend to outweigh any extra costs. The OECD has shown these positive impacts to be greatest in Switzerland, the USA and the UK.

The position we have now reached is that there are broadly agreed multilateral rules governing trade in goods, which have some linked extension into services, investment flows and procurement, but that there is limited appetite to extend liberalization. There is more appetite for, but also considerable resistance to, liberalization on a more restricted basis in groupings like TTIP. And there is no appetite at all to extend liberalization in the area where benefits are potentially the greatest: migration.

The other major future challenge to trade policy, broadly defined, is to create a set of rules that governs competition between enterprises that originate in quite different traditions of corporate governance. There are different kinds of capitalism even within a tightly drawn group like the EU – from the highly competitive and volatile Anglo-Saxon model, to the long-term 'Rhenish' model of Germany and Holland, and the state-influenced enterprises of Italy and France. There has been convergence and also the evolution of common EU rules for competition and takeovers, state aid and public procurement, which have proved remarkably effective in buttressing the single market.

However, the challenge at a global level is much bigger. Western liberal capitalism, even the French variant, is being eclipsed by what can best be described as state capitalism, within which state-owned enterprises dominate. The Chinese state is the biggest shareholder in almost all of the country's 150 biggest companies, and state enterprises account for around 60 per cent of the Chinese stock market. The figure is thought to be around 40 per cent in Russia and Brazil, and state companies remain powerful in India, Saudi Arabia, Korea, Indonesia and other emerging powers. In asset terms, state companies totally dominate the oil and gas sector (Exxon and Shell don't even make the top ten) and utilities (companies like Dubai Ports World, but also EDF in France) and play a big role in telecommunications (China Mobile), finance (mainly through the sovereign wealth funds of China, the UAE, Norway, Saudi Arabia, Singapore and Kuwait) and some industries (such as SABIC in chemicals, Brazilian Vale in mining).

This is not the place for a long discussion on the merits and demerits of this form of ownership. Suffice it to say that compared to other models, state capitalists can take a long-term view, have access to (usually cheap) capital for large-scale investment, and can align company and national interests. But they can also more easily succumb to cronyism, corruption, misdirection of investment and inefficient but well-connected management. And they are a declining force. After 2007 the state enterprises in the world's top 500 firms lost 35 per cent of their value as against a rise of 5 per cent for global shares as a whole. Nonetheless, Aldo Musacchio and Sergio Lazzarini have described how state-owned companies are often now reinventing themselves through improved governance. Growing numbers of governments are looking to part-privatization, as in Mexico, or to mimicking markets. Many would welcome the introduction into WTO rules of market disciplines around public procurement, trade-distorting subsidies, and cartels and monopolies. We are beginning to see, with the possible plurilateral agreement on public procurement, the outlines at least of a genuine global competitive regime of the kind pioneered in the EU.

Internet Governance and E-commerce

Nothing embodies global interconnectedness so much as the internet. The communications revolution based on digital computer technology effectively became global in 1990 with the World Wide Web, followed shortly after by the advent of the browser. The number of users had climbed to 350 million by 2000 and is now estimated at 2.4 billion, 600 million in China alone. A growing amount of trade is conducted within and between countries via e-commerce; international finance is underpinned by the vast computing power and global communications systems of banks, insurance companies and hedge funds; cross-border mail has largely been displaced by email. This depth of integration is why a reversal of globalization seems so much less thinkable than in 1913.

Yet efficient technology does not by itself guarantee that information will flow freely across frontiers. The nineteenth century saw immense strides in communications technology – transoceanic cables and telegraph, rapid and reliable maritime and rail travel – but warring governments managed to reverse the advances in living standards brought by innovation and markets.

It is a popular myth that the internet is unregulated and 'just happens'. Certainly, in its early days the system operated as a 'bottom-up', messy and unruly self-regulating system. But from the outset there were standard-setting bodies like the World Wide Web Consortium, engineering standards and protocols agreed via the Internet Engineering Task Force, and the Internet Corporation for Assigned Names and Numbers (ICANN) which oversees the system of domain names. These are, for the most part, still models of open, democratic decision-making, independent of government, though the US government had until very recently a role in checking the accuracy of changes to ICANN's addressing. And, of course, internet technology originated in data network research for the Pentagon.

There are now major challenges. The first is a fundamental one: to ensure that the internet evolves as an open global system, vastly increasing access to information and enabling people to communicate with like-minded people anywhere, rather than becoming another instrument of state control. The Chinese have demonstrated, through a vast technological effort, that it is possible to censor and guide the internet, and also develop a formidable cyber-security capacity for offensive as well as defensive purposes. The so-called Great Firewall can eliminate 'undesirable' websites like Twitter and Facebook, monitor domestic users and screen out politically threatening messages, while allowing the prodigious growth of a 'national' internet with a wide range of commercially valuable or personally useful services. Chinese software also helps other governments create firewalls of their own. Russia and Saudi Arabia have developed variants of the Chinese approach. Other countries, like North Korea and Turkmenistan, simply outlaw the internet altogether.

Until recently, the USA and the EU held the moral high ground in shaping the debate about the future of the internet, championing a free and open global system. In fact, the debate has never been totally black and white, as even the most permissive Western countries have recognized the desirability of filtering out hardcore pornography. But moral authority has been dented by the exposure by Edward Snowden of large-scale intelligence surveillance via the internet. Indeed, the US National Security Agency (NSA) and the UK's GCHQ have seen such surveillance as crucial to national security. There is, of course, a big difference between surveillance and censorship as applied through the Great Firewall. And there are varying degrees of intrusiveness in surveillance. Overall, surveillance to detect and monitor terrorist activity, with appropriate safeguards, is rather easier to defend than is eavesdropping on friendly heads of government. Nonetheless, the US government came under pressure to relinquish its role in ICANN. The European Commission is putting forward revised data protection legislation which strengthens privacy rights, including data held on EU citizens in the USA. Overall, most Americans and Brits seem less exercised by data piracy than Germans and other Europeans who have had experience of totalitarian rule.

There is an overlapping debate on how to widen commercial use of the internet in order to generate trade. One of the main objectives within the EU single market is to create a 'digital single market', which is shorthand for a whole set of proposals designed to make e-commerce easier to transact across the EU. These include agreement on data protection, consumer protection for digital transactions, agreed rules on copyright, financial settlement arrangements and dispute settlement procedures. In 2015 I gave the annual Schuman Lecture in Brussels, endorsing and championing the digital single market. Beyond the slogans, however, the issues are immensely complex and will take years to negotiate. The TTIP negotiations aim to carry through the digital single market to a transatlantic level.

One so far largely submerged issue is the monopoly power exercised through the internet by US-owned platforms such as Microsoft, Google and Amazon, all of which have been subject to European Commission investigations into abuse of monopoly. It is right in principle that market dominance should be studied and if necessary curbed, but the European Commission has proved a rather unwieldy institution manoeuvring slowly in a world of rapidly changing technology. Some member states, notably Germany, see the issue as one of 'digital sovereignty'. But digital protectionism would almost certainly be a backward step and for countries like the UK the future lies in giving maximum scope to the new digital economy and writing international rules to sustain it.

Collective Globalization: Global Warming

One of the biggest tests of the strength and durability of the process of closer integration is the ability of states, and individual actors within them, to coordinate in order to deal with major externalities or market failures through regulation or other intervention. We have seen that, even after the shock of the global crisis, there is still a willingness to coordinate over common rules governing trade, investment and communications.

A bigger test is management of the 'commons', notably environmental resources, both 'sources' of national wealth, like forests, fish stocks and water supplies, and 'sinks' for absorbing pollution, like the atmosphere. The issue of sustainability on a cross-border and global basis has been recognized for a generation or more and found its best expression in the Brundtland Report,

Our Common Future. Having worked with the Norwegian prime minister, Gro Harlem Brundtland, and Sir Sonny Ramphal, the Commonwealth Secretary General, to prepare the report, I have some pride in its partial authorship and regard it as the best statement of what 'sustainable development' actually means.

Governments have acknowledged the challenge in general terms, and there is a plethora of international agreements for managing the 'commons', some of which, like the Montreal Protocol to protect the ozone layer, the treatment of Antarctica as a common space, and cooperation over satellite communications, have been broadly respected. But the biggest challenge, over climate change, has produced over the thirty years or so during which a scientific consensus has existed little more than a collective acknowledgement that there is a major but unresolved problem.

The warming effect of man-made atmospheric emissions is basic science and there have been persistent warnings of potentially catastrophic consequences from an overwhelming majority of qualified scientists. The economics is less secure than the science, but reputable and properly qualified research from Nick Stern, William Nordhaus and others suggests that the economic cost of limiting global temperature increases to non-catastrophic levels is modest, relative to the costs averted, provided that abatement is concerted and quick. Nordhaus, for example, argues that the cost of limiting the increase in temperature to 2°C would be around 1.5 per cent of GDP, were all major countries to participate.

There are, of course, massive uncertainties. The feedback loops in nature could slow down climate change, but they could also accelerate it (the emission of methane from warming Arctic tundra is a possible trigger, for example). The assumptions underlying the economics can produce a wide range of outcomes. But it is simply prudent and sensible to deal with the risk of major and irreversible damage by behaving cautiously. At the level of both rhetoric and intellectual reasoning, most governments appear to accept the nature of the problem and the need for collective action. A succession of conferences – Kyoto, Johannesburg, Copenhagen, Warsaw – has reiterated concern, albeit with varying degrees of commitment to action, from some to none. And in the EU at least there has been some collective action in the form of agreed long-term carbon emission limits and a system of carbon trading, reinforcing varying levels of national commitment. The Paris, global negotiations, in December 2015 were seen as a significant advance, though ambitious targets depend on national governments to implement them.

There are various reasons why the response has been somewhat lame. Overall these are mainly to do with domestic politics. Even in Western countries, like the UK or Germany, where there is a high level of awareness and respect for the science and a general political commitment to act and even to play a global leadership role, there is resistance to strong carbon abatement measures. The coalition government broadly endorsed a continuation of the policies developed under Ed Miliband as climate change minister in the Labour government, with the UK taking a leadership role in the EU, and Chris Huhne and Ed Davey were able to secure ambitious long-term commitments at EU level. But there was growing resistance to onshore wind farms on aesthetic grounds and from ministers influenced by climate-change sceptics. There has been resistance from the owners of potentially stranded carbon-intensive assets, including carbon-intensive power systems, energy-intensive industries and petrol-based motor vehicles, and from those whose jobs are at risk. Indeed, I faced strong pressure from engineering and process industries, such as steel, aluminium, glass and cement, that were already struggling with recession, to stop unilateral UK action that would make them uncompetitive and lead to 'carbon leakage' overseas. I led the efforts in government to secure compensation for these energy-intensive industries – notably steel – and achieved partial success. These problems set clear limits on unilateral action.

There is, in addition, a short-term cost to using renewable energy, and in the shadow of a major economic crisis in which living standards have been squeezed there was no great appetite for inflicting that cost on voters. George Osborne was increasingly hostile to environmental measures that had negative price or revenue impacts, and there was a major division on this issue with the Lib Dems in government. Despite that, considerable progress was made through the industrial strategy in, for example, attracting Siemens to manufacture wind turbines in Hull, and in promoting collaboration with and within the car industry on new low-carbon engine technology. Put more generally, most of us discount the long-term future quite heavily, whatever nice words we may use abut safeguarding future generations. Woody Allen's sardonic quip, 'What have future generations ever done for me?' is actually quite a profound insight into behaviour.

Even if the prospect of major catastrophe were to generate a sufficient sense of urgency, there are two fundamental problems to overcome. The first is that rapid growth and development, as experienced in China, India and other emerging economies, is energy- and fossil fuel-intensive. Poverty may fall, a desirable outcome, but at the expense of large carbon emissions, an undesirable outcome. Even then, with a rapid expansion of coal burning, the CO_2 emissions per head in China are still below those of the UK, the eurozone and Japan, let alone the USA, where they are about three times greater. India's are around one third of Chinese levels. Quite plausibly, the leaders of those countries could advance a strong moral, social and political case for resisting ceilings on their growth unless rich countries agree to emission reductions far more draconian than they are currently willing to contemplate. The Paris negotiations did however lead to some reconciliation of these positions.

The second problem, which flows from the first, is the complexity of reaching agreement on meaningful and enforceable emission control when there are differences on the distributional principles underlying such a system. Climate-change campaigners have a broad framework, 'contract and converge', which is logically the only way to proceed but is not meaningful without politically credible numbers. The central problem is that even with challenging assumptions about improvements in energy efficiency, BP estimates that over the next twenty years there could be energy consumption growth of around 35 per cent, and growth in CO_2 emissions of 25 per cent, even allowing for renewable energy growth of well over 300 per cent. Yet overall CO_2 emissions have to be cut in order to limit global temperature increases to below 2°C. Some encouragement may be derived from the fact that in 2014, for the first time in forty years, annual emissions actually stabilized as a consequence of big strides in energy efficiency in China and a shift from coal to gas in the USA. But serious risks of destabilizing climate change remain unless there is global agreement not just on targets but on practical policies much more radical than are currently in train.

A sense of despair is often expressed at the failure of global conferences on climate change to produce results and this is frequently attributed to a failure of intergovernmental coordination and the limits of global governance. In fact, the problem is a different one: the ministers and officials who negotiate on these matters are often far ahead of their domestic constituencies in their sense of global responsibility. There is a genuine problem of creating a politically persuasive narrative around the need for any serious action, especially when there is a wide range of views, as there was in the coalition, ranging from deeply committed Lib Dems to Conservatives who dismissed the idea of man-made climate change out of hand. The first step is to win the political argument about the seriousness of the climate threat relative to the short-term costs, which is not straightforward, especially in countries that have learned to live with and prosper under such obvious and massive threats as nuclear war.

It also means selling a positive and practical agenda based around job-creating green technologies, as is happening in the emerging UK supply chains for offshore wind, as well as taxes and charges that incorporate environmental costs, large-scale investment in scientific research and the development of alternative fuels, energy conservation systems and climate-change adaptations. Examples include the British experiment with carbon capture and storage, the Catapult centre based in Glasgow, low-carbon car engines, and the strengthening of institutions like the Green Investment Bank that can demonstrate the economic and environmental value of long-term investments. Difficult though these challenges are, we should not underestimate the progress that is being made in Europe, including the UK, Japan and, to a lesser degree, in China and the USA.

Financial and Economic Policy Coordination

Throughout the post-war period of deeper and wider economic integration, both globally and regionally, there has been a debate as to the effectiveness of policy coordination to take account of 'spillovers': the impact of one country's monetary and fiscal policies, or micro-level interventions, on another. The greater the degree of integration, the bigger the spillover, either for good or for ill, and the desirability of coordination.

The financial crisis and its damaging aftermath have led to a good deal of heart-searching as to the strength and effectiveness of coordination mechanisms. In relation to banking, there have been moves towards common capital standards under the umbrella of Basel 3 and a global regulatory body, the Financial Stability Board, as well as a partial banking union in the eurozone. But as I described in chapter two, there has also been a degree of regulatory divergence.

In relation to the coordination of macroeconomic policy, the eurozone crisis has concentrated minds, to a degree, on mechanisms for managing imbalances within a monetary union. It has led to enhanced monetary powers for a coordinating central bank, the ECB, though the coordination is currently heavily biased towards control by German conservatism in monetary and fiscal policy. For the rest of the world, with floating exchange rates as between the USA, the eurozone, the UK, China, Japan and other major economies, there is an adjustment mechanism that does not require explicit coordination. However, the build-up of imbalances in savings and investment, particularly in relation to China and the USA, was an indirect cause of the financial crisis and the potentially devastating, deflationary consequences evoked the most effective cooperative response of the post-war era. Major economies agreed an ambitious package of expansionary and unorthodox monetary policy, together with a moderate fiscal stimulus. The emergency action achieved its objective, stabilized the world economy, and allowed rapid growth to proceed in the main emerging economies.

Five years on, two major, related, international coordination problems are looming. The first is that the era of unorthodox cheap money generated by low interest rates and QE in major Western economies is coming to an end. There has been anxiety in some countries that this could unleash a flood of money flows, attracted by higher yields, back into the USA but destabilize other parts of the world. That is already beginning to happen.

Secondly, the search for yield attracted a lot of capital to some emerging markets which have, as a consequence, been able to run large current account deficits: Turkey (4.5 per cent of GDP in 2015), Indonesia (around 2 per cent), Brazil (4 per cent), Colombia (6.5 per cent), South Africa (5.3 per cent). The UK, Canada and Australia all have substantial deficits, of over 3 per cent, too. Corresponding surpluses have existed in the main oil-producing states, notably Saudi Arabia, the eurozone (mainly Germany), China, South Korea, Taiwan and Singapore. The concern is that a sudden change of sentiment, amplified by the herd mentality of investors, could create a new cycle of financial crises centred on emerging and rapidly growing economies. In 2014 and 2015 there was evidence of significant capital outflows from China, Russia and other emerging economies, and this could well build in seriousness.

The obvious and recognized mechanism for resolving such coordination problems is the IMF. Its role has, however, shrunk relative to the scale of global capital flows (US$370 billion in quotas versus many trillions of dollars), but it remains important and has played a key role in the eurozone crisis. Yet at a time when quota enlargement is crucial to managing the next wave of payment problems, the US Congress blocked an agreement to double quotas. The Republican right objected to the principle of enlargement of a global multilateral institution and to enhanced voting powers for emerging economies, notably China. President Obama was able to negotiate a compromise but the capacity of governments collectively to respond to a future crisis has been weakened. And this is merely one of many examples of the difficulties of strengthening global governance in the face of resistant national politics.

Part Two
The UK after the Crisis

Boom, Bust and Recovery

I write about UK economic policy from the standpoint and vantage point of having helped to make it in the five years from 2010, and of having been a leading opposition critic before that. I will try here to be as objective as possible, but inevitably I carry the burden of personal baggage as well as the advantage of inside knowledge. I also try to straddle the worlds of minister, party politician and economist, all of whose preoccupations and language are different.

The various phases of the financial crisis have created a sharp contrast with the experiences of other developed economies. In the three decades before the financial crisis, the UK was a star performer. In the period 1980–97, following the tribulations of the 1970s, the UK grew at 2.9 per cent per annum – higher than for the twentieth century as a whole, which averaged 2.7 per cent per annum. This period of growth – considerably faster than Germany and France and a little less than the USA and Japan – was widely attributed to the reforms of the Thatcher era, though it was also a period of macroeconomic instability with the boom and bust cycle culminating in the sterling crisis of 1991.

Then, between 1997 and 2007, there was a remarkable period of both rapid and stable growth: 3.2 per cent on average, faster than the USA and far in excess of the eurozone economies, let alone Japan, which was then mired in the aftermath of the 1989 banking crisis. Gordon Brown celebrated his fifty quarters of growth by claiming it was the best economic performance since the Hanoverians. The question that lingers politically is this: was it, indeed, a golden age, brutally but unfortunately terminated by a global financial crisis well beyond the control of the UK policy-makers? Or was it a fool's paradise based on several elements of unsustainable growth: household consumption linked to a booming housing market and growing personal debt; excessive government spending and lack of attention to an emerging budget deficit; a bloated, internationally focused, banking sector exposing the economy to global systemic risk; and a neglect of the role of exports and import substitution in driving growth, in part because of an overvalued exchange rate? While this debate is now a question for economic historians, it matters enormously in terms of who carries the historic blame for the crisis and for judging whether the post-crisis recovery has truly broken the mould of the past.

I have never believed that it was helpful to identify a principal villain whom we could blame for the crisis. Responsibility was widely distributed. There was complacency among pre-crash ministers, Gordon Brown and his Treasury team, who failed to appreciate the significance of personal indebtedness in relation to income, which rose to the highest level historically recorded and the highest in the Western world, along with an extraordinary boom in house prices, and who showed extraordinary deference to the City and to the banks in particular. Their Conservative predecessors carry the responsibility for having unleashed financial sector deregulation with major unforeseen consequences. The Bank of England believed it was successfully managing inflation, but it totally ignored asset inflation. Then, when disaster struck, it appeared to have no contingency plans to deal with lack of confidence in banks. The financial regulator, the Financial Services Authority (FSA), had developed a complex bureaucratic system of regulating banks, but failed to supervise them adequately so that several mortgage-lenders (Northern Rock, HBOS, Bradford

& Bingley, Dunfermline Building Society) engaged in imprudent commercial and domestic lending, leading to collapse. Major British global banks, notably RBS, developed fatal systemic weaknesses. Above all, there were bankers whose greed and stupidity has been exposed in innumerable reports, domestic and international. RBS expanded to become the world's largest bank on one measure, and it collapsed with catastrophic consequences.

All of these issues were discussed extensively in *The Storm* and I do not need to rehearse them in detail again. Suffice it to say that while errors of omission and commission led to Britain being particularly exposed to the financial crisis – the scale and structure of UK-based global banks, the extent of personal indebtedness and housing inflation – it was, after all, a global financial crisis. I have also acknowledged that whatever criticism attaches to the Labour government for the hubris and complacency leading up to the crisis, both it and the Bank of England dealt with the unprecedented and alarming series of events around the crisis in a sensible way, which minimized the damage. Banks were provided with emergency liquidity and effectively taken over when they failed, so as to maintain the functioning of the financial system. As with the other major countries' authorities, expansionary and creative monetary policy was used to sustain demand; large fiscal deficits caused in part by collapsing revenue were sensibly accommodated, along with a modest, temporary fiscal stimulus; and cooperative rather than nationalistic solutions were sought, with the UK playing a leadership role – mostly good policy, apart from a decision to curb government capital spending when it was most needed to offset recession.

However, while it is both fair and satisfying to be able to apportion blame and credit in an even-handed and nuanced way, the world of politics is less forgiving and demands simpler answers. The political question that still reverberates is whether the long-term damage, and the legacy problem of public deficits and debt, are primarily down to the banking collapse or whether they originated in careless, profligate management of the public finances in the years leading up to the 2008 crisis.

The Conservatives have consistently argued that it was the latter, and that no doubt helped in convincing a sufficient number of voters to give them an overall commons majority in 2015, for the first time since 1992. The evidence is less compelling. In the 2007/8 budget, before the Northern Rock crisis, which provided the first sign of an impending financial crash, the government's estimated current budget deficit was close to 1 per cent of GDP for that year and public debt was 37 per cent of GDP. Both were at that stage broadly compatible with the government's own fiscal rules, aiming to balance the current budget over the cycle and to meet a 'sustainable investment rule' of debt to GDP of under 40 per cent. Unfortunately for Labour's subsequent reputation, the deficit and debt position was already deteriorating, albeit from what appeared to be a strong position.

Much mischief has been made over the numbers and what they meant. The then government claimed that it was continuing to pursue 'prudence with a purpose', while the Conservatives talked about a 'huge' deficit and a failure 'to fix the roof while the sun was shining'. It is useful to go back for a balanced assessment to the Institute of Fiscal Studies' analysis of January 2009. It broadly concluded that Labour entered the recession in 2007/8 with public finances in a better shape than they had inherited in 1996/7, but in a worse shape than when the Conservatives entered recession in 1989/90. The debt position (net debt to GDP) was the second best in the G7 and better than Labour had inherited, but it was deteriorating (Figure 7.1), whereas most developed countries were strengthening their position at this time. On the measure of balance set out in the coalition agreement, the budget before the crisis was almost in balance and was in a better position than Labour had inherited (Figure 7.2). As the main Lib Dem spokesman on economic matters, I sought, both at the time and subsequently, to communicate this nuanced judgement. But in the heat and noise of political battle any subtleties were lost.

Where the Labour government was subject to particular criticism was that its overall public borrowing pre-crisis, even when defined in structural terms, was one of the largest in the developed world. The reason was that the government had been increasing public investment, financed by borrowing, from 0.5 per cent of GDP to over 2 per cent of GDP, reversing the sharp cut in public investment in the Conservative years. As I have argued elsewhere, it is economically foolish to treat investment and recurring current spending in the same way and the yo-yo in investment under successive governments has done great harm to the construction industry and to infrastructure planning. The big cut in public investment that took effect in 2012/13 was the latest and most severe example of this phenomenon (Figure 7.3).

The critics still say that the Labour government in pre-crisis days should have been better prepared for budgetary shocks. And because there was no independent oversight of fiscal policy before the establishment by the coalition of the Office for Budget Responsibility, those critics say that the government deluded itself and the public about the strength of its position. Indeed, there were commentators arguing for some years that there was a structural deficit in the budget, over and above the economic cycle. The Institute for Fiscal Studies consistently argued from 2005 on that there should be a small fiscal tightening, of around 0.5–1 per cent of GDP for just that reason, and Conservative critics of budget policy argued, usually in non-specific terms, that that was what was required. Had their advice been heeded, however, it would have made little difference to the scale of post-crisis fiscal problems since the pre-crisis structural deficit was so small.

Subsequently, the OECD has retrospectively recalculated the structural deficit pre-crisis and come up with a much higher number, as much as 5 per cent of GDP. David Smith of the *Sunday Times* is among those who regard this as conclusive evidence of overspending. However, the retrospective recalculation of the structural deficit is based on the fact that a bank collapse showed the economy to be structurally over-dependent on banking and housing, whereas the banking crisis was not anticipated before it happened. The Labour government should, of course, have been more aware of these risks, as some of us argued at the time. But Conservatives and others who now claim the moral high ground were among those who were apologists for the banking industry and inflated house prices and saw no risk in either.

The rather arcane arguments about what is 'structural' and what is 'cyclical', and how these are measured, are not just of interest to professional economists. Essentially, budget surpluses and deficits should cancel each other out over the cyclical fluctuations of an economy around a trend – what the Labour government called the 'Golden Rule' – and any persistent surplus or deficit is deemed to be 'structural'. These concepts are, however, easier to describe in the abstract than in reality, and after rather than before the event. Thus the promised timetables for fiscal consolidation made in the 2015 election were based on precise estimates of what is required to eliminate the structural deficit before 2018, yet the distinction between structural and cyclical is based on guesswork and is subject to a wide range of error.

As we can see in Figure 7.4, there is a range from 0 to 6 per cent of GDP for estimates of the output gap from which the structural deficit is calculated. The output gap measures the spare capacity in the economy. Where there is a lot of spare capacity beyond that which is estimated by the OBR, as some of the analyses indicate, there is less need for fiscal tightening. On the other hand, there are some estimates that suggest that the tightening is not enough. But the range of error is truly enormous. The government works from the OBR estimates, which happen to be fairly close to the middle of the range, but these then lock the government into a more conservative fiscal policy than would be recommended by, say, the IMF. And that suggests, above all, that policy has to be flexible and pragmatic, recognizing that those driving the economy are trying to steer a car without the ability to see through the windscreen and with a rear-view mirror that is very dirty.

———

The other area where there is live debate around historical matters concerns the length and depth of the post-crisis recession and the speed of recovery. The contraction of GDP in the UK was estimated to be 7.2 per cent between Q2 2008 (the fall of Lehman Brothers) and Q3 2009, the biggest of any major economy (though Greece experienced contraction of a higher order of magnitude, around 25 per cent). The UK shock was more serious than any post-war recession, and even than the 1929–31 period when output fell by 6 per cent, though in terms of jobs the interwar period was much worse. Unemployment rose to 17 per cent in 1932 as against a peak of 8.5 per cent in 2010. Subsequent statistical revisions, as in February 2014, have suggested that the contraction was 6 per cent, not 7.2 per cent, and there may be more revisions.

What is striking is the time it has taken to get recovery going. GDP finally reached its pre-recession peak in the final quarter of 2014, six years (or twenty-four quarters) after the onset of the crisis. The British experience contrasts with the USA, which reached its pre-recession peak in half that time and has been growing consistently ever since, and also with Germany, where the recession was deeper than the USA but which enjoyed a strong recovery, reaching its pre-recession peak at the same time as the USA. By contrast, the rest of the eurozone, after a shallow post-crisis recession, recovered somewhat, but has stagnated since the beginning of 2011 and has never recovered its pre-crisis production level. The eurozone countries had the additional burden, not shared by the UK, of trying to achieve major structural adjustment within a fixed exchange rate system.

The question for the UK is why recovery took so long? Those mainly apologists for the Blair/Brown Labour government of 2005–10 believe that a fundamentally sound economy was blown off-course by the crisis of 2008, and argue that the prolonged pain was unnecessary, a conscious policy choice by the coalition government. A more sophisticated version of this view is that a more aggressively Keynesian set of policies – postponing or ignoring deficit reduction policies in the belief that higher growth would automatically correct them – would have produced a quicker exit from recession than reliance on loose monetary policy. The counter-view is that deeper factors inhibited the recovery: the structural nature of the fiscal deficit; the overhang of public and/ or private debt; damaged banking and credit transmission; and permanent loss of capacity in terms of skills and other productive capacity. There were also external factors: a slump in export demand in the eurozone market and rising commodity prices which cut real incomes and consumption. I shall review all these factors below.

But with ten quarters of successive growth by autumn 2015, no one doubts that a recovery has now taken place. Expectations among a range of forecasters is in the range 2.2–2.9 per cent in 2016 slowing from 2.8 per cent in 2015. There is a broad consensus among institutional forecasters, such as the OECD and the IMF, that the UK has had the strongest growth, and strongest growth forecasts, of any major developed economy. Some turnaround from two years ago! Growth has been driven primarily by household consumption. Yet there has been only a delayed increase in real wages (by roughly 3 per cent in 2015), and living standards towards the end of 2015, measured by real disposable income per head, were roughly at the same position as pre-crisis, according to the Institute of Fiscal Studies. There has been a stronger link with rising house prices and easier mortgage availability, which have generated greater confidence and a sense of enhanced personal wealth, together with a general inclination to spend a little more and reduce the levels of savings built up in crisis times. Indeed, one of the objectives of very low interest rates has been to encourage such spending.

Other demand drivers of growth have been less strong. Overall, investment in the economy fell by a quarter from Q1 2008 to Q4 2009, and within that investment by the private business sector by 27 per cent. Investment has grown steadily since – by 5 per cent in 2015 – but is still well below the pre-crisis peak and, as a share of GDP, is at the lowest level for over half a century. The trade balance has remained largely unchanged, with weak export growth, partly because of weak demand in the euro area, and weak import growth; but the current deficit, at around 5 per cent of GDP, is the largest of any major economy. This is a reminder that while there is undeniably a recovery taking place, it is seriously unbalanced.

So, how meaningful and secure is the recovery? A strict definition of recovery is one that doesn't just resume growth but recovers lost ground – that is, lost output. In previous recessions, that is what happened in the UK. But on this occasion, when output passed its pre-crisis peak, the economy was still around 15 per cent below what it would have been if the long-term pre-crisis trend had continued. As for the future trajectory, the impressive growth numbers of recent months disguise the latent constraints, about which there was depressingly little discussion in the 2015 election.

————

There has been and will be a whole set of factors, legacies of the financial crisis, that will act as a brake on a full recovery. Historical experience of financial crises suggests that the negative legacies are much more profound than the traditional cycles experienced in the post-war period. Carmen Reinhart and Kenneth Rogoff's study of many such crises suggests that on average there is a 6 per cent loss of output, relative to trend, from crisis point to output trough, three to four years later, and that a decade after the crisis the loss remained the same. Seven years after the UK crisis there are still factors inhibiting full recovery: the need to end unorthodox monetary policy (very low interest rates and QE), which have stimulated growth and acted as a life support system but will have to be reversed, posing a serious challenge to indebted households and companies. The Bank of England has been coy about when this might happen – less explicit than the US Federal Reserve, perhaps noting that the Fed has had to keep postponing interest rate rises. There is also a residual structural deficit in the budget and a higher level of public and private debt than has been seen as comfortable in peacetime and outside periods of crisis. Furthermore, the process of deleveraging of banks is taking a long time despite all the government's efforts to stimulate new lending – with continuing negative net lending to SMEs.

It is far from clear at the moment whether each of these factors will be temporary, permitting a full recovery, or will act as a continuing brake. Japan has demonstrated how prolonged stagnation, interrupted by short bursts of growth, can become self-perpetuating. The factors noted above make it clear that there is a risk of this happening in the UK. However, the longer and stronger the UK period of recovery is, the less likely it is to founder.

Over and above the factors inhibiting strong recovery, there are doubts about its sustainability because of structural imbalances: 'the wrong kind of recovery'. Several separate points can be made. First, there is the reliance on demand led by consumption rather than investment. Consumption as a share of GDP rose to 23 per cent in 2013, higher than at any time since the 1950s. The investment share fell to 13.5 per cent, having fallen from around 15 per cent pre-crisis. It was as much as 22 per cent in the late 1980s and early 1990s. In the early stages of recovery it is not unusual for consumption to precede investment: that is the 'accelerator' in the standard theory of the trade cycle. But arguably, a greater willingness to use public investment could have 'crowded in' private investment, as has happened on a modest scale with the Regional Growth Fund and Green Investment Bank. The offer of guarantees has been an acknowledgement that the state has an important role in sharing and reducing risk in order to stimulate investment. The use of capital allowances to support private investment was another. But when the private sector lacks confidence to invest, public investment should be used more actively. The Conservative approach to fiscal policy meant that this didn't happen.

Secondly, there has been a reliance on domestic rather than

overseas demand. Export growth has been weak despite, until recently, a more competitive exchange rate. There is a danger of this problem becoming more serious as recovery leads to market expectations of interest rate rises, attracting overseas capital and driving up the exchange rate further, thus losing any competitive advantage for exporters. It is difficult to be definitive about when an exchange rate is 'over-' or 'under-' valued. But the standard (purchasing power parity) measures suggest that overvaluation is becoming a serious problem for industries involved in trade.

With a current account deficit already close to 5 per cent of GDP and a trade in goods deficit of 7 per cent of GDP, the economy starts its recovery with a substantial external imbalance. This does not matter in the traditional sense of a 'balance of payments crisis', since there is a free floating exchange rate. But it matters nonetheless since exports, or internationally tradable goods and services more generally, especially manufacturing, are the main source of productivity growth. The coalition government's response to this problem was to emphasize export promotion. I did raise publicly and privately the question of whether there should be a policy for the exchange rate, but this would have complicated the role of the Bank of England's Monetary Policy Committee and there was little support for any kind of exchange rate intervention in the Bank or the Treasury.

A third source of imbalance is that represented by housing infla-tion: 10 per cent across the UK and over 20 per cent in London in 2014 with little slowing in 2015. There is a short-term benefit of higher house prices increasing the wealth of owner-occupiers and hence their willingness to spend. There is an incentive to developers to build on land with planning permission. But there is also a range of negative economic and social consequences: increasing the indebtedness and exposure to interest rate rises of households dependent on mortgages, with increasing multi-ples to mortgage debt to income; further movement away from bank lending for business investment towards domestic property acquisition, because mortgages are secured against a seemingly ever-appreciating asset; knock-on effects such as raising the cost of living in the rental market; and a bigger affordability gap for those on middle and lower earnings and younger people.

These imbalances represent long-standing problems. For two decades Britain has been near the bottom of the OECD range for fixed investment, for example, and the decade before the crisis was also characterized by a weak trade account, a housing boom and strong regional disparities. Until they are countered, the prospects for a genuine sustained recovery from the crisis are limited.

There is a particular feature of the recovery that casts some light on the question of whether it is now secure or is potentially mired in deeper structural problems: the so-called 'productivity puzzle'. Britain has seen impressive recovery in employment. But labour productivity remained, in mid-2015, 15 per cent below pre-crisis levels, and 20 per cent below where it was at an equivalent stage of the cycle in earlier recessions. On 2013 figures, UK productivity is also around 30 per cent lower than in France, Germany or the USA in GDP per hours worked, and 17 per cent lower than the whole of the G7. In relation to the G7 it is 20 per cent lower in GDP per worker, and 40 per cent lower than in the USA. Britain started the recession behind other G7 countries and the differential has widened.

Employment in 2015 reached a forty-year high, with working age employment of 73 per cent and unemployment at 5.6 per cent, one of the lowest figures in the developed world. At first sight, this is a good example of classical economics at work and an endorsement of flexible British labour markets. What appears to have happened is that falling real wages, because of continued inflation on top of severe wage restraint, caused employers to replace capital with labour. Pay was sacrificed for jobs. This experience represents a strong rebuttal of those who clamour for US-style 'hire and fire' legislation with minimal recourse to the law in cases of 'unfair' dismissal or discrimination.

But the productivity puzzle remains. And it remains important since, as Paul Krugman has put it, 'productivity isn't everything but in the long run it is almost everything'. During the coalition I did seek to provoke public debate around the proposition that UK labour markets were, perhaps, too flexible and that we needed to address the chronic insecurity of employment. As a result we passed legislation dealing with one of the main abuses of zero-hour contracts – exclusivity contracts – but the dominant view was not to put at risk the real achievement of rising employment and falling unemployment.

Various explanations have been offered for poor productivity, some prosaic and statistical, others suggesting deeper forces at work. One point, brought out in a study by Charles Goodhart of Morgan Stanley, is that a very high percentage – around 80 per cent – of the increase in employment since the crisis has been in self-employment, roughly half of it part-time. Some self-employment is genuinely entrepreneurial and reflects new patterns of working in the IT and creative industry sectors. But a lot is disguided unemployment. Also for the year to mid-2015, the part-time share in employment fell sharply, along with unemployment, but the proportion of part-timers wanting but unable to find a full-time job – around 18 per cent – rose. So, poor productivity may partly reflect the fact that true employment is overstated.

Other explanations for the puzzle are more sector-specific. Ian McCafferty argues that much of the poor productivity performance can be put down to a few particular industries, without the need to invoke a wider problem. The banking industry now 'produces' less and has an army of regulators to police it, which may be necessary but makes it less productive. North Sea oil fields have seen declining production performance in recent years, requiring more people to extract the same amount of oil and gas. Airport security – large numbers of people searching bags – has affected labour productivity there. These particular factors are collectively large and are likely to drag down productivity for some time.

Another set of explanations relates to the slow pace of recovery. John Van Reenen at the LSE has argued that lack of investment following a fall in demand is at the root of the problem. Over the decade before the crisis-investment was growing at 3 per cent per annum and had that trend continued, capital per worker would now be around 30 per cent higher than it is. But the problem is almost certainly more deep-rooted than the disruption to investment. Business investment was growing strongly in 2014 and 2015, but productivity was not. Indeed, Jonathan Haskel and his colleagues have argued that we are merely seeing a short-term blip in a longer-term story of weak 'total factor productivity', caused by long-term neglect of R&D and skills development. That is almost certainly a major factor and, far from being a puzzle, has been extensively discussed over the years.

One other explanation of the productivity puzzle, linked to the crisis itself, has been suggested by Goldman Sachs and by Ben Broadbent at the Bank of England: that productivity has been impaired by the damage done to the banking system. Credit is not flowing, as it should, to start-ups and high-potential firms seeking capital to expand. Banks have also been reluctant to expose losses by pulling the plug on 'zombie' companies, which would be forced into insolvency under normal conditions. The new conservatism of the banks and the demands of regulators to reduce risk exposure have discouraged lending to exporters and to companies offering intellectual property rather than strong physical collateral – property – as security. The same set of factors helps to explain why export performance has been poor. The conclusion of this compelling analysis is clear: 'recovery' will not just plough ahead, taking up 'slack' in the economy. It will only become secure when banks are sufficiently restructured and reformed to support the economy. All of this suggests that the productivity puzzle will not easily be resolved and that recovery will require tackling some deep-rooted problems in banking as well as long-standing underinvestment in R&D and skills.

———

The analysis above also has a strong bearing on the debate about austerity policies. One view can, very loosely, be caricatured as cyclical in character and rejects austerity – deficit and/or debt reduction in the public sector – as unnecessary and undesirable. Advocates of this view argue that the 2008/9 recession was fundamentally no different from any other. It required, and requires, expansionary demand management policies, notably deficit finance, to utilize spare capacity. On this view, the austerity policies of the coalition government retarded recovery and caused unnecessary suffering. The term Keynesian is loosely applied to this way of thinking, though, of course, Keynes himself was addressing the very different conditions of the inter-war period. The Labour opposition sought to make this case, but struggled to explain why the predicted double- or triple-dip recession never happened and why recovery occurred without the necessary fiscal stimulus. The success of the SNP, however, suggests that in some parts of the UK at least a relentless anti-austerity message struck a chord.

The opposite, also caricatured, point of view is that the post-crisis recession was the inevitable consequence of a deeper structural problem which, depending on who is making the case, is represented by a badly damaged, dysfunctional banking system which inhibits demand from being translated into the supply of goods and services, and/or by an 'overhang' of public and private debt which inhibits investment. In an extreme (Austrian) view of this argument, demand stimulus is counterproductive without addressing the underlying causes.

In the UK the debate has been much less polarized than these caricatures suggest, and the coalition government used insights from both sides of the argument. (By contrast, in the eurozone, the German economic orthodoxy is less compromising and much closer to the Austrian view.) The idea that the government was obsessed by Plan A – rapid deficit reduction to the exclusion of growth – owes more to tribal political debate than to reality. I wrote a pamphlet in 2011 about Plan A+ which was my interpretation of government policy at the time and which emphasized its flexibility and also the various ways that growth-enhancing measures should, and often did, complement deficit reduction. The pamphlet did, however, cause a rift between George Osborne and myself, and some difficult negotiations were required to camouflage our disagreements over borrowing for government capital spending.

In reality, the more interesting policy debates have been within rather than between the extremes, in particular about the respective roles of monetary and fiscal policy in supporting demand, and about the effectiveness of particular policy instruments (like QE) or the balance within budgetary policy (tax or spend, current versus capital spending). Similarly the structural approach can involve either *dirigiste* solutions – radical reorganization of the banking sector, or a variety of interventions to promote investment and raise productivity – or radical free-market solutions of the kind originally advanced by Hayek and others of the Austrian school, who believed that investment would revive only when wage and regulatory costs had fallen sufficiently to restore returns on capital.

Putting these important qualifications on one side, there has been a serious austerity debate both within the coalition and with external critics. My own arguments were set out in a series of public exchanges with Robert Skidelsky, Keynes's biographer, who set out a Keynesian criticism of the government's planned fiscal consolidation. Ed Balls's pithy phrase, cutting 'too much too soon', captured the argument. In the event, the warnings about the consequences of the speed of consolidation proved to be overdone. The predicted double- or triple-dip recession never happened. Although the coalition initially hoped to proceed faster with fiscal consolidation than the seven-year plan announced by Alistair Darling in his 2010 budget, in practice the seven-year timetable proved to be too ambitious rather than not ambitious enough.

There is still, however, lingering criticism that if the coalition had taken a less rushed and more measured approach to the deficit at the outset, recovery would have taken place sooner and permitted the Darling deficit reduction schedule to be met. The issue that proved to be very divisive was the £11 billion fiscal tightening introduced in the early months of the coalition – a mixture of spending cuts and reversing the cut in VAT, designed, in 2008, to stimulate demand in the depths of the post-crisis recession. It involved a change in my own judgement about the urgency of fiscal measures and was agreed during the coalition negotiations, prompted by events in the eurozone as markets started to panic over the Greek problem.

My own recollection of events is coloured by several conversations at the time with the permanent secretary to the Treasury and the Cabinet Secretary, among others, who communicated the concerns of the Governor, Mervyn King, who was anxious not to be directly involved. The argument they made was that, with the biggest fiscal deficit of any major economy, the UK could hardly avoid some kind of contagion effect. We had no reason to fear a sterling crisis since the currency was floating and a further devaluation, beyond the 25 per cent or so post-crisis, would not be damaging in itself. We had more reason to fear a loss of creditor confidence, resulting in higher bond yields which would negatively affect the wider economy.

I also bought the argument that fiscal consolidation – deficit reduction – would be difficult to implement, unpleasant and unpopular in any event, and that an early commitment, validated by an external crisis, could create the necessary momentum. Much was made of this 'U-turn' because the emergency package was essentially what George Osborne had called for in advance of the Greek crisis. But in the potentially febrile atmosphere of the time it was a rational response. Those of us involved in the discussion were aware of the risks of undermining an incipient recovery by precipitate fiscal tightening. But bringing forward a consolidation of only around 0.7 per cent of GDP, offset by a commitment to continued aggressive monetary policy, including QE, by the Governor, meant that the risks were reasonably low.

By mid-parliament, with recovery now clearly happening

alongside fiscal consolidation, Skidelsky summarized the continuing Keynesian critique by arguing that although 'George Osborne did not cause the recession . . . he has not caused the recovery'. 'Britain has been lifted off the rocks by the global upturn.' 'Fiscal austerity slowed and weakened the recovery, and monetary looseness ensured that it would be highly unbalanced and therefore fragile.'

Let me take the criticisms in turn. First, there is little evidence to suggest that, as the economy recovered, the UK was lifted by the world economy. Net exports did not increase at all during the recovery phase. The acceleration in UK GDP growth during 2013 far outstripped that in other leading economies, following several successive years in which the opposite was the case. Whatever caused the recovery, it was internally, not externally, driven.

As for the argument that fiscal contraction had earlier slowed and weakened the economy, the Bank of England's analysis directly contradicts that assertion. It concluded that fiscal consolidation was a minor factor in explaining the slowness of recovery after 2010. The main causal factor was the squeeze on real household incomes and spending, caused by imported inflation, notably fuel costs. Moreover, in practice, the government operated a Keynesian, counter-cyclical budget policy, allowing the budget deficit to rise when the economy slowed in 2011 and 2012. I made a point, in parliamentary debates on the economy, of praising the Chancellor's Keynesian policy and pragmatism, knowing that it was ideologically inconvenient for both the Chancellor and his critics to acknowledge the fact. In truth, fiscal austerity was, to a significant degree, a myth. Fiscal consolidation happened much more gradually than planned or than critics claimed. In practice, despite the ambition at the outset to achieve the elimination of the structural deficit before the end of the 2010–15 parliament, the government delivered roughly half of that.

Skidelsky and other Keynesian critics almost certainly exaggerated the importance of fiscal policy in any event, since they drew parallels with a period in history when conditions were crucially different. Keynes's own analysis was in a period when the banks were stable and functioned normally. The inter-war crisis, at least in the UK, was not a banking crisis. This has practical implications for the way a fiscal stimulus, or contraction, operates. When the credit transmission system has broken down (at least the part of it connecting credit to SMEs), the income multiplier from any stimulus is much lower. In Keynes's General Theory, income multipliers of two or three were assumed. The IMF recently calculated a figure in the current context as 0.4 for tax cuts and government current spending, and 1.0 for capital projects.

There is more force in the criticism that a reliance on monetary policy has had negative side effects, notably on house prices, so unbalancing the economy. However, this criticism contradicts an earlier Keynesian criticism of monetary policy, that it has little or no effect. In the early stages of the crisis, critics argued that expansionary monetary policy was 'like pushing on a piece of string', because of a theoretical problem identified by Keynes that there is a lower band to interest rates. Nominal interest rates cannot go below zero. (This is not strictly true: in the Alice in Wonderland world of monetary policy, savers can be penalized with negative interest rates, and have been in some European countries.) In the early years of the coalition, however, with inflation over the target rate of 2 per cent, short-term interest rates were clearly negative in real terms. And with long-term interest rates (gilt yields) at around 2 per cent, they were zero to negative also. The policy of QE, gilt purchases by central banks, also had the effect of driving up gilt prices and driving down yields (that is, interest rates). Keynes himself attached considerable importance to such policies, but recognized their limits.

The limits of interest rate policy led the UK (and other monetary authorities, notably in the USA) to pump money directly into the economy via gilt sales to non-bank financial institutions, such as pension funds. The aim was to reduce long-term interest rates and increase the flow of money and credit, via banks, thus stimulating household and corporate spending, and inflation, in order to head off deflation. The Bank of England believes it cut long-term interest rates by 1 per cent in the first round of QE and that, while the impact on credit was partly nullified by aggressive bank deleveraging, the impact overall was to raise GDP by 2.5–3.5 per cent above what it would otherwise have been.

We also discussed in government the 'what if' question: should monetary policy fail to lift the economy, what do we do next? I raised with the Chancellor in early 2011, when the outlook was particularly bleak, the possibility of directly creating money by monetizing the deficit: covering the deficit by borrowing from the Bank of England rather than bond markets. Although I received no encouragement – and others who raised the issue publicly, like Lord Turner, were slapped down – I have no doubt that there were contingency plans in the Treasury and the Bank.

The combination of low or negative short-term interest rates and QE did, however, have a range of effects that are not fully understood and which are disputed. Skidelsky argues that if less weight had been placed on monetary policy, the recovery would have been less unbalanced. This is, at first sight, plausible, but less so if we pursue the argument in detail. Among the effects of loose monetary policy have been low long-term interest rates, which support private investment, and exchange rate depreciation, which is exactly the right signal for economic rebalancing (now being reversed as markets expect a tightening of monetary policy).

It is certainly true that there have been adverse distributional effects. The wealth embedded in property and shares is heavily skewed to the wealthy. It is, however, too simple to blame the surge in house prices on loose monetary policy. The fact that the increase in credit supply flowed into housing rather than business investment and exports was not inevitable but due to particular UK interventions which created or aggravated any such bias.

These included prudential capital requirements which penalized lending to SMEs; the Funding for Lending Scheme, which helped mortgage-lenders in particular (until the scheme was restricted to business); and interventions like Help to Buy, which were specifically designed to boost the housing market. I was critical in government of these interventions, but the prevailing view in the Treasury and the Bank of England was that a boost to house prices would stimulate the economy.

The emphasis of policy could and should have been different. Adam Posen, then a member of the Monetary Policy Committee, and others argued that the Bank of England should have acquired a wider range of assets, such as corporate bonds and securitized bundles of small business loans. Infrastructure project bonds were another possible asset class that would have boosted investment. I supported Posen's argument in discussions with the Treasury and the Governor. However, the Governor rejected these options as akin to government borrowing, which was a political choice, not to be achieved indirectly via the Bank of England. And he was also worried about the quality of the balance sheet of the Bank of England, which Posen and I felt was a somewhat recondite distraction from the real world. But the fiscal versus monetary policy debate had less to do with ideological dialectic than with mundane technical issues of statistical classification, such as what is classified as government borrowing.

The question that government critics posed remains as to why more slack could not have been cut to allow for higher levels of government capital spending, with its relatively high multiplier effects, or the kinds of QE rejected as borrowing by the Bank of England? Here, the critics are right. After all, such borrowing would not impact on the main target of government fiscal policy, reducing the structural current deficit in the budget. Here, economics dissolves into a metaphysical debate around acts of faith and market confidence: the nervous reaction of the Treasury, acting on advice from contacts in the bond markets, that there is a 'cliff edge' beyond which the cumulative total of government borrowing triggers a fall into a void with, in practice, a sharp rise in gilt yields (long-term interest rates), thus aborting recovery. This proposition is inherently untestable, and although I broadly accepted it in May 2010, I became progressively more frustrated as it was wheeled out to dismiss each and every departure from approved, orthodox, policy.

Indeed, the 'cliff edge' theory became increasingly less plausible as the economy recovered. Treasury ministers and officials continued nonetheless to remind us of the lurking damage reflected in the loss of AAA rating and a differential in long-term interest rates with Germany of around 1 per cent. Nonetheless, I had some gentle fun later in the parliament pointing out to Conservative Cabinet colleagues that British bond yields had actually risen above those of the despised Hollande administration in France – which they saw as a basket case, scarcely better than Greece – for exactly the opposite reason to that advanced by the Treasury (higher UK yields signalled recovery, not crisis). I believed that it was a major policy error by the coalition to carry through the cuts in capital spending announced by the Labour government in 2010, but hitting the economy hard in 2012 (new capital investment virtually stopped) at the worst possible time. I return to the issue of curbs on capital spending in the next chapter.

———

To summarize, the broad anti-austerity critique of government and the invocation of Keynes do not stand up to scrutiny. The nature of the recent crisis, resulting from a banking collapse with major structural damage, including a large structural deficit, simply did not permit the kind of expansive fiscal policy favoured by the critics. The government's patience and trust in monetary policy have been rewarded with a recovery, albeit one that is unbalanced and that relies excessively on property inflation in one corner of England.

There are, however, two criticisms that do have real force and that have been made by myself and others both in government and outside over the last five years. The first is that while some very useful, practical micro-interventions have been made to support business lending in the SME sector, such as the British Business Bank, far too little was done at a strategic level – through the Bank of England's regulatory controls or through the government and RBS – to correct the bias towards property-based lending and against productive business. I subscribe to the analysis of Goldman Sachs that this factor, more than any other, explains the unbalanced nature of the recovery.

The second valid criticism is that the unavoidable fiscal discipline required to reduce the structural fiscal deficit morphed into a generalized constraint on overall borrowing which has cramped public investment unnecessarily. The government did, at the margin, favour capital over current spending. Nonetheless, the draconian cuts that took full effect in 2012 were damaging. Greater flexibility in allowing borrowing for capital projects would have accelerated recovery by 'crowding in' private investment, and would certainly have ensured a better balance in the economy and would have reduced the risk of the recovery hitting bottlenecks as a result of lack of infrastructure in future.

I pursue this issue at more length in looking at future fiscal policy in the next chapter.

8

Life after Cheap Money

It is premature to talk about recovery when the economy is still on a life-support system. Loose monetary policy may have been the key element in keeping the stricken patient alive after the financial crisis, but as recovery strengthens, the issue of when and how to disconnect the life-support system becomes pressing. This is an issue both for the UK and the USA, but not yet for the eurozone and Japan where recovery is less nimble. And the UK is still some way behind the USA.

We are currently a long way from normal. Official interest rates, at 0.5 per cent, are at the lowest level for centuries. Market rates are the lowest for thousands of years, argues Andrew Haldane of the Bank of England. Long-term, risk-free interest rates are just under 2 per cent. With an economy growing at 2.5–3 per cent and inflation at the target rate of 2 per cent, we would expect 'normal' short rates to be closer to 5 per cent and, to maintain a positive yield curve, long rates of around 6 per cent. What we mean by 'normal' here is the kind of return people have historically expected for setting aside savings. Either there is a very big adjustment to come or there has been a historic shift to a 'new normal'.

Abnormally low interest rates aren't the only legacy problem. As a result of QE, the Bank of England now 'owns' £375 billion of gilts, which is about 30 per cent of the total stock in existence (the remainder being government debt held by financial institutions). If the recovery runs into difficulty and Japanese-style stagnation threatens again, then further QE may be required. But even if it is not needed, there is the tricky issue of what to do about the existing stock. On one hand, it could be 'unwound' (bought back by the government from the Bank of England), pushing up long-term interest rates and reversing the stimulus of QE. Given the continued deficit reduction commitment, that would be a seriously deflationary option and one to be avoided for the foreseeable future. On the other hand, there is no reason why the Bank of England should not continue to hold its stock of gilts. These could be rolled over, issuing more debt in order to do so – but the debt would still have to be serviced.

Or the QE debt could be cancelled. That sounds attractive and may indeed be an option if there is need for a future economic stimulus. But there would be consequences. Bank reserves have been created by QE and cancelling them could force a contraction of lending. These are somewhat arcane issues, currently of interest to a technical few; but they matter. And the speed of withdrawal may be more important than the fact of it. A rapid change of direction could have a dramatic effect on bond and equity prices and on banks' liquidity. The Bank of England has said it will start selling back bonds to the government when interest rates reach 2 per cent but that assumes a much stronger economy.

———

One basic question is whether the whole framework of monetary policy-making needs to be reopened. At present there is an independent body, the Monetary Policy Committee (MPC) of the Bank of England, to set interest rates in order to achieve price stability, on the basis of an explicit inflation mandate set by the Chancellor. Its introduction in 1997 was widely welcomed (I made my parliamentary maiden speech in support of it). To this day there is no demand to re-politicize interest rate setting and take away the Bank's operational independence. But the context is very different. The problem back in 1997 was that after the preceding quarter of a century inflation appeared endemic, and politicians' appetite for countervailing monetary policy could not be relied on. That now looks like rather a remote problem.

Questions can, moreover, legitimately be raised as to whether the mandate of 2 per cent CPI inflation is a sensible one in the light of experience. In the decade before the financial crisis, the MPC met its inflation target, along with healthy growth in the economy. What it did not do was either identify as a threat, or deal with, rampant inflation in asset markets, notably housing (though there was some tightening of interest rates, from 3.5 per cent to 5.5 per cent between 2004 and 2008, reflecting growing inflationary pressure in general). The Bank of England is now in a different place and is equipped with macro-prudential tools to deal with inflationary bubbles in asset markets.

The banking collapse and the recession that followed it fundamentally changed the nature of monetary policy. There was a real threat of deflation. Interest rates were cut to 0.5 per cent, the lowest level deemed practical, and the Chancellor, Alistair Darling, also authorized the use of QE. The Bank of England has disregarded short-term increases in inflation on the basis that the main threat was one of deflation. In the post-crisis period, 2010–13, CPI inflation was consistently over 3 per cent and on two occasions exceeded 5 per cent, due mainly to the impact of falling sterling and rising external (mainly oil) costs. The MPC has been struggling to understand and model the new post-crisis world. It seriously misjudged the trajectory of unemployment and wrongly expected a resurfacing of wage inflation. The Bank of England has undoubtedly acted in a sensible and proper way, taking into account the enormous risks to the economy, but in the process it has disregarded the inflation mandate. In practice, the MPC has been tracking growth as well as inflation.

The argument has subsequently been made that this change should be formalized into a new mandate. Samuel Brittan argued for many years, pre-crisis, that stability should apply both to growth and to inflation. In practice, a nominal GDP target of 5 per cent captures what the Bank of England has been trying to achieve, both pre- and post-crisis. But, to be meaningful, the target would have to be forward-looking, based on forecasts. The argument for making the change is that it is a more explicit and honest statement of what governments want to achieve. While it would not eliminate price fluctuations or business cycles, it would do better at achieving price and growth stability together, and it would generally make it easier to manage the real world of shocks. It would not be a radical change, but it should improve outcomes.

The immediate issue facing the MPC is whether to start the process of raising interest rates sooner rather than later. In June 2013 the Governor issued forward guidance to the effect that interest rates could be expected to rise once unemployment fell below 7 per cent, as a measure of spare capacity and therefore of inflation potential in the economy. In practice, unemployment has already fallen well below 7 per cent – it is now well under 6 per cent – but inflation has also fallen and was zero in May 2015, mainly reflecting the impact of falling energy and other commodity prices, as well as appreciation of sterling. While this sequence of events has caused some embarrassment to the Governor, and the Bank seems to have given up assessing 'slack' in the labour market, it does not fundamentally change the validity of his warning that interest rates should start to increase gradually as the economy strengthens.

There are strong reasons for moving to higher rates as soon as is possible without pitching the economy back into recession. The current position is highly abnormal. Low interest rates, and negative real rates, are a serious disincentive to saving and, while it has been necessary to encourage people to spend in the short run, a long-term, balanced recovery requires a revival of contractual saving. Moreover, the current conditions under which some companies and households can borrow very cheaply and others with great difficulty – in particular, the disparity between cheap domestic mortgages and expensive SME credit – seriously distort the economy.

Several arguments have been advanced for holding back interest rate increases. The first is the impact on highly indebted households. One of the defining features of the UK financial crisis was the exceptional level of household debt to income, very largely due to mortgage borrowing during the housing boom. It reached 170 per cent, far in excess of other countries, with the exception of Spain. Since the crisis, households have repaid debt and borrowing has been difficult, so the ratio has fallen back to around 145 per cent, but now it is rising again and is forecast by the OBR to return to peak levels at the end of the decade (Figure 8.1). The Resolution Foundation estimates that one in five households already has difficulty making mortgage payments, and that will double if interest rates rise to 3 per cent, a higher proportion than in the early 1990s when there was a serious repossession problem. If income growth is also affected negatively, affordability impacts will be compounded. However, there is no economic case for allowing the management of the economy to be held hostage to some past reckless mortgage-lending. Many savers are also suffering distress. Moreover, banks can, and can be required to, offer relief or part-ownership arrangements in order to stave off default. The mortgage issue becomes more dangerous for individuals when house prices also fall, leading to negative equity – although from a wider economic and social point of view, falling house prices may be very desirable. So the household debt argument against interest rate increases is a poor one.

Moreover the problems presented by an overheated housing market can be dealt with in other ways, through targeted macroprudential tools, such as fixing maximum loan to value and loan to income ratios. The Bank has begun to use these, albeit very timidly. The current recommended limit of 4.5 for the loan to income ratio is considerably in excess of what would traditionally be regarded as prudent lending. And the Governor has ruled out restrictions on buy-to-let mortgages and unsecured credit. No doubt he has judged that the Bank of England could make itself politically unpoular if it was seen to hit property owners. However, there is now an understanding, which did not exist pre-crisis, that it is the Bank of England's responsibility to act on short-term mortgage demand in the housing market and that macro-prudential tools rather than interest rates represent the best mechanism for dealing with property bubbles.

A further concern is that higher interest rates would inhibit export growth, because of the impact of international differentials in interest rates (and expectations of interest rate changes through forward markets) on capital flows, and thence on the exchange rate. The pound appreciated by 12 per cent in the two years from mid 2013 to mid 2015 – by 6 per cent in real terms against all currencies and allowing for inflation. The IMF judged recently that sterling was 5–10 per cent overvalued, and there were growing complaints from manufacturers about loss of competitiveness and eroding margins on exports, a serious warning that the recovery was unbalanced. The interaction between interest rates and exchange rates is complex. A reduction in domestic inflation should reduce pressure to increase interest rates, and this in turn would ease pressure on the exchange rate. But we have had prolonged 'overshooting' before, with exchange rates far above the level needed to maintain external balance.

There would be strong resistance by the Bank of England to targeting the exchange rate as well as inflation, and there would be legitimate objections to using one policy measure, that of interest rates, for two objectives. But this raises the separate issue of whether exchange rate management is back on the agenda and how it would be done. Central bank intervention in foreign exchange markets – selling sterling assets and buying dollar or euro assets – is one obvious mechanism. But it has not been tested in a major open economy like the UK. I expressed concern in government about the UK's passive approach to the exchange rate. I remain concerned that serious damage could be done to export industries.

Whatever the specific impacts on housing or the exchange rate, the Bank of England will soon be faced with a decision about raising rates. This will be a crucial move. A move to monetary tightening would affect one of the principles governing the government's response to the crisis: that loose monetary policy is a necessary concomitant of fiscal tightening. Yet the government is contemplating an acceleration of fiscal tightening at a time when monetary policy is also likely to tighten. There is a theoretically attractive option, advocated by Lord Turner among others, of reconciling a move to higher interest rates with deficit reduction, by covering the budget deficit by the government: simply 'printing money'. The idea of 'helicopter money' has been advocated for deflationary emergencies by Milton Friedman, among others, but there are obvious practical problems of knowing when to stop and ensuring that the government does not abuse the printing presses, as so many historically have done. As I mentioned in the previous chapter, I favoured the use of deficit monetization in government in early 2011 when business and consumer confidence was very weak and the recovery had stalled. But that was, and is, very much a remedy for emergencies. That leads to the issue of how to manage future fiscal policy.

———

The often emotional arguments around austerity and fiscal responsibility mask some highly technical debates about what fiscal austerity and responsibility actually mean. The devil is usually in the detail and different definitions of fiscal objectives have enormously different real-world implications.

The last Labour government had a clearly defined set of fiscal objectives which, like the Bank of England's inflation targeting, attracted praise at the time from international organizations like the IMF and OECD. These reflected international good practice and were broadly sensible objectives for 'normal' conditions. The aim was to have a balanced current budget (that is, revenue, mainly tax, offsetting recurrent spending on services and transfer payments), but balanced over the economic cycle. The government would also borrow for investment, typically 3 per cent of GDP, under the so-called 'Golden Rule'. There was also a 'Supplementary Investment Rule' limiting net investment to 40 per cent of GDP. The objective was close to the Maastricht rules for monetary union, which state that there should be a 3 per cent of GDP limit on deficits, without distinguishing capital and current spending and not specifying cyclical variation.

The impression has been created by that government's critics that the post-1997 period was an orgy of government spending and high taxation. The Labour party has signally failed to dispel that impression, although in fact current spending and government spending remained comfortably below 40 per cent of GDP, in marked contrast to the high spending, high tax era of the 1970s (Figure 8.3).

In practice, however, the cycle proved impossible to define before the event, and in the absence of any independent body to test and verify the assumptions made by government, the credibility of fiscal policy declined. It was easier to let the deficit drift up than to act in the opposite direction. By the time of the 2008 crisis, most serious independent commentators believed there should have been a small surplus. The Institute for Fiscal Studies argued at the time, as I did in an annual lecture to the Royal Economic Society, that there should have been a fiscal tightening of £5–10 billion, though no one, as I recall, argued for radical fiscal tightening at that stage.

The crisis changed everything. There was a major structural element: a collapse of government revenue from the banking industry, including tax on bankers' bonuses, and from the housing market, together with emergency outlays to support collapsing banks. And the cyclical effect of deep recession meant that social security spending rose and tax income from individuals and companies fell. Together with borrowing for capital spending, overall government borrowing surged to 10.2 per cent of GDP in 2009/10, a post-war record.

There was broad political and professional agreement that it would have been economically damaging – indeed stupid – to have sought to eliminate the cyclical deficit at a time of deep recession. But there had to be a plan to eliminate the structural deficit over a reasonable time period, since this deficit, by definition, does not disappear as the economy recovers. A parallel can be drawn with, let us say, an oil-exporting country that finds itself with a large budget deficit because of a collapse in the price of oil or the oil running out. The British banking sector operates in a similar way to the oil sector in OPEC countries, bringing in large amounts of revenue but leaving the country exposed to the risk of a price collapse. With hindsight, of course, it would have been better to have treated the tax earnings of the City as a windfall, rather than as a regular source of tax revenue, but not even critics of the government anticipated that the banking sector, and its tax revenue, would collapse.

I described in the last chapter the debate inside and outside government about the speed of structural deficit reduction. The argument for pursuing a shorter timescale revolved around policy credibility: a shorter time period, with government accepting responsibility for completing its task within the lifetime of a parliament, would be easier to sell to lenders, thus reducing borrowing costs. The counter-argument was that rapid deficit reduction would slow growth, and critics claimed that postponement of fiscal tightening from the outset would have reduced the costs of the crisis. These backward-looking arguments are, in any event, frustratingly unresolvable because we do not know the counterfactual: what would have happened to borrowing costs had the government been more relaxed about the deficit and how much that would have mattered.

Looking to the future, the new Conservative government was initially committed to 'complete the job' before 2017/18, as the coalition had agreed in principle. The aim was ambitious, since reducing the structural deficit by about half has taken seven years and the plan was to deal with the next half in three years. The officially estimated current structural deficit in the 2015 budget was 2.5 per cent of GDP for 2015/16, but as explained in chapter seven there is a wide range of estimates of what the structural, as opposed to the cyclical, element is. The commitment to proceed along these lines was incorporated in a Charter of Budget Responsibility agreed by parliament in January 2015. The Charter did, however, build in flexibility, at the insistence of the Lib Dems. The three-year time period was defined as a rolling objective, so the new government could remain within the letter and spirit of the Charter by rolling the target date forward to 2018/19, which would be altogether more sensible and realistic. The OECD has also recommended a postponement. I made a personal contribution to the internal debate by insisting on the word 'aim' rather than 'target' in the Charter. In the event, in the July 2015 budget the Chancellor wisely opted for a year's postponement. One of the lessons of the coalition is the value of flexibility, and the Conservative government will do well to remember that new shocks or the impact of monetary tightening might require further flexibility in timing. The July budget suggests that that lesson, at least, is now understood, but the proposal to legislate to make fiscal surpluses binding suggests the opposite, an intention to abandon fiscal flexibility.

One cause of genuine uncertainty is how much of the deficit is structural and how much cyclical. There are widely differing estimates and, as I described earlier, there has been a lot of retrospective statistical revision. Pessimists argue that there is little genuine spare capacity (output gap) left in the economy, so all the remaining deficit is structural, requiring greater fiscal consolidation or a longer period of time. Other analysts, including the IMF, argue that there is more spare capacity. If that is the case, the structural element is much smaller and the task of eliminating the structural deficit is largely complete. The government is reliant on the independent OBR to arbitrate over what is a highly speculative set of numbers. The current government fiscal objectives are based on OBR numbers for an output gap a little below the middle of the range of independent forecasts, at just over 2 per cent. When it came into office, the new government launched a draconian three-year spending review involving deep cuts in benefits and unprotected departmental spending, based on the assumption that 'the deficit' had to be removed in three (later, four) years. However, the notion of what a 'deficit' means has substantionally changed.

———————

One of the problems with the public debate about the 'deficit' is that different people use the same word to mean quite different things. The coalition agreement was quite clear that the objective of fiscal consolidation was to deal with the 'current structural deficit'. One of my contributions to the negotiations was to be clear, in writing, that that was what I and my colleagues were signing up for. Yet it was clear from the outset that the Conservative side of the coalition, and the Treasury, felt this was too narrow an approach. They wanted to peg back all forms of government borrowing, whether for current or capital spending, or for cyclical or structural reasons. Over the period of the coalition, Treasury papers and speeches referred to the deficit as synonymous with government borrowing, and this became the language of the economic commentariat. The difference, in practice, is large: between 2.5 and 5 per cent of GDP in 2014/15. Alarmingly, the Conservative government has switched from the former to the latter, with little debate.

The reasoning behind the Treasury approach had several strands. It was an extension of the 'cliff edge' theory about financial markets: that bond markets look at total government borrowing rather than particular components of it when deciding whether to panic. Like the 'cliff edge' theory in general, it is impossible to test the proposition, and if it is real it has an element of self-fulfilling prophecy about it. In any event, it was never put to the test. The fact that the structural deficit cannot be measured accurately and consistently, while government borrowing is a real-world rather than a theoretical construct, adds to the sense that markets primarily care about borrowing.

A second strand in the argument was the belief that what mattered was total public debt rather than the structural current deficit (though obviously the latter adds cumulatively to the former). After the government was formed, the Treasury introduced a 'second fiscal rule', the commitment to reduce the debt to GDP ratio, which made no distinction between different reasons for borrowing. In fact, the idea of having a supplementary debt rule was not new; the Labour government also had one, albeit in very different circumstances.

I believe this shifting of emphasis, from structural deficit to debt, was and is misconceived. The most serious consequence of the emphasis on debt rather than current deficits was that it prejudiced the Treasury against capital spending. In fact, there is a long-standing Treasury aversion to government borrowing for investment purposes. This bias explains such questionable innovations as the large-scale use of the Private Finance Initiative (PFI), designed to take hospital building and similar construction projects off the government balance sheet, and a history of starving state enterprises such as the Royal Mail of investment capital. I experienced at first hand from Treasury ministers and officials the deep scepticism that there are such things as good, investable public sector projects. I suspect that one of the underlying reasons is a theoretical belief, originating in previous boom years, that public investment 'crowds out' private investment. This thinking lingered even in a period when it was palpably wrong. In the context in which we were operating, public investment was more likely to 'crowd in' private investment. That was implicitly acknowledged in some of the successful interventions of the coalition that I oversaw: the Regional Growth Fund, the Green Investment Bank and the British Business Bank. But there was a reluctance to go far down this road, despite the fact that the cost of borrowing was close to zero in real terms. Yet in recession conditions capital spending has a much higher income and expenditure multiplier, creating jobs and growth, than any other form of tax changes or public spending. Thus a big boost in public investment should have been, and should be, a no-brainer.

There are, moreover, good mechanisms for identifying and

appraising productive investment in areas like transport and tele-communications infrastructure, science and skills. One inhibiting factor is a system of classifying spending as 'current' or 'capital' that does not correspond closely to common or economic sense. It may well be, as the Social Market Foundation has argued, that investment in the form of current spending on science and inno-vation, skills training or childcare, will be more productive than capital spending on Japanese-style 'roads to nowhere' or public buildings. But sadly I saw no sign of a willingness in the Treasury to probe these issues.

For this reason, capital investment has usually been the poor relation of government spending and the first to be cut. Some drastic cuts in capital spending were announced in the latter days of the Labour government, which became fully effective two years later, after the election, when all public investment stopped (sta-tistically, net investment was negative in 2012). That was a time when the depths of a recession most required infrastructure and capital projects, not least to offset the collapse in private house building, commercial property development, and bank-financed PFIs, which were casualties of the financial crisis. Instead, govern-ment cuts compounded the problem.

To give some credit to George Osborne, he did move some way to rebalance capital and current spending, though capital spending remained severely rationed (notwithstanding cynical complaints from the Treasury that they could never find good capital projects – a largely artificial problem caused by cumber-some and short-term public financing rules). But while he clearly grasped the relative importance of capital investment, he was unwilling to relax the severe overall constraints on borrowing because of concerns over public debt.

I have explained already the origins of the so-called second fiscal rule, which had the aim of reducing the then rising share of public net debt to GDP by 2015. The practical significance of it was that it imposed a constraint on all forms of spending, since capital spending also adds to debt in the short term, even if it produces a stream of income that reduces debt to GDP in the longer term.

There are perfectly good reasons to be concerned about the stock of government debt and the sustainability of it, just as there are good reasons to be concerned about household debt and the debt of companies and financial institutions. Indeed, converting government debt into private debt doesn't reduce the debt overhang in the economy, however much it helps improve the government's balance sheet. The OBR predicts that the net debt to GDP ratio will have fallen to 60 per cent by the end of the parliament, from 80 per cent, but that household debt will be back to the 2008 peak of around 170 per cent of GDP. Overall indebtedness remains unchanged and, just as before the crisis, household indebtedness will become the bigger problem.

Long before the financial crisis erupted, the European Union set a public – gross – debt to GDP target of 60 per cent for its member states, in preparation for monetary union – though at least part of the motivation was the fear of highly indebted countries defaulting and offloading their debts on to other eurozone members, rather than sustainability as such. The Latin American sovereign debt crisis of the early 1980s was also a warning of how public debt can become unsustainable.

Until the financial crisis, the UK operated well within the 40 per cent net debt to GDP benchmark and the Labour government frequently drew attention to its performance as a mark of its fiscal virtue. The ratio was 37 per cent at the end of 2007/8. The enormous fiscal deficit post-crisis, together with the costs of stabilizing the banks, transformed the position for the worse and the debt to GDP ratio rose quickly, to 71 per cent at the end of 2011/12. The ratio was close to 80 per cent at the end of 2014/15 and expected by the OBR to peak at this level and fall through the rest of the decade, as anticipated in the second fiscal rule.

One of the most fundamental policy questions over the next few years will be how much we should worry about the public debt legacy of the crisis. The debate about austerity has shifted from the speed of deficit reduction to the degree to which public spending, and investment, should be squeezed to achieve a bigger or faster reduction in the overhang of debt. A key point made by fiscal conservatives is that debt-servicing costs become more onerous the higher the stock of debt – the fact that in 2015/16 debt interest will be a predicted £33 billion, equivalent to the defence budget.

While it is quite legitimate to worry about public debt management, there are good reasons for not allowing it to dominate economic policy. At the time of the crisis I was among those who pointed out that throughout its modern history Britain had lived comfortably enough with debt to GDP ratios well in excess of 100 per cent, the product of wars, from the Napoleonic to the Korean, previous economic crises, particularly in the inter-war period, colonial expansion and bail-outs from slave owners to banks. Economic performance did not seem to have been greatly impaired as a consequence, though Britain did engineer a default on debt to the USA in the 1930s and a *de facto* default via high inflation in the 1970s – policies that would be difficult for a weaker Britain, such as today's, to achieve. (See Figure 8.2).

It is worth noting that, at the beginning of the 1930s, public debt was 180 per cent of GDP, almost twice present levels, and debt service was over 8 per cent of GDP, compared with 3 per cent today, rising to an expected 4 per cent in five years' time. As a share of public spending, debt service, at around 7 per cent, has been steadily declining since the 1929/30 crisis, when it touched 30 per cent, and only fell to single digits after the turn of the century. As a result of expansionary monetary policies, and a boom in housing supply, the economy grew strongly from 1933 onwards, and this in itself improved the debt ratio and servicing obligation, until the war added much more debt, which was subsequently worked down by a combination of growth and inflation. This experience does not support the view that high levels of public debt stand in the way of growth.

Markets do look at comparisons. As it happens, government

borrowing as a percentage of GDP, as well as the net debt ratio, are almost identical in the USA and the UK. Other countries have operated with far higher levels of public debt, notably Japan, and while Japan in recent years has hardly been a role model of good economic management, it is perfectly able to sustain its debt because Japanese savers are willing to lend to the government at very low rates of interest. And that is the point: the cost of borrowing. At present, UK gilt rates are below 2 per cent and recently have been negative in real terms. The government should have been able to refinance its existing stock of debt, as well as new debt, very cheaply. To the extent that cheap borrowing costs are a result of the market's response to prudent deficit reduction, past austerity makes austerity less necessary in future.

There is also a basic point about the elementary maths, which is that the debt ratio is as much about the denominator as the numerator. Reducing debt – the numerator – does not help if the means to achieve it, curbing productive public expenditure, damages growth – reducing the denominator. Put more positively, sensible borrowing to enable productive investment to proceed can make debt more sustainable, not less.

One counter-argument that weighed heavily with the Chancellor and his officials was the academic evidence available from one much-quoted paper by Reinhart and Rogoff, that beyond a certain critical threshold – 90 per cent – higher debt ratios contribute to lower growth rates. However, there is now a mounting volume of critical literature that dismisses the Reinhart–Rogoff work as based on calculation errors and shows that re-running the data produces the opposite result: that highly indebted countries have relatively strong growth performance. Moreover, even those who accept the data argue that the causation is the wrong way round: poor growth results in greater problems of indebtedness. And the IMF, which five years ago was seen as a leading advocate of fiscal austerity, now argues that debt ratios should be allowed to decline 'organically' with growth, or through revenue windfalls, not by cutting public investment or raising taxes in ways that impair growth. Significantly, Kenneth Rogoff, unlike his protégé the Chancellor, is now an advocate of immersed public investment in the UK.

I recognized throughout the coalition government the need for fiscal discipline and for debt reduction. But I was never reconciled to Treasury orthodoxy on borrowing for public investment, or on public debt. I found myself, with my special adviser Giles Wilkes, in a lonely minority, not least because my senior Lib Dem colleagues in the Quad accepted the Treasury view. At the end of the parliament, my party did agree to support more public investment through borrowing, as did the Labour party. But this was too late to affect the policies of the coalition and there is now little chance of the Conservative government reopening this issue. We will be told that public debt must be curbed to protect the interests of the next generation. But the next generation will not thank us if they inherit a poorer economy that has neglected investment in infrastructure, skills and research and other productivity-enhancing measures.

———————

The 2015 election also opened up a change of emphasis on the extent of cuts in current public spending. In the autumn statement of 2013 the Chancellor indicated that he wished to see a growing structural surplus on the current budget, going considerably beyond the assumptions in the coalition agreement. There was no agreement within the coalition on this issue and the commitment hardened into Conservative policy for the new parliament.

In order to achieve further fiscal consolidation, the first choice to be made is between tax increases and spending cuts. Under the coalition the split was 10:90, roughly speaking. Those on the Labour opposition who criticized this, not unreasonably, as disproportionately skewed to public spending cuts were also those who complained most strenuously about tax increases, notably the VAT measures in 2010. Some of us would have preferred a better balance, and in the 2015 election my party campaigned on the platform that the future split should be around 45:55. The Chancellor, however, assumed in his own plans that 100 per cent of continuing fiscal consolidation would be achieved through further spending cuts, with additional cuts to finance promised through tax cuts. This assumption lasted only a few weeks and in the July budget the Chancellor sensibly acknowledged the need for tax rises as well, raising an extra £47 billion over the life of the parliament, via taxes on dividends and insurance premiums, vehicle excise duty and cuts in pension tax relief, and raising the share of tax in GDP from 35.7 to 36.8 per cent in 2020/21: still low by comparative and historical standards.

The OBR produced forecasts for government borrowing and spending that involved the elimination of all government borrowing, for capital as well as current spending, by 2019/20. A further fiscal consolidation of around 4.5 per cent of GDP – as opposed to the 2.2 per cent of GDP on the coalition's assumptions – was assumed to be necessary to 'finish the job' of deficit reduction. Even after the tax increases and allowing more borrowing by extending the target date for balancing the budget, cuts of £35 billion in welfare spending, and departmental spending cuts rising to £20 billion per annum in 2019/20 were planned. This may seem modest in relation to total current spending of around £690 billion predicted for 2015/16. But of that total, £272 billion was to be set aside for debt interest, state pensions and other items considered untouchable, and another £230 billion was to be used up by protected spending like the NHS, schools and foreign aid. Cuts were to be concentrated on unprotected departments and the unprotected welfare budget – tax credits, housing benefit, disability benefits and child benefit, where the Chancellor envisaged a further £12 billion per annum in cuts. Despite a retreat on working tax credits, that objective remains.

The spending review concluded in November 2015 actually involved deep real cuts albeit less than initially expected: by 17 per cent for example in my former department – BIS – as against

the threatened 25 to 40 per cent. Since elements of those departmental budgets are already ring-fenced (science for example), the
actual cuts for the remainder of departmental spending will be
deeper. A last moment revision in OBR forecasts with more optimistic revenue assumptions and higher taxes – an apprenticeship
levy and council tax – has eased the pressure. There will still be
painful consequences for central and local government services
and for government activities that contribute to improving productivity, such as skills, innovation, transport and energy.

In practice, there may have to be a further rethink of the
assumptions about the speed and extent of consolidation, the
split between tax changes and spending cuts, and the protection
of some areas of government spending at the expense of others.
There will also be a revival of the austerity debate, since if the next
few years see a return to higher interest rates, as well as continued
deficit reduction, there could be a sharp slowdown in growth.

————————

I have discussed at some length above the conflicting data around
recovery and what it means for unemployment, wages and productivity. There are, however, several policy issues that still need
to be addressed. One question is whether we are in danger of
being trapped in a low-wage, low-productivity, but high-employ-
ment, economy. A related set of questions is whether, in order
to move to a higher-wage, higher-productivity, but still high-
employment, economy, more needs to be done beyond demand
management in the form of supply-side measures to ensure that
workers share in the recovery.

There is much political controversy around the decline that
has taken place in living standards. The decline is sometimes presented as a shocking discovery, but it is an entirely predictable
consequence of the costs of the financial crisis and the loss of
output. In the UK, average weekly wages fell 8 per cent in the six
years after April 2008 (albeit with a recovery of around 3 per cent
the nadir). This was essentially because wages grew by around

1.6 per cent per annum from 2008 to 2014, but that was more than offset by inflation of over 3.9 per cent. But the fall in real incomes was lower, by 2–3 per cent, because disposable income was boosted by tax cuts (lifting the tax threshold) and in-work benefits (by the end of 2015 real incomes were back above pre-crisis peaks). Averages, however, disguise a lot of variation between different groups. Young workers and the self-employed have been hit particularly hard, while workers in settled employment (for over a year) have seen significant increases in real wages over several years. Taken as a whole, however, this crisis has hit real wages, once inflation is taken into account, more severely than at any time on record, including the inter-war period.

Policy reform is being promoted from two opposite ends of the political spectrum. One argues that it is too difficult to dismiss workers and that this inhibits firms from taking on employees. There was during my period in office a modest shift in terms governing unfair dismissal in order to reduce the numbers of cases going to tribunals. It now requires two years of employment, rather than one, before a case can be brought, while measures introduced elsewhere in government radically to increase tribunal fees have almost certainly tipped the balance too far against workers. But I firmly resisted recommendations from the Conservatives for so-called 'no-fault dismissal', making it easy to hire and fire without the existing safeguards. The very smooth workings of labour markets in the UK and the unexpected fall in unemployment have made these demands largely irrelevant. They would have added to worker insecurity and increased reluctance to spend, making the crisis worse.

A radically different approach is to say that weak labour market conditions and depressed real wages have actually caused low productivity, by making it more attractive for firms to hire labour than to invest in new machinery. The implication is that recovery will not in itself raise productivity; that will only happen when growing labour scarcity pushes up wages and forces firms to invest.

There is not, however, any evidence to suggest that there is some systemic factor at work holding down wages relative to other sources of income (such as profit or rent). The UK labour share in GDP has remained broadly stable for the last forty years, fluctuating around 70 per cent, unlike in France, the USA and Germany, where it has fallen. Nor do low-paid workers appear to suffer relative to others. Thanks in significant part to the minimum wage, the ratio of the minimum wage to the median is currently as low as it has ever been. It even narrowed through the crisis period, although the minimum wage, like wages in general, fell in real terms. I managed, with some difficulty, to preserve the independent Low Pay Commission's remit for setting the basic minimum wage based on economic considerations, in the face of pressure from the Chancellor and the leader of the opposition who wanted to politicize the decision.

The July 2015 budget has radically changed that set of assumptions, with a mandated increase in the minimum wage of 40 per cent (by £2.50) over the next five years for workers over 24. While politically adroit, this move could create serious damage. There was to be an offsetting deep cut in tax credits worth £8 billion, twice the value of the wage increase leaving low-earning families significantly worse off – but that policy is now in abeyance. Many beneficiaries of the 'living wage' are not actually poor but second or third earners in households that are on average or above-average incomes. Another reason for concern is that, as the Low Pay Commission has warned, there could be substantial job losses in companies that are only just profitable at current minimum wage rates and which cannot pass on higher costs to their customers. By 2020 the 'national living wage' will be 55 per cent of median earnings as against 47 per cent in 2013. In the current climate of tightening labour markets, that may not be of great concern and could boost productivity. But if the economy slows and unemployment rises again, the high minimum wage could have very damaging effects on employment.

There is also a perception that workers have suffered exceptional levels of insecurity in the crisis period. There are undoubtedly many insecure workers on short-term contracts and many others who are frustrated by lack of hours. I took action against abuses of zero-hour contracts and asked BIS to study the wider issues around employment contracts and job security. But the survey evidence suggests that the UK has fewer part-time workers than continental economies like Germany, that fewer workers are frustrated by lack of hours, and that overall levels of work dissatisfaction have not risen.

The sensible course of action, therefore, is the one pursued under the coalition: to maintain the framework of basic labour rights; to maintain and support the minimum wage and toughen enforcement where it is weak; and to deal with abuses around job insecurity as and when there is evidence. Real wages will then rise as productivity rises. So the task of government is to concentrate on measures that can raise productivity by stimulating investment and innovation, improve skills training and support high-productivity growth sectors through the industrial strategy. But, before moving to those issues, I deal with two related obstacles to a sustainable, high-productivity economy: the national obsession with residential property, and a damaged and dysfunctional banking sector.

The British Housing Obsession

The Governor of the Bank of England, no less, has warned that the housing market is the 'biggest risk to recovery'. The IMF has added its weight to these concerns, warning that the UK is one of several countries, which also include Canada, Australia, Belgium, Norway and Sweden, that are at risk from another housing crash, 'with prices well above average for a majority of countries'.

We in the UK have just emerged from the aftermath of a financial crisis that had a housing price boom at its heart. There was a near quadrupling of house and land prices in a little over a decade, from the trough of the previous downturn to the peak in 2008, with mortgage borrowing leading to historically high levels of personal debt in relation to earnings.

As the quote from the IMF makes clear, the UK is not unique. In the run-up to the financial crisis, there was also a major boom in house prices in the USA, though not as extreme as in the UK, and it was the exposure of financial institutions to derivatives based on the housing market and state-backed mortgage institutions like Fannie Mae and Freddie Mac that was the immediate cause of the financial contagion. However, the US housing market has largely adjusted, albeit with regional variations. Prices there have largely returned to pre-boom levels in real terms.

That is not the case in the UK. After a limited adjustment, prices, and price to earnings ratios, have returned to peak, pre-crash levels. With average annual price increases of 10 per cent in 2014, and 20 per cent in London, followed by 6 per cent nationally in 2015, the UK housing market has been heading towards stratospheric levels. Other countries that experienced a major housing boom and bust, like Spain and Ireland, have, unlike the UK, seen a collapse in house prices and a market adjustment. Germany, by contrast, experienced neither boom nor bust; in real terms, German house prices have been almost stable over the last thirty-five years, with little cyclical variation – indeed, they have fallen slightly despite a rising population (Figure 9.1).

What is unique about the UK is that after the crisis supply collapsed along with demand and has also failed to respond to recovery in demand. Britain suffers from a damaging combination of rising demand and severely constricted supply, with a falling supply of new homes over the long term. By way of comparison, over the decade 2004–13, the UK provided 0.4 new homes for every additional head of population, while Spain, Italy, France and Holland all provided more than one. Demand is driven by demographic factors (ageing, family break-ups, regional and national net migration), the growth of second-home ownership (especially in rural areas of natural beauty), investment demand (buy-to-let, speculative purchase in periods of high housing inflation, overseas property investment, especially in London), and the cost and availability of mortgages. This list is mainly one of factors pushing demand in one direction over the long term, but it is availability of credit that creates effective demand and was crucial to the 1997–2008 housing boom, and the subsequent fall and recent rapid recovery. Demand has also been fuelled by a variety of subsidies like Help to Buy and the Funding for Lending Scheme of the Bank of England. These factors are all interrelated. The willingness of banks to lend for owner-occupation or investment, and the willingness of borrowers to borrow, are based in significant measure on price expectations.

It is the lack of supply that has been so remarkable and damaging (Figure 9.2). At the post-war peak in the late 1960s, over 400,000 homes were being built every year, for a UK population significantly smaller than today's (which, of course, reflects the urgency given at the time to the reduction of overcrowding and slum clearance). Of those, roughly 250,000 were privately built and the rest council houses. With the drastic decline in council-house building in the late 1970s and 1980s, only partially replaced by housing associations, total construction settled in the 1990s into a range of 175,000 to 250,000 houses per year, of which around 30,000 were 'social' housing, the rest private.

There was concern at the time that supply was seriously deficient. Estimates based on Kate Barker's analysis of the housing market, made before the crash, suggest that 250,000 to 300,000 new homes per year are needed to stabilize the market in real terms – in other words, to maintain a stable relationship between price and earnings at a level considered affordable across the income spectrum, except for those with low and insecure incomes, for whom social housing is designed. Yet the UK population has grown by 7 per cent over the last decade, the equivalent of over 150,000 homes. After the 2008 crash, building levels fell again to just over 100,000 per year. More precisely, the year before the crash – 2007 – which was the best for a decade, saw 143,000 houses started and 137,000 completed. By 2010 this had fallen to 107,000 completed. By 2014 there was a revival to 141,000 completions, 30,000 of which were social housing. The government's aspirational figure for 2015 was just under 150,000, which is still well below the minimum estimate of what is needed to stabilize prices. Some of that, too, is to supply the luxury market in London for overseas investors, rather than the UK domestic market.

In this way, the UK experience (or rather the British experience, since Northern Ireland functions in a largely separate Irish market) is unusual. The situation also varies enormously from one part of the country to another. It is a very different picture from the inter-war experience, when the UK recovered strongly from the shock of 1929/31 on the back of a boom in housing supply. Houses built by the private sector surged from 130,000 in 1931 to almost 300,000 in 1934. What was different? Then, around one thousand mutually owned, not-for-profit building societies, which were untouched by the crisis, were willing to lend. Interest rates were negative in real terms, as now, but credit was not restricted. Credit was also available for large numbers of small builders who were relatively unconstrained by the banks or by planning constrictions in the absence of green-belt designations.

Trying to understand the contemporary supply-side story involves getting beyond the simple and popular explanations. The current conventional wisdom is that the crucial long-term constraint on supply lies with planning restrictions and with the availability of land for housing development. That message was reinforced by the announcement around the July 2015 budget that further planning powers would be stripped from recalcitrant local councils. There undoubtedly is a problem with the slowness of planning system and also with lack of housing land and it does need tackling. But the post-war planning regime existed when housing supply was at twice or more of present levels. There are also an estimated 400,000 units of housing for which planning permission has been granted but that have not been built.

This leads to the second, short-term explanation: that developers have lacked the certainty of demand needed to proceed with development. That was the rationale behind the coalition government's schemes to encourage mortgage-lending and specifically the Help to Buy scheme. The first stage of Help to Buy provided government support for mortgages of up to £600,000 for newly built houses, allowing a 70 per cent mortgage to be extended to 90 per cent. The scheme had a contingent cost of £3–5 billion and was designed to help the cash-strapped rather than the needy. But beyond that it did little harm, matching additional demand to additional supply.

But an extension of the scheme to guarantee mortgages for any house purchase up to £600,000 and not just first-buys fuelled demand with only a tenuous link to supply. Among the few supporters of the scheme, Charles Goodhart argued that it should stimulate supply but should also be carefully managed by linking it to the Bank of England's macro-prudential policy tools so as to manage demand, up and down as necessary. I earned considerable ill will with the Chancellor, the architect of the scheme, by criticizing it in public. But I was in good company. Other critics have argued that the policy, at taxpayers' expense, raises prices higher than they would otherwise be. Criticisms ranged from the polite comments of the IMF ('This may lead to even higher prices which may reduce affordability of housing') to the more brutal criticisms of the Institute of Directors ('The world must have gone mad'), Conservative-leaning think-tanks such as the Adam Smith Institute ('This will worsen Britain's housing crisis') and Policy Exchange ('risks detonating a bomb under the UK economy'), and the *Daily Mail*, which would normally defend any policy favouring owner-occupiers ('the making of another subprime disaster'). Dario Perkins of Lombard Street Research points out that previous interventions for stimulating demand in the housing market, such as the delay in the abolition of mortgage tax relief in 1988 and the cut in interest rates in 2005, had dramatic effects on house prices, resulting as much from their effects on buyer psychology as from their direct impacts.

The problem is one of supply, not (except in the depths of the post-crisis recession) lack of demand. There are several supply-side problems. First, the banking crisis has seriously affected credit to SMEs in the building industry. We have had a ludicrous position where banks will lend to purchase houses but not to build them. The consequence is that the supply of houses is now more dependent on large builders that have access to equity and debt markets. Two decades ago, 50 per cent of new builds were by companies contributing up to five hundred units, and the level was only a little lower in 2009. But since the market crashed, the bigger builders have accounted for 70 per cent of supply. The coalition government eventually recognized this problem and provided some limited support for loans to small builders.

Second, and a related point, there is a serious lack of diversity in UK supply. There is virtually no self-build, as opposed to 40 per cent of supply in the USA and over 60 per cent in Germany, France, Italy and Sweden; and there is a highly constrained supply of social housing, amounting to approximately 30,000 per year (overwhelmingly housing association dwellings). We have in the UK a fundamentally irrational approach to public support for housing, where demand is increasingly subsidized via housing benefit to private landlords costing £9.3 billion per annum in (up from £3.4 billion in 1998), and schemes like Help to Buy, which cost £1.5 billion per annum. Conversely, house building via housing associations is losing the small amount of subsidy it received (£1.1 billion in 2014, down from £2.3 billion in 2010). The Conservative government has also decided to force housing associations to cut rents, which will reduce the housing benefit subsidy to social landlords but will also reduce their ability to generate surpluses to build new homes. Overall, the subsidies for demand currently amount to over £25 billion, while those for supply come to barely £1 billion.

Third, the concentration of the house-building industry in the hands of a relatively small number of companies, with a similar approach to the market, and this has also exposed weaknesses in the model of development. In practice, developers and builders are not necessarily the same, and they may have different degrees of appetite to proceed and different degrees of access to finance. Landowners in turn may operate to a different agenda, especially as the vast majority of development sites – around 90 per cent – are reported to have been bought up by financial institutions or cash-rich individuals seeking to speculate on land prices. Public bodies, including some councils, also own large swathes of land. A study by Savills estate agents – not, it must be said, totally disinterested – suggests that there is land already in public ownership that could accommodate two million homes: over half owned by councils, 600,000 by central government and 300,000 by the NHS.

What appears to be happening is that the interaction between these different interests has resulted in a muted response to increased demand and prices. Owners of land may benefit in the early stages of recovery if land prices anticipate a future boom and move up sharply, and landowners can aggravate scarcity by with- holding land for speculative gain. These expectations are captured in option agreements, whereby landowners can capture the gain from rising land prices after they have agreed to sell. Developers who have to acquire land in a rising market may find their mar- gins squeezed and their risks increased in the time lag between buying the land and selling homes, unless prices continue to rise. Developers can seek to mitigate these risks by acquiring their own land-banks. But the best insurance for an individual developer is to limit their commitment to new building so as to ensure that they are not caught out in the next downturn with houses they can't sell.

A final complication is that the UK does not have a nationally integrated housing market but many local variations, ranging from raging inflation in many parts of London to virtually none in the North East. Within regions, too, there are big variations, as between, say, Hull and Bradford, and York and Harrogate. In the south-east of England, rising housing and land prices are now producing a supply response and the key problem is the lack of land coming through for development, aggravating the boom in prices. But in much of the Midlands and the north, and in Scotland, developable land is available and price increases are still muted. It is not yet profitable to build because the margins between house prices and the cost of site development and build- ing are not big enough. A yawning gap is opening up between regions where there is rapid economic and job growth but hous- ing is unaffordable for those on average incomes, and regions where housing is more affordable but jobs and growth in eco- nomic activity are not yet plentiful. In both cases, for different reasons, supply is inhibited.

It is worth raising the rather basic question of what 'supply' means. We tend to think of it in terms of the number of homes.

But Danny Dorling suggests that this gives a false impression, since if we look at living space per individual, housing is more abundant than at any other time in history. We enjoy more and more space. However, space is highly unequally distributed. Many low-income families are seriously overcrowded in socially or privately rented accommodation, while millions of others under-occupy, often because (like the author) they continue to live in family-sized houses when their children have left home, or because they keep a second home in the country or a flat in the city. Suburbanites (again, like the author) also have gardens, and suburban communities are heavily, and understandably, resistant to gardens being built over to create more accommodation space. The idea of charging for space has become policy with the introduction of the spare-room subsidy, or 'bedroom tax', for recipients of housing benefit. The idea of applying this concept in the owner-occupied sector, however, is unlikely to happen this side of a revolution, even though seven million owner-occupied houses have two or more spare bedrooms and 25 million, one spare. Under-occupation has grown 25 per cent in a decade. The Chancellor's recent decision to increase the threshold for inheritance tax to £1 million will make it worse, persuading older owner-occupiers to hold on to under-occupied housing until death.

Why should the severely dysfunctional British housing market should matter so much. Such a market serves the interests of a large and important section of the population very well. Home-owners make up 65 per cent of households and even though the proportion is falling because of affordability issues, down from 71 per cent a decade ago, there is a substantial majority who benefit, at least on paper, from property price appreciation. The older segment (my generation) has an asset unencumbered by mortgage debt, which represents a pot of savings, which is appreciating in value unlike many other forms of saving. It can be used to trade down to a smaller property or a property in another part of the country at a profit, or can be used as collateral for personal borrowing. And for younger mortgage borrowers, net asset values are accumulating – there is no negative equity problem so long as prices rise – permitting upward movement on the housing ladder, using equity for the next deposit. Indeed, the enhanced wealth and confidence of owner-occupiers was perhaps the single most important factor triggering the recovery. And it has also given banks the confidence to lend not just for house purchase but to those businesses that can offer a home or other property as collateral.

So, what is the problem? It is clear that even the beneficiaries are aware that there is a problem. Public opinion surveys conducted by YouGov for Shelter show that even for those unencumbered by mortgages, only 28 per cent want house prices to rise further and 67 per cent want to see either stability or a fall. At the last peak of the market before 2010, the British Social Attitudes Survey suggested that 45 per cent felt prices were 'too high', 4 per cent 'too low', and the rest 'about right'.

One reason for this ambiguous response is that even if rising prices produce net wealth, large numbers of house purchasers – especially those who entered the market recently – are highly vulnerable to rising servicing costs if or when interest rates return to historic normality. The Resolution Foundation has calculated that if interest rates rise from the current 0.5 per cent to 4 per cent, then 1.2 million would be spending half of their income on debt service and 6 million more than a quarter. One third of all mortgage debt in London is held by households that have borrowed more than four times their income (the figure for the rest of the country is 9 per cent). The traditional bank and building society definition of safe lending was a multiple of three. I recall invoking this principle on a radio call-in show, only to be assailed by listeners and the press on the basis that it would make some house purchases unaffordable – oblivious to the danger of rising house prices also affecting affordability. Indeed, a feature of the market at present is that while mortgage lenders have been much more careful than before the crash in lending on high loan to value ratios, the proportion of high loan to income ratios has been rising steadily, especially in London.

The hard-headed cynic may say 'so what?' If borrowers are overextended, 'that is their problem'. They could downsize or move somewhere else if they can't keep up with their debt servicing. It only matters systemically if large numbers default on their payments, leading to problems for the lenders. The banks, however, have the option of extending mortgage repayment periods, moving borrowers on to an interest-only basis and as a last resort repossessing, which is a serious problem – for them – only in a falling market. Since the crash, tough stress tests are now applied and banks have reserves to deal with a price crash of up to 35 per cent. Systemic risk will become an issue only in the event of a major price crash. Servicing problems are currently much more of a worry to indebted households than to banks.

Thus the central issue, at least at present, is not systemic economic stability but the social impact of abnormally high house prices. The reason why even many owner-occupiers appear to regard rising prices as a problem is that those adversely affected are not some separate species of humanity but include their children and grandchildren. The Bank of Mum and Dad can help alleviate the intergenerational impact – and Mum and Dad can accommodate their offspring for longer, or help by providing an inheritance – but these arrangements are not always feasible or welcome, and do not apply in many cases, especially for families that never got on the property ladder in the first place.

The social impacts are becoming painfully apparent in several specific ways. First, despite the Conservatives' strong ideological commitment to owner-occupation and a variety of costly inducements, owner-occupation is falling, quite sharply. Indeed, it is falling for the first time in a century. For 18- to 34-year-olds owner-occupation has fallen by a third since 2003, and by 18 per cent for 35- to 44-year-olds. The reason is simple: affordability. With each successive housing boom the ratio of house price to income – the best measure of affordability – has risen (Figure 9.3). In 1997 the price to earnings ratio for an average family was between three and five, rising to over six in London. On normal prudent lending criteria, a family with one principal earner could just about afford to buy in the cheaper parts of the country or at the cheap end of the London market. By 2012 the ratio had reached five to seven in the north of England, making purchase difficult except at the bottom end of the market, and six to eight in the south, rising to ten or more in London, creating an enormous affordability barrier to all except high-income two-earner, mainly professional, families. The position has deteriorated since. On one estimate, the proportion of private tenants priced out of home ownership rose from 2.5 million in 2010 to 3.8 million in 2015.

But, of course, the people have to live somewhere. The social housing stock is itself declining, mainly because of Right to Buy (much of the sold stock ending up with buy-to-let landlords), such that after 2003 there was a fall in social tenancy of 21 per cent for the 25- to 34-year-olds age group and 18 per cent for 35- to 44-year-olds. The Conservatives' plans to extend Right to Buy to housing associations will accelerate the process further since one for one replacement is extremely difficult (as councils have discovered), and the finances of housing associations will deteriorate unless they are fully compensated, at great cost to the Exchequer. Even making a genuine attempt to be politically detached about the new Conservative government, extending Right to Buy is a terrible idea.

The displaced population has been absorbed into private rented accommodation, up by 90 per cent for 25- to 34-year-olds and by 132 per cent for 35- to 44-year-olds over the period 2003–13, with young people under twenty-five almost entirely in this sector. A Price Waterhouse Cooper study in July 2015 suggests that by 2025 over half of under 40s will be renting privately. To some degree the growth, or revival, in renting is to be welcomed because of the mobility it helps generate and because the weakness of the British rental sector, relative to, say, that of Germany, has often been seen as a problem. David Blanchflower has produced empirical evidence to show that there is a strong connection between the scale of the rented sector and low levels of unemployment. However, this movement of the young into private renting is often involuntary, with young families, whose numbers in private rented property have doubled in a decade, subject to high levels of instability. Forced moves lead from one short tenancy to another, with a dearth of the long-term seven- to ten-year agreements institutionalized in continental Europe. Inevitably, the high and rising prices of property are transmitted into the rental market. Indeed, a recent survey by Savills shows that mortgaged owner-occupiers pay less than tenants for comparable property, though that is a function of historically low interest rates and will be reversed if interest rates rise to 3 per cent. The same affordability issues apply in the private rented market and low-income families survive there almost entirely because of housing benefit, the cost of which to the state has doubled in the last decade despite measures such as the benefit cap which has undoubtedly caused hardship, including homelessness and forced migration from high-rent areas.

It would be a mistake, however, to regard housing problems as simply social in character. The dysfunctional property market has powerful negative economic consequences. Many countries suffer from cyclical instability caused by price fluctuations in a major commodity. In the UK, arguably, property, and particularly domestic property, performs a similar role. Fred Harrison has argued that there is a long-term property cycle of around seventeen years which is highly correlated with the wider economic cycle. In an upswing, confidence grows, encouraging consumption, and there is an associated boom in home improvements, while increased building spills over into construction products and furnishings. Certainly, the three booms and busts experienced by my generation – in 1974/5, 2001/2 and 2008/9 – fit that pattern. The IMF is even concerned that serious property bubbles in major economies, or synchronized property bubbles in several significant economies, could destabilize the world economy.

Also damaging is the increase over a long period of time in house prices, in relation to other ways of accumulating capital. It has transformed property into an attractive, relatively low-risk investment for both households and lenders. For households, owning a more valuable primary residence or buying a second home for letting has been a better investment than shares or a pension fund. Britain's one million buy-to-let landlords have made an estimated 16 per cent compound annual return over the last twenty years, as against 6.5 per cent for shares, and banks are happy to lend to them (with a massive 40 per cent increase since the 2008 crisis). But investing in existing property – as opposed to new – property contributes little to the productive capacity of the economy. Continued housing inflation then vindicates the decision to invest in property (Figure 9.4). A decision by George Osborne to remove upper rate tax relief and charge higher stamp duty on buy-to-let property will however discourage new buy-to-let investors.

Banks, similarly, will lend against domestic property much more willingly than to businesses that cannot offer comparable collateral. Depreciating machinery, export orders, intellectual property or a good business plan are, by contrast, higher risk, more difficult to value or more uncertain, and are therefore likely to attract higher borrowing costs or no credit at all. The risk weights applied by regulators reinforce this bias. Reputedly, a bank will typically have to set aside five times more capital for an SME loan than for a mortgage. The distortion in lending patterns that this produces is immensely damaging. Only around 12 per cent of UK bank lending in 2009 went to companies in ways that had nothing to do with property. Over 50 per cent was advanced for domestic mortgages, and overall about three quarters of bank lending was linked to the property market. A study by Jordà, Taylor and Schularick shows that the share of bank lending accounted for by property jumped from 16 per cent in 1928 to 63 per cent in 2007. It is likely that the proportion has since grown further.

It is tempting, but facile, to deplore the behaviour of banks and individuals. Under current incentive structures and policies, their behaviour is wholly rational. It is rational for banks to invest in unproductive, but safe mortgage-lending and to deny credit to creative industries, manufacturers and other exporters. It is rational for individuals owning property and land to speculate that prices will keep rising, rather than to invest in new businesses. It is rational to be a NIMBY and to restrict other people's opportunities to own a home if it devalues one's own investment in property. Rational – but ruinous to the prospects of sustained, balanced recovery.

So what is to be done? It is clear from the above that there is a variety of different factors at work on both the demand and supply side, and that some of these are deep-rooted and have become embedded in the behaviour of individuals, companies and financial institutions. There is no 'silver bullet'. By common consent, the main, and most difficult, policy issues are on the supply side, but it is important to look at demand, too, especially in the short term when demand management can make a difference. When a fire is raging out of control, it is important to ensure that water is being used to put it out, not petrol.

———

The adoption of macro-prudential policies by the Bank of England is a useful step forward. But its first major application – in 2014, in an attempt to act as a brake on the current house price boom – was hardly draconian. The regulator announced that no more than 15 per cent of new mortgages should be at or above a loan to income multiple of 4.5. But since only 11 per cent of new mortgages fall into this category, the restriction has had little overall impact, except possibly in London where 19 per cent of mortgages come within this limit. In addition, there is a stronger bank stress test (against an interest rate of 3.5 per cent) and more intrusive testing of borrowers (who now have to be stress-tested against an interest rate of 7 per cent). The Bank has expressed specific concern over buy-to-let lending by banks but taken no action yet.

The most obvious next step to moderate demand would be to scrap the Help to Buy scheme. Since it is the brainchild of the Chancellor, that isn't going to happen under a Conservative government. But hopefully the policy can now reflect changed conditions, scaling back the limit from £600,000 to £250,000, and its use confined to parts of the country where the market is still sufficiently depressed to discourage development. Other demand-affecting policies are in the pipeline: inevitable increases in interest rates, and tougher capital requirements for banks to hold more capital against mortgages.

All of these factors should dampen demand and hopefully stop, or even reverse, recent price increases. There is, however, the longer-term issue of how to reduce the incentive to see housing as a more attractive investment than other forms of saving and as a profitable opportunity to speculate on future capital gains.

Tax is the obvious way of achieving this. Although owner-occupiers no longer benefit from interest rate relief on mortgages, buy-to-let landlords have been able to claim interest relief as a business expense (until the Chancellor's 2015 decision to restrict this relief to the standard rate). Moving away from interest tax relief is a broader tax reform, but is urgent in the case of property. Another route would be reform of council tax to make it more closely aligned with property prices. In the absence of revaluation or a move to a flat percentage tax on estimated values of the kind operated in some US cities and European countries, council tax is a very blunt instrument. John Muellbauer has produced a very plausible plan for council tax reform which would combine greater fairness and economic efficiency. Politicians of all parties have, however, run a mile from any reform of council tax that could produce losers – like revaluation to correct the distortions introduced by valuations made a quarter of a century ago.

One tentative move in that direction was the so-called 'mansion tax' on high-value property which I originally proposed in 2009. The form adopted by my party had a series of new council tax bands for properties currently worth over £2 million, to correct the anomaly that high-value properties pay a much lower rate of tax, as a percentage of value, than do modest homes. The proposal came close to fruition because George Osborne accepted the trade-off that I put to him of a 'mansion tax' in return for a 40 per cent top rate of income tax. The prime minister vetoed the idea, however, and a politically weaker compromise was agreed by the Quad, including a 45 per cent top rate and higher stamp duty on expensive homes. Subsequently, and with the Labour party also adopting a 'mansion tax', a formidable campaign was launched on behalf of wealthy property owners, mainly in London, which understandably had some political impact. Post-election, the proposal is no longer live.

Another approach would be capital gains tax on primary residences (it currently applies only to second homes), probably as part of a more comprehensive reform of property taxes, including inheritance tax. But as politicians know to their cost, tax reform is much more popular with academics and think-tanks than with the public, whose attention is soon drawn to the potential losers, such as the asset-rich, income-poor 'little old lady' who is invariably raised as an insuperable obstacle to fairer and more sensible property taxation. But it must be part of any meaningful housing policy reform.

———————

On the supply side, the planning system is invariably blamed for the lack of development land for new building. Some planning reforms have been attempted and there is modest evidence of a speeding up of decisions and a higher proportion of appeals by applicants being upheld. But most of these changes relate to change of use within developed, built-up areas, which account for under 10 per cent of the land. Half of built-up areas are accounted for by gardens and parks, but this area is being slowly eroded, and other changes, such as permitting the conversion of retail, office and industrial space to housing, are in some areas leading to unbalanced communities, with homes but no jobs, and greater pressure to travel further for work and shopping. Lord Adonis has agreed that some large low density London estates which councils could redevelop but their residents will resist losing green space as much as suburban owner occupiers.

A taboo subject is the green belt. There have been entirely sensible economic and environmental reasons for preventing urban sprawl, which lacks the infrastructure of planned communities, and also for preserving areas of natural beauty and ecological diversity for the wider public good. However, much of the land protected from development is farmland which has little amenity or environmental value and perpetuates enormous disparities between agricultural and development land prices. In reality, gardens and parks in urban areas contribute far more to public amenity and to species diversity than does the green belt.

Various ideas have been promoted for opening up parts of the green belt for development without destroying its original purpose. One is a revival of garden cities, on the post-war model of Hatfield, Welwyn and, later, Milton Keynes: properly planned with high environmental standards and good public transport infrastructure. A variant of this idea, promoted by Lord Matthew Taylor, is for smaller, planned communities built around existing villages, thus helping to save and support local shops, pubs and village schools. But both of these will not just happen randomly or as a result of developers acquiring plots of land. It requires a development agency or interventionist council to acquire and assemble the land and to prepare the infrastructure – a quite different approach from 'freeing up the planning system'. The London Olympics was a recent example of this approach being successfully employed on a tight timetable.

Planning isn't just about land. The industrial strategy that I introduced under the coalition government prioritised the construction industry. At present, it is ill-equipped to expand supply rapidly. There is a chronic shortage of skilled labour, a product of short-sighted training and employment practices in the industry, which is being met partly through immigration and belatedly through a revival of apprenticeships. New building techniques, like off-site assembly, lag behind continental practice, adding to costs. There is some innovative work taking place incorporating new information technology into building design and planning, but this has yet to penetrate beyond the leading firms. At least there is now a structure bringing the industry together to address these issues.

A related question is how to reform a land market that is highly volatile and appears to work against increasing housing supply. Philosophically, there are two approaches. One is to free up planning controls and sell off public sector land, thereby increasing supply by bringing more land on to the market and helping to stabilize prices. The other approach is more interventionist: using public bodies to acquire land-banks for development purposes, if necessary using compulsory purchase, which can then be released counter-cyclically; using public land sales to extract early building commitments; and redrawing green belt maps to open up areas of low priority for development. In fact, the two approaches are complementary. The difficulties lie less in philosophical differences than in policy decentralization. The coalition government rightly emphasized decentralized local planning, but inevitably some councils will be more activist than others, and all are prey to local vested interests resisting development that appears to undermine local property values. The state cannot mandate development, but it can ensure that in all the areas where it has discretion – including the approval of local plans, appeals and the establishment of garden city development authorities – there is a meaningful presumption of sustainable development.

One mechanism for bringing more land into development at low cost could be the use of Community Land Auctions, an idea originally put forward by Tim Leunig. In effect, councils are allowed or encouraged to run reverse auctions to acquire mainly agricultural land with development potential but without development approval. The land can then be used directly for building or for sale with planning approval. There are tricky issues here in terms of the conflicting roles of councils – extracting revenue for auctions, acquiring development land, granting planning approval – which is why the idea has so far not got beyond the pilot stage.

Another complication is the need to fund infrastructure, including amenities like public open space and schools, and quality standards beyond those that developers would be inclined to provide (gardens, for example). These factors have to be incorporated in the land price. The coalition government introduced the Community Infrastructure Levy (CIL) as a more transparent alternative to the negotiated, unpredictable Section 106 agreements, and although some developers complain that it is a cost burden (along with the obligations to provide social housing and high environmental standards), it is an improvement. But since these costs are a deterrent to development, it becomes all the more important to ensure that land is available at cheaper prices.

While there are many ideas for improving the working of land markets and freeing up the use of land, there is nothing at present to force the transformation of land with planning permission into development, unless public agencies carry out the development themselves. Taxation is one means. Taxes, or penalty charges, have been proposed on unused land-banks. In practice, however, it would be difficult to distinguish cases where landowners or developers are holding back development for speculative reasons from those that are not proceeding because high costs make development unprofitable (for example, where expensive site reclamation or decontamination is involved) or because local demand is insufficient. The counter-argument would be that, if those are the reasons, the developer could sell on the site at a lower price to someone who would develop it.

A more comprehensive approach, which does not involve arbitrary decisions based on the presumed motives of developers, is the use of land taxation. This is an old idea going back to the Liberal government before the First World War, but it has encountered strong political resistance, not least because of lack of certainty about the liability of particular landowners and the practicalities of valuation and collection. But it must surely be right in principle that there is a tax penalty for the under-utilization of land. One specific way forward would be the replacement of business rates on developed and improved property by taxation of the underlying site value.

Drawing these threads together, there are, effectively, only two forms of new housing becoming available. One is owner-occupied housing, dependent largely on a badly functioning land market and a small number of major developers producing currently short of 150,000 houses per year. The other is social housing, mostly provided by those housing associations that have a strong enough balance sheet to borrow and develop, and that have access to developable land via quotas imposed on private developers by local authorities or through their own activities in the land market. These amount to a fairly steady 30,000 per year. There is a danger at present that the policies of the Conservative government will reduce social housing supply. Furthermore, councils and developers will now be required to provide more 'starter homes' at a 20 per cent discount to the market for first time buyers, and if the subsidy element comes from 'planning gain' it will probably be at the expense of social housing for lower income groups rather than adding to supply.

So if supply needs to double, where could the additional capacity come from? One option, already discussed, is for development corporations to create a new generation of planned communities. The model is already proven and it is estimated that there is a potential for 30,000 to 40,000 houses per year in this form, if there is the will to face down local opposition in rural areas. The Conservative government has now embraced the idea of directly comissioning building on public sector land but hasn't yet shown how this will work. Another option is to make it easier for self-build on the continental model, and the coalition government introduced a programme to facilitate self-build, which essentially involves flexibility over design and building standards and easy connections to utilities.

Councils could play a much greater role, as they did in the early post-war era, using land that they own to commission builders to proceed with development for sale or affordable rent. The council's role would be that of enabler and commissioner, using the balance sheet of the local authority to borrow. This is an area where borrowing caps, which have already been lifted for other forms of local authority development, should be lifted as a matter of urgency. The government's rhetoric about radical devolution to local government makes this an obvious step to take. But the Treasury's obsession with curbing all forms of public borrowing for investment however essential – discussed in the next chapter – is a serious road block.

Financial institutions such as pension funds have long expressed an interest in funding long-term investment in housing, mainly for private rental, and have already financed substantial student accommodation. Government guarantees are available – up to £6.5 billion, as well as a Build to Rent fund of £1 billion for low-cost finance – and after years of frustrating discussion there is some sign of real progress. Projects are evolving, resulting in professionally managed projects of good quality. Roughly 10,000 homes are agreed in principle, led by developments in Southampton and Manchester, with another 30,000 in prospect.

It is, however, difficult to see how major progress can be made without significant additional public investment either to finance development directly or to act as a catalyst for private development. Shelter suggests that an annual commitment of an extra £3 billion per year could finance an extra 50,000 homes per year, costing barely one tenth of the current housing benefit bill. Unfortunately, Treasury orthodoxy and Conservative ideology strongly resisted this during the coalition and are now more deeply entrenched. Indeed, the overall lack of political consensus around housing policy means that it is likely to remain a disaster area. Timidity in supply measures together with inexorably rising demand will lead inevitably to growing property wealth for older homeowners and growing hardship for younger renters.

British Banking after the Banking Crash

The story of the global and British banking crash was told in *The Storm*, and the global consequences were discussed in chapter two above. I am concerned here with the aftermath in the UK: the short-term and long-term damage done; the regulatory moves to create a more stable, safer banking and financial services sector; and the long-term cultural issues highlighted by the crisis and its legacy. There has been antisocial behaviour ranging up to and including fraud, extreme rewards, and a bias against long-term financing of productive business. But a new and healthier, more diverse and competitive banking industry is also starting to emerge.

I write from the perspective of someone who commented on, usually to criticize, British banking in the decade before the crisis and who then spent five years helping to reform the banks, working with them and redesigning the architecture of business banking. There were genuine achievements from the Vickers reforms to the establishment of the British Business Bank, but there were massive frustrations, from the slow progress in reforming RBS and continued net negative lending to SMEs, to the failure of the system to lay a finger on the most egregious villains of the banking crisis. I was often accused of banker-bashing, though nothing that I said or did was remotely as painful as what the banks did to themselves. I admired some of the skills of the leading bankers, whom I came to know, without ever understanding their need for extreme rewards. I always felt more comfortable with the mutuals; indeed, I may never have become involved in banking at all had I not been roped in to lead a (successful) campaign – Save Our Building Societies – to stop the demutualization of the leading societies, notably Nationwide. These factors clearly influence my analysis of the sector.

My starting point is that Britain had, and still has, exceptional representation among the world's largest banks (Figure 10.1). At the time of the financial crisis, RBS was, depending on how it is measured (by balance sheet or capital), either the biggest or the third biggest bank in the world. HSBC was of similar size. Barclays and Lloyds were also in the big league. Total net banking assets for these four banks as a share of GDP were around 450 per cent, far higher than the average of fourteen major advanced countries (around 200 per cent of GDP) or key economies like the USA (100 per cent of GDP), and higher even than Switzerland. When two of the banks collapsed and had to be rescued (and Barclays, almost, as well), there were enormous and disproportionate repercussions for the UK. Since the financial crisis, the UK global banks have shrunk relative to their overseas competitors. On the league table drawn up by *Banker* magazine, four US and Chinese banks now rank ahead of HSBC, Barclays has slipped to thirteenth place and RBS to eighteenth. But the banking sector as a whole remains disproportionately large as a share of the UK economy.

There is an argument that has raged ever since as to whether this experience and its consequences are the responsibility of the bankers themselves, particularly in the case of RBS, or their boards and shareholders, or the regulators that failed to supervise them, or the politicians who indulged them. There are now enough post-mortems and reviews on the record to provide answers to those questions, from the Banking Commission which I participated in with David Davis and John McFall, to the more comprehensive Parliamentary Commission on Banking Standards, chaired by Andrew Tyrie. With hindsight, however, it was a mistake not to have had a full judicial inquiry which could have produced a definitive set of conclusions – though I understand, following the interminable and costly Saville and Chilcot inquiries, why that model has lost its appeal.

The practical, forward-looking question is whether it is in the UK's national interest to have such a large, concentrated, globally based banking sector, or financial services sector. I raised this issue in chapter two in the wider context of economies with a large financial sector where there was evidence that the costs may outweigh the benefits. The issue is profoundly important for the UK. Should we look to defend these institutions and their global reach as a wealth-creating national asset, or to curb them as a liability on account of their exposure to systemic risk and instability?

There are some definitional issues here. The UK financial services industry is complex. It has major sub-sectors like insurance with a different maturity structure of assets and liabilities from the banks and facing different kinds of risks. Some of the UK financial services sector is wholly domestic, like building societies and personal financial advice, and some almost entirely international, like the commodity and foreign exchange markets. Even within banking there are UK-based banks that are largely global in character and focus (HSBC, Standard Chartered); others that are largely domestic, albeit with overseas operations (Lloyds and RBS); and overseas banks that operate here, of which there are 250, owning half the country's banking assets. The overseas banks in turn have subsidiaries here: some are in offshore activities based in the City; others in the domestic market (like Santander and Handelsbanken); and some, like the US investment banks, operate globally but have significant UK corporate business. London has a dominant position in cross-border lending, foreign exchange markets and interest rate derivatives, and is important, next to the USA, for hedge fund and private equity assets. That is why sweeping references to the value – or not – of UK financial services are misleading at best.

If we try to reduce these varied activities to the income generated by the sector (fees and spreads and also capital income), a French economist, Guillaume Bazot, has calculated that the UK financial services sector in 2000 accounted for around 8 per cent of GDP, a little more than Germany and France and a little less than the USA. (All were around 3–4 per cent in 1960.) But in the following decade, the UK share grew to over 12 per cent, while the others remained roughly the same. It is this surge in relative exposure of the UK to financial services that lies at the heart of the debate: the big rise in City employment, tax revenue and associated risk in the run-up to the crash. Globalization of finance is not, clearly, a UK phenomenon alone. The share of bank assets to GDP for fourteen major economies quadrupled after around 1960 from a level that had been roughly stable for a century before. But in the UK the expansion was extreme and insecurely based. As a share of GDP, banking assets in the UK are five times bigger than in the USA and greater than in smaller countries with a large banking sector like Ireland and Switzerland, exposing the wider economy to more systemic risk.

Not to be discouraged, Mark Carney, the Governor of the Bank of England, made a controversial intervention declaring that the City of London is once again 'open for business'. He predicted, and welcomed, the historic trend of financial deepening that saw UK bank assets grow from 40 per cent of GDP in 1913 to 400 per cent now, and which 'by 2050 could exceed nine times GDP, and that is to say nothing of the potentially rapid growth of banking and shadow banking based in London'. He continued that 'some would react with horror'. I did, and do.

There are, of course, some rational arguments for wanting an expanding financial centre in London. There are employment and tax benefits, though many of the foreign banks including Deutsche Bank, JP Morgan and Goldmans arbitrage via tax havens to pay little UK corporate tax. British global banks may have networks that benefit British exporters (which is part of HSBC's appeal), but the dire state of British exports and export finance (as against Germany, with less centralized banking) does not suggest that this is a major factor.

The arguments for being worried about the scenario described by the Governor are several. One is the disconnect between the finance sector and the domestic economy. I have likened the role of the City to the oil and mining industry in many poor countries: a 'dual economy' enclave, generating, of course, some jobs and taxes, but for the most part segregated from the national economy except for adding cyclical instability and structural problems, such as an overvalued exchange rate. A comparative study by the Bank for International Settlements showed that there was a negative relationship between the growth of the finance sector and overall economic performance. The link I referred to in the previous chapter between bank lending and property collateral has been at the expense of high-productivity investment, including innovative companies involved in intellectual property and exports. The question left by the financial crisis is whether prudential regulation now makes the banks safer and whether conduct has improved with an end to antisocial behaviour.

In the event, the Conservative government after May 2015 has adopted a much more conciliatory approach to the banks. At the Lord Mayor's Banquet in June 2015, the Chancellor promoted a 'new settlement'. He criticized the large fines imposed on the banks and argued for Britain to be the headquarters for global banks, softening and, then, phasing out the annual bank levy on balance sheets, which was of concern to HSBC in particular. (The rationale of the levy is to force banks to pay, in the manner of insurance, for the risks they pose to the UK taxpayer and the proposed substitute, a surcharge on profits, will be easier to evade). The removal of a tough Financial Conduct regulator, Martin Wheatley, who threatened to 'shoot first and ask questions later', followed by the dropping of the FCA enquiry into bank culture was a significant concession to the banks. For his part Mr Carney offered to reverse the process of increasing financial regulation through a Fair and Effective Markets Review, replacing market abuse rules by a voluntary code of conduct. There had been cross party agreement for senior bank executives to be made personally responsible for the conduct of their banks – in relation, for example, to the Libor and Forex markets – but the proposal is now to be weakened. Other rules, like extending the application of the Bribery Act to the sector, have been shelved.

The main lesson of the 2008 crisis is that the structure of banking was systemically fragile. The years since then have been used by regulators in the UK and elsewhere to make the banks safer by requiring them to hold more capital (equity) in reserve and also more liquidity, since lack of liquidity to meet emergency requirements, as occurred with Northern Rock, for example, can quickly evolve into a solvency crisis. Banks are now much better capitalized. But the process of getting there may have aggravated weaknesses in the real economy. Banks can raise new capital by going to their shareholders for new issues, which is difficult at reasonable cost under current uncertain market conditions (or, in the case of RBS, involves taxpayers' money), or by deleveraging (reducing their lending exposure), which is essentially what they have done. Greater stability, through raising capital, has been bought at the expense of lending to smaller companies, undermining sustainable growth. Hence my own criticism of the 'capital Taliban' and the Chancellor's reference to 'the stability of the graveyard'.

There is a clear tension between the end of stability and the means to achieve it. That tension is reflected in an ongoing debate over the leverage ratio, since a rapid move to higher ratios would have a significant impact on lending. The tension between greater financial stability and more productive lending was heightened by a parallel move to change the risk weights attached to capital so as to penalize 'risky' lending. The risk weights, internationally agreed, have had the effect of penalizing activities like exporting, or financing start-ups or companies whose business model rests on difficult-to-value intellectual property. At the same time they reinforced 'safe' lending, such as mortgage-lending. But as Martin Wolf has pointed out, 'the labelling of a particular form of activity as relatively safe makes over-lending more probable. Its relatively low level of riskiness is a self-denying prophecy: the market response will itself make it false.' That is precisely what is now occurring: a domestic property bubble, especially in London, and the semi-starvation of SMEs seeking to expand and export.

Superimposed on capital requirements has been major structural reform. The UK has gone further than any other major economy in reforming bank structure. I was among those who believed that what was required post-crash was not simply a rescue of the banks, but an attack on the complexity of the big banks which have internally conflicting values and objectives. A key problem is the intermingling of high-risk, high-reward investment banking, so-called 'casino banking', and retail banking, including most business banking.

I referred in chapter two to the wider context of structural reform in banking. The radical option, harking back to the US reforms post-1929 under the Glass–Steagall Act, was a legal splitting of these banks and I have always been attracted to that. In the event, the Chancellor and I, who were given responsibility to respond to this problem under the coalition agreement, agreed to seek the advice of an independent body that we established, the Vickers Commission. It recommended, on cost-benefit grounds, an intermediate position: the ring-fencing of retail from investment banking. The aim was to prevent conflicts of interest, objectives and culture between the different kinds of banking. More radical options were rejected on the basis that there would be large hidden costs, mainly in the form of disentangling complex IT systems, in splitting up banks completely. Ring-fencing was strengthened, 'electrified', as the legislation went through parliament, so that full separation remains an option if ring-fencing fails. There has been criticism that ring-fencing has not gone far enough to curb reckless behaviour, but the continuing fierce lobbying of the banks to dilute the policy suggests that it has had an impact on behaviour already. Banks are also lobbying hard against the levy on bank assets, though, quite apart from the revenue benefit, there is a compelling argument for requiring the banks to pay for the implicit subsidy they continue to enjoy.

Ring-fencing does not, of itself, solve the problem of banks that are too-big-to-fail and which depend on an implicit taxpayer guarantee, though it helps to isolate the component parts and to identify the risk to the system. Additional measures are now required in the form of 'living wills' and resolution mechanisms to convert debt into loss-absorbing equity capital in crisis conditions, so that investors rather than taxpayers bear the risk. Some comfort is derived from the successful management of crisis in the Co-op Bank. It was not bailed out by the taxpayer, but capital shortfalls, of around £1.5 billion, were found by the Co-op group and its bond-holders without the bank itself collapsing and without wider knock-on effects. The only policy issue I faced was whether the introduction of private equity as part of the rescue made the Co-op Bank incapable of adhering to its ethical mandate and would affect its mutual branding. No strong case was made that it did. But in any event the Co-op Bank is a financial minnow in global terms when compared with Barclays, HSBC, RBS, Lloyds or even Santander.

The strength of the new regulatory structure is being stress-tested in simulated, laboratory conditions, but we simply do not know how it would cope with a real-world crash involving the simultaneous collapse of investment banking and a generalized slump in house prices, together with unknown unknowns of the kind that proliferate rapidly in the finance sector. One potential source of weakness identified by Avinash Persaud is that the banks have devised a new way of meeting their capital requirements, by issuing securities known as 'contingent convertibles' or 'CoCo' bonds, which can be called in and converted into risk capital (equity) if necessary. Were these held by, say, pension funds, there would be confidence that there was a sufficiently deep pool of liquid assets to meet an emergency. But they are being snapped up instead by hedge funds and shadow banks which are lightly regulated and essentially short-term in their behaviour and could, if they were to fail, leave banks with a serious problem. I, for one, do not believe the system is safe, though it is safer than it was in 2008.

A parallel structural reform has been the creation within RBS of a 'bad bank' to hold and gradually run off non-core assets and non-performing, mainly commercial, property loans, and a 'good bank' of healthy retail and commercial banking and investment banking business, the last being shrunk and in order to be ring-fenced in due course. The split is not a formal one and it follows a pattern established much earlier with Northern Rock, where the 'good bank' has become Virgin Money. The model was established successfully in the wake of the Scandinavian banking crisis in the early 1990s and there is a legitimate criticism over the fact that it took our government five years to get around to it.

The structural issues are linked to the cultural, or conduct, issues. These were exhaustively covered by the Parliamentary Commission on Banking Standards in June 2013. Bankers are not inherently wicked people and a generation ago were widely respected for their integrity and criticized, if at all, for being rather boring and colourless. Something happened in the intervening period to make them into a vilified profession characterized, certainly at a senior management level, by 'insufficient personal responsibility' (to quote the Commission), leading to 'profound loss of trust' born of 'profound lapses in banking standards'.

One important change had been the adoption of stretching financial targets to achieve high short-term rates of return on shareholders' equity. This was, in turn, a consequence of the liberalization and globalization of financial markets and the lack of securely rooted, long-term national and local banking of the kind that survived in Germany but was, in the UK, undermined by the demutualization of building societies. It may not excuse, but it helps to explain, the conduct of the likes of Fred Goodwin and Bob Diamond, to understand that their shareholders expected higher returns than were available from 'boring' UK banking and required some combination of high-risk investment banking, a strategy of international acquisitions, and squeezing higher margins from domestic and business customers through aggressive salesmanship. The egregious mis-selling of personal protection insurance (PPI) or credit default swaps to small businesses by branch managers turned salesmen, the market manipulation, as in the Libor and Forex scandals, the predatory lending, the excessive leverage underpinning acquisitions of questionable value, and the bonus-fuelled trading in derivatives, all these did not happen by accident. They are inherent in the business model used by the leading banks.

I got a flavour of the dynamics involved several years before the crisis when I acquired a reputation in the industry for attacking the leading banks. I criticized them for undermining relationship banking through aggressive selling of financial products and for fuelling what, even to the untutored eye, appeared to be a dangerous house price spiral. I recall meeting the chief executive of HBOS, James Crosby, who, having helped to undermine the mutual ethos of the Halifax and the conservative reputation of the Bank of Scotland, was leading the charge into high loan to value mortgages. He fully recognized the possible consequences of what was happening in the industry, but said that if he didn't lend aggressively, his shareholders would replace him with someone who would. About the same time, I met the members of the board of Lloyds, then still a venerated bank with a reputation for restraint, who explained that their shareholders were dissatisfied with modest returns and were propelling them into growth through acquisition. The seeds of the disastrous HBOS-Lloyds merger were sown well before the shotgun marriage. I have no doubt that the RBS acquisition of ABN Amro similarly originated in short-term market pressures as much as in Fred Goodwin's reported megalomania. It is easy to blame the bankers, but I recall that at the time that I was criticizing and being invited to meet leading bankers prior to the crash, I also had occasional meetings with key members of the Bank of England's Monetary Policy Committee who either did not accept that there was a problem or took the view that it was nothing to do with them. This was a consequence of the divisions within the 'tripartite system' of Treasury, Bank of England and Financial Services Authority, which George Osborne identified as a key weakness and legislated for in the early days of the coalition.

The post-crisis regulatory response – forcing banks to hold more equity, or near equity, and ending the implicit taxpayer subsidy – should have the effect of either turning banks back into safer, relatively low-risk, low-reward utilities or, for those who need the adrenalin, genuinely high-risk, high-reward hedge fund-type institutions, which can fail. The recent adoption of more narrowly focused and more conservative business models by RBS and Lloyds, and at Barclays under Antony Jenkins, does not indicate that saints have replaced sinners, merely that regulatory changes have dampened expectations of future returns. But low-risk, low-return banking is perhaps better undertaken by institutions that are not driven by stock market compulsion: mutual and cooperative banks (though these are not perfect, as the Dunfermline Building Society and the Co-op Bank have shown) or other public interest entities. The Swedish Handelsbanken is another excellent model, developing long-term relationship banking for business, but it relies on steady organic growth and is so far a small player. Regulation has to make it as easy as possible for such entities to enter the market and to grow.

There have been, in addition, welcome changes in UK and EU regulation and practice that are dealing with some of the excesses around remuneration. I introduced reforms to align top executive pay with the interests of shareholders through legislation requiring a binding shareholder vote on remuneration. This is helping to reduce the 'agency' problem of managers enriching themselves at the expense of their owners and awarding themselves high pay regardless of performance. But these reforms will only work in the banking sector if shareholders themselves have expectations that are compatible with stable, safe banking. And some of the more extreme payouts in banking, which set the bar for others, occurred in partnerships (leading investment banks) or private companies not subject to the corporate governance disciplines of listed public companies.

Remuneration abuses have essentially been of several kinds. There are the very large payments in investment banking, usually in the form of bonuses, often as a result of short-term profits achieved through highly leveraged growth. Such rewards have aroused anger not simply because they are so large but because the activities that underpinned them put their institutions at risk and were ultimately underpinned by taxpayer guarantees. The regulatory response has often been counterproductive, mixing up symptom and cause. The attempts by the EU to cap bonus payments have simply had the effect of converting discretionary bonuses, which do relate, albeit haphazardly, to performance, into very high fixed salaries, which leave institutions less able to respond flexibly to shocks. The better approach, which the British FSA pursued, but not very radically, is to require that bonuses be paid in stock which matures after five to ten years, forcing traders to take a longer-term view of their activities.

Another manifestation of abuse has been the incentive schemes in retail (including commercial) banking for front-line staff, which led many employees to forfeit trust by activities that they knew to be inappropriate for their customers. This is a classic economic problem of asymmetric information: sellers with superior knowledge of a complex product taking advantage of the purchaser. There is now a tougher regulatory regime under the Financial Conduct Authority (FCA), though the head, Martin Wheatley, has been removed, reportedly for being too tough. The main way in which such abuses are being dealt with is via enforced compensation schemes, as with PPI, but these have been protracted, costly and, in the case of swap mis-selling which crippled numerous small companies, very limited. They merely deal with problems after the event. The only way of preventing such abuses recurring in future is to outlaw sales-based bonuses, as Handelsbanken has done. A softer but also sensible approach is to professionalize banking so that individual misdeeds can be pursued by professional bodies, as is the case for doctors, nurses and professional accountants. In the banks themselves, or at least those that take the need for cultural change seriously, the kinds of measures that are significant include obligatory training in codes of conduct, regular, personal, signed statements by senior managers acknowledging responsibility for implementing the codes, and, in retail banking, rewards linked to customer satisfaction.

The remedy of the regulatory authorities for various abuses has been large fines on the banks. The Forex scandal, for example, involving large-scale collusion between traders in the US$5 trillion per day market, resulted in US$10 billion of institutional fines in May 2015, on top of earlier fines. Such fines sound draconian, but they only work in competitive markets when they are passed back to bankers and shareholders, and not passed on to consumers. Globally, 'regulatory revenge' has led to an estimated £200 billion (US$300 billion) in fines, to a point where legal risk is now becoming serious. The Chancellor indicated in his June 2015 Mansion House speech that he believed the process had gone too far. Moreover, collective fines do not address the issue of individual accountability to the criminal law or codes of professional ethics. It is striking that, in the wake of one of the greatest financial disasters in history, virtually no banker has gone to jail and few have been financially penalized, except through mass redundancies which bore little relation to individual culpability. My own ministerial responsibility in respect of overseeing the enforcement of the laws related to director disqualification proved to be very limited. No case was judged to meet the legal tests, and the most serious cases, relating to RBS, had to be passed to the Scottish authorities, which found no legal basis for action. In the case of HBOS, an official report by the FCA is still unpublished six years after the bank crashed, costing the taxpayer £20 billion and 40,000 employees their jobs.

There has been a lot of sound and fury, but so far little pain to those who directly caused the disaster. The moves to criminalize reckless behaviour taken by the coalition government are an advance, but unless the recommendations of the Parliamentary Commission on Banking Standards and the standards review of Sir Richard Lambert are followed through, cynicism will become firmly embedded and will lead to deeper problems in future. Mr Carney's launch this year of the Fair and Effective Markets Review was intended to establish senior executives' personal responsibility for their banks, but it will rely on voluntary, not legal, enforcement. Under the Conservative government there is a retreat from attempts to change bank culture.

———

My biggest preoccupation in government was the dearth of lending by the banks to SMEs. This factor undoubtedly inhibited business recovery. Surveys of small business suggest that the difficulty and the cost of obtaining credit loomed large throughout the period of coalition government and have continued. While bigger companies have access to debt and equity markets, SMEs depend largely on banks.

There were, and remain, several overlapping problems, some of long standing. There is the uncompetitive structure of the industry, dominated by a handful of commercial banks. The British business lending marketplace contrasts strikingly and unfavourably with Germany in particular, where there are many specialist lenders for the *Mittelstand* and small business sector, operating on a long-term relationship basis. There is also a serious lack of long-term 'patient capital' (loan as well as equity) for growing medium-sized companies. Indeed, this gap in the lending market has been identified since the 1920s (the 'Macmillan gap'), but addressed only fitfully since. Previous, successful interventions like the 3i's disappeared through privatization. Although the

German KfW served as an example to follow, successive governments failed to pursue the issue further.

The banking crisis made the position worse. The collapse of commercial and domestic property markets led to insolvencies and bad debt, or the withdrawal of credit from companies whose collateral was reassessed negatively. The tougher regulatory requirements for capital led to banks disengaging from SMEs judged to be relatively high-risk, and from risky firms within the generality of SMEs: start-ups, exporters, manufacturers, creative industries – in other words, precisely those companies needed for rebalancing the economy. A combination of companies trying to deleverage by running down their overdraft facilities or paying off loans, and banks also trying to deleverage, resulted in substantial negative net lending by the banks, continuing up to and including 2014. Banks claimed that there was 'lack of demand', SMEs that there was a credit famine. Both were true in part.

The Labour government's initial response was to offer partial guarantees to the banks to cover elements of risk for marginal loans. These schemes played a positive role and continue to operate. When the coalition government was formed there was broad consensus that more should be done. The leading bankers, led by John Varley of Barclays, offered an agreement, the so-called Project Merlin Agreement, under which leading banks would commit themselves to gross lending targets (that is, overall new lending, not taking into account repayments). The motivation was in part to head off government plans for net lending targets, which I had been advocating, and to stop ministers constantly berating the banks over their poor lending performance to business. The banks also offered a £3 billion fund to meet the gap in long-term patient capital, and the Business Growth Fund is now performing a useful role in that market.

The gross lending targets were largely met, but the net figures remained negative and there was frustration on both sides. The criticism of banks continued, though it was clear that some were making a serious effort to increase lending to SMEs and to repair relationship banking because of worries about their reputation. Lloyds and Santander in particular were active in this regard. Others, notably RBS, seemed to do little.

I endeavoured to make the case to the Chancellor and his officials for using RBS as a lending platform for SMEs, operating at higher levels of risk than the bank was applying and offering incentives to the CEO to prioritize SME lending. Nothing transpired from this. The Treasury view was that it would affect the share price and compromise any early move to privatize RBS, and would probably trigger legal action by minority shareholders.

I then tried a different approach, establishing a dedicated state-owned business bank that would act as a catalyst for new forms of SME lending that would bypass the major banks, like peer-to-peer lending and asset finance, and would provide leverage enabling challenger banks to grow more rapidly. The Chancellor agreed to the project, and provided £1 billion of start-up capital – provided I agreed to support his proposal for a new class of enterprise that diluted employee rights in return for shareholdings. His scheme was widely criticized, and had few takers, but I regarded the trade as a good one, coalition working at its best.

The British Business Bank was launched after the usual long delays over EU state-aid clearance, and by the end of the parliament had advanced around £1 billion in existing schemes (loan guarantees), operated a new start-up loan scheme, acted as a catalyst for peer-to-peer and crowd-funding platforms, funded asset finance and invoice discounters, and launched a project to help challenger banks expand by securitizing their SME loan books. Bank net lending remained negative, but was reviving and a more competitive and diverse industry was emerging.

———

Although it is not a panacea, more genuine competition improves the position of personal and business customers and reduces the opportunities for cartel-like behaviour (though competition does not necessarily improve systemic stability, as the USA has demonstrated throughout its banking history, in contrast to the hitherto more stable but concentrated UK market). The immediate aftermath of the financial crash was to reduce competition: the withdrawal of overseas banks (Icelandic and Irish) from retail or business lending, the disappearance of failed institutions (Northern Rock, Dunfermline Building Society, Bradford and Bingley), and the process of deleveraging and withdrawal from markets seen as unprofitable. Britain has long had a highly concentrated banking sector, at least in the UK retail and business market. The names have changed (no more Martin's or Midland); takeovers have changed structures and brands (RBS-NatWest, Lloyds-TSB and Halifax-Bank of Scotland, Santander-Abbey); and there are some banking activities with lots of choice and players, such as mortgage-lending from the main banks and local building societies.

But in two key markets there is still a high concentration. The big four banks have almost 85 per cent of current accounts and a similar percentage of lending to SMEs. As to the first of these, there are some new entrants – notably Metro, Tesco and Virgin – offering deposit-taking services, as do building societies. Metro is the first new banking house for a century. The key constraint on competition has long been the hassle factor of closing one account and opening another, with all the problems of reconnecting direct debits and standing orders. We are, however, moving towards full convertibility, including the ability to transfer account numbers. The deeper problem is that behind the complexities of charges and tariffs, which purport to represent competition, the main banks all offer a similar service in a similar way and have near-identical business models, at the heart of which is a free current account. The Competition and Markets Authority (CMA) investigated consumer competition in 2015 but added little new.

A more economically damaging block to competition is in the market for SME lending. Fifteen years ago the Cruickshank Report identified excessive charges and profits, and a near cartel of bigger banks, as damaging to business. I secured a parliamentary debate in 2001 demanding action on Cruickshank, but the then Chancellor, Gordon Brown, declined to implement the main recommendations, including a regulator for the payments clearing system.

Some important steps are now being taken to improve the competitive landscape. The clearing network, which is a monopoly, is now being brought under regulatory supervision, as Cruickshank recommended, so as to prevent new entrants being subjected to capricious and unreasonable connection charges. The licensing regime for new banks has been simplified and shortened in order to encourage new lenders. Legislation has been passed requiring banks to refer rejected loans to other banks. Credit-risk data is being shared. RBS is splitting off a challenger bank, Williams and Glyn, following EU rulings, albeit very slowly.

The big four still dominate, but Santander has built up its SME lending operation. Handelsbanken is expanding rapidly but prudently. New lenders, like Aldermore, with asset finance, Shawbrook, Close Brothers, the various invoice discounters and other specialist lenders, are growing. A major new departure is 'alternative finance': peer-to-peer lending through internet-based platforms, like Funding Circle, RateSetter and Zopa, part of a wider phenomenon of crowd-funding involving both debt and equity. Most of these institutions add to diversity and competition in lending but are not full banks (deposit takers). The British Business Bank has been an increasingly important catalyst for all this activity.

Much more needs to be done to create a genuinely diverse system of banking. Unlike the USA, Germany and Switzerland, the UK has little genuine local banking apart from a few small building society hold-outs, the Airdrie Savings Bank in Scotland, and a few small challenger banks like Cambridge & Counties. Small community banks have the advantage of local knowledge, but there are major obstacles such as the costs of creating an IT platform, of regulation, and of obtaining expertise. Community

Development Finance Institutions (CDFIs) and credit unions have struggled to operate at scale. There are some potential ways forward, like off-the-peg IT ('bank in a box') platforms and a task for the British Business Bank will be to help develop these.

There is, of course, a large elephant in the room called RBS, 82 per cent owned by the taxpayer. When the bank was effectively nationalized, there were two views about its future. One was the prevailing, and continuing, orthodoxy, strongly supported by the Chancellor and his officials, that it should remain 'at arms' length' from the government and pursue a commercial approach to lending and restructuring, with a view to returning to private ownership as soon as possible. The second, my own preference, was for the state to be an active owner, setting it lending objectives to support business growth and restructuring (dismembering) it in order to achieve a more competitive banking industry.

In the event, neither set of objectives was achieved. That frustrating outcome may reflect much deeper problems than at Lloyds, which is already selling off its 40 per cent state share, has already achieved a divestment, of TSB, and is expanding its net business lending, all in marked contrast to RBS. It took some years for the RBS management to restructure the bank, selling off some overseas operations, and to identify and isolate the large amount of non-recoverable loans, ranging from derivatives in the investment banking arm and the legacy of the ABN Amro takeover to loans on failed commercial property investments by the Ulster Bank. It took over five years to get to the point of setting up a 'bad bank' within RBS to contain this portfolio.

It is now clear, however, that the Conservative government is firmly committed to a rapid, step-by-step sell-off of RBS shares, even if this means selling at below the price originally paid by the state in the bail-out. The bigger disappointment is that so little has been done to restructure the bank in the interests of banking competition, rather than asset disposal. Its one helpful divestment has been the creation of Williams and Glyn as a stand-alone business, but this was mandated by the European

Commission six years ago and will not come fully into effect until the end of 2016. The bank argues that the IT issues are so difficult that faster or further progress on divestment would be impossibly costly. It is not as if there is a shortage of ideas for further restructuring. Conservative critics like John Redwood and David Davis argued for the break-up of the bank into competing entities. The New Economics Foundation has argued for radical decentralization to 150 or so community-based banking units with the kind of devolved decision-making enjoyed by Handelsbanken. They also argue for continued public ownership in order to ensure a social purpose.

In conclusion, the banking collapse and rescue of 2008 was a deeply traumatic experience for the economy. Enormous damage was done, and continues to be done, because of the impact on the credit transmission system and the fiscal impact on government. The disaster was also an opportunity for reflection and reform. There has been some questioning of the merits of an overweight banking sector and several leading banks, notably RBS, have scaled back their global ambitions. But the prevailing orthodoxy remains worryingly uncritical of the dangers. There has been some structural reform following the Vickers Report on ring-fencing retail and investment banking activities and a strengthening of capital reserves – indeed, it is more radical in the UK than elsewhere – but big, complex banks continue to dominate the industry. Banks are safer, but not wholly safe, and there are dangers ahead: known unknowns, like a major fall in house prices and the return of major recession, as well as unknown unknowns. There are tentative signs of a change in banking culture towards more socially responsible behaviour, but there is a vast legacy problem of mis-selling and abuse, leading to large fines and 'regulatory revenge', and the Conservative government has drawn a line under attempts to impose bank 'culture'.

Most encouragingly, there is an upsurge in challenger banks, and the British Business Bank is at the heart of these innovations. It remains to be seen, however, whether this will lead to a genuinely diverse and competitive banking market that can, above all, offer a range of financial products to growing businesses, along with risk capital and long-term patient capital. In short, the storm has passed – for now. Repairs have been made and the SS British Banking has been made seaworthy. But there remain questions around British finance in the context of long-term growth, which leads me to a review of some of these fundamentals.

Getting the Long-Term Fundamentals Right

The financial crisis has concentrated the minds of policy-makers on the immediate: the avoidance of disaster and the restarting of growth by whatever means. The economic policy debate in both the political and academic worlds has centred almost exclusively around short-term demand management issues, rather than on how, as a country, we can raise long-term productivity and create sustainable growth. The most passionate argument in the early stages of the last parliament revolved around the speed of the first round of fiscal consolidation, of well under 1 per cent of GDP. Largely ignored was the more important question of why governments of different persuasions, including mine, were so easily persuaded to make damaging cuts in long-term government capital investment, at the wrong time. Most of my government colleagues and many commentators also saw the surge in house prices as a positive signal of growing confidence, rather than as a warning sign of long-term economic and social damage.

The 2015 election campaign encapsulated all that was bad about the political treatment of economic policy: a bit more or less government borrowing; austerity, treated as a matter of taste, like the temperature control in the shower; varying degrees of stupidity in the treatment of the housing crisis; and complete indifference to the question of how Britain can manage to earn a living in a world where skills, knowledge, creativity and innovative use of technology are at a premium, and where there are billions of poor, or formerly poor, people jostling in the same global marketplace.

That said, I am pleasantly surprised by how much the government of which I was part succeeded in doing by way of badly needed and overdue long-term reform. To take one example, although I and my Lib Dem colleagues disagreed with the Conservatives on particulars, there was a large degree of consensus on the need to simplify the benefit system and reward work. My colleague Steve Webb piloted through far-reaching pension reforms for the next generation, and a necessary, albeit unpopular, reform of public sector pensions was also undertaken. But the consensus rested on a careful balance and the need to avoid a vindictive approach to benefit claimants, which were undoubtedly features of the 'bedroom tax' and a crass, insensitive system of testing work capability for the disabled. The balance has now been lost in the proposed post-coalition cuts in welfare, which, if carried through, will penalize the working poor and create additional disincentives to work.

And to take another example, in my corner of government, where consensus broadly prevailed, I oversaw the launching of an industrial strategy, a radical overhaul of university financing, the resurrection and reform of apprenticeships, the carrying through of long-promised commercialization in the Royal Mail, bank restructuring and the creation of new banks, as well as the launching of the British Business Bank and the Green Investment Bank, copyright reform, the reform of executive pay and corporate governance and a lot else. This experience persuades me that it is possible to swim against a tide of pessimism and low expectations.

With that experience in mind, I address in conclusion three broad issues. One revolves around the question of whence the country will derive its jobs and wealth in an increasingly competitive international environment. A second is how to maintain the UK's generally liberal response to globalization – openness in relation to trade, investment and, until recently, migration – in the face of growing scepticism and a possible backlash against an open economy. And third, there is the issue of income and wealth inequality, which is not just an issue for politicians of the left but for anyone concerned about social cohesion.

This is by no means an exhaustive list. I have already, in earlier chapters, discussed how best to deal with the legacy issues around fiscal and monetary policy, with the problems presented by an overweight, dysfunctional banking sector, and with the chronic failures in the housing market. I am aware of having spent little time on the massively important issue of climate change and how Britain should adapt its energy and transport policy to deal with it. I have little to say about how we refashion an over-centralized state, an issue forced on to the agenda by Scotland. I have almost nothing to say about how new, digitally based economic structures intersect with issues of privacy, civil liberties and national security. And although I deal extensively with cross-border issues and the phenomenon of globalization, I see this through the eyes of an economic policy-maker rather than in strategic or military terms. These areas of omission or de-emphasis reflect both ignorance on my part and a wish to avoid encyclopedic length.

———

Until the financial crisis in 2008 there was broad optimism that the UK was doing well in terms of growth relative to other advanced economies. The introspection and declinist mood of the 1960s and 70s seemed to have gone away. But the crisis has brought back with a vengeance all the worries about a distorted economy subject to boom and bust cycles in property markets and an overweight banking sector. We have been reminded that the UK has relatively low productivity, inadequate investment relative to competitors, poor export performance relative to domestic consumption growth, low R&D and innovation spend, and a hollowed-out manufacturing sector. These features pre-dated the crisis and are well analysed *inter alia* by the LSE Growth Commission. But they have now been reinforced by the near collapse of the banking sector and signs that, while recovery from the crisis is happening, it is unbalanced and is not likely to be self-correcting. The seemingly remorseless decline in Britain's trading performance (Figure 11.1) is a symptom of this problem.

The concept of industrial strategy has emerged in response to all this and reflects several ideas. The first is long-termism: an attempt to overcome some of the impediments and uncertainties described above through long-term planning, especially in areas like advanced manufacturing, energy and physical infrastructure, where investment cycles are long and new technologies may be long in gestation. There are strong elements in the UK business culture that reward short-term performance and devalue a strategic approach to innovation and investment: the rewards for investment managers based on short-term changes in share prices; the ease of takeovers and share buy-backs; the rewards earned on the trading floors of banks compared with those of industrial managers and engineers; the difficulties of smaller, growth firms in raising long-term patient capital. It is striking that we look to foreign-owned companies to remedy these defects – Indian, Japanese, German, Chinese, French – where traditions of family ownership or government sponsorship provide stability. And although US companies come from the same Anglo-Saxon stable, the new generation of giant internet-based companies is able through scale and reach to transcend short-term pressures.

Public policy mimics this short-termism. Quarterly GDP figures build or break reputations as easily as quarterly and half-yearly results can do for companies. The annual or twice yearly budgets, three-year spending reviews and a Treasury obsessed by short-term cash management, a parliamentary cycle lasting at best five years, all of these create uncertainty in areas where a settled view is necessary, such as regulatory regimes for utilities and infrastructure planning. These are by no means uniquely British issues: the US Congress has created budget chaos. And even the famously stable Japanese system is now subject to frequent changes of direction and government.

The second element in the idea of industrial strategy is a sense of partnership between public and private sector, recognizing that there are major market failures and externalities from, for example, training and R&D, which necessitate government involvement. We achieved agreement across government and with business on a framework for dealing with long-term issues of this kind. But there are ideologues who will always argue that the costs of government will exceed the market failure it is trying to address. One of the uncertainties surrounding the Conservative government is how far it will succumb to the arguments of these ideologues, who will enjoy quiet support in a Treasury that always fears loss of control of the economic agenda and will see an opportunity for further cuts. So far, the industrial strategy has survived but lacks energy and commitment.

———

And third, linked to the above, there is a sectoral approach. This has proved a little controversial with those who fear a return to 'picking winners' and, rightly, point to disruptive technologies which make traditional demarcations redundant. However, that is an argument for flexibility and adaptability, rather than for doing nothing. The simple fact is that all governments have an industrial policy, intentional or otherwise, based on choices that are made through government procurement and the allocation of support for training or research or trade promotion. These choices should be made on a strategic basis, with all the necessary qualifications about technological and market uncertainty, rather than randomly.

The coalition government arrived at an industrial policy as a result of a series of events. I was obliged in the early days of the government, and in the first round of cuts, to cancel promised government support for the expansion of Sheffield Forgemasters, a well-regarded specialist steel company. The cancellation provoked outrage in Sheffield, and was politically damaging to Nick Clegg, a Sheffield MP. I heard strong arguments for and against the expansion, but I was suspicious of the intensive political lobbying and the project was seemingly disembodied from any wider strategic framework. Another highly controversial decision was made by the Department of Transport, to award a railway rolling-stock contract to Siemens, which would mostly import the trains, rather than to Bombardier to make them in Derby. There was little doubt that the decision was made on merit, but it further exposed the lack of strategic thinking in government about supply chains and manufacturing. I had inherited from Peter Mandelson an embryonic structure, the Automotive Council, which brought together the various car companies to look strategically at common problems facing the industry. I was further encouraged by Michael Heseltine, who had a base in BIS as a roving adviser to government, and I wrote to the prime minister advocating this approach. The idea fell on fertile soil.

I announced in September 2012 the introduction of a new industrial strategy with a particular sectoral focus. Strategies were then developed for eleven sectors, which broadly represent knowledge-intensive goods and services that are internationally traded (advanced manufacturing, including aerospace, automotive and life sciences, professional and business services, information and communications, and higher education treated as an export), and enabling sectors such as energy and energy supply chains and construction. These have been augmented by others (creative industries, railway supply chains) and by groups formed spontaneously within industries (chemicals, electrical industries, and energy-intensive foundation industries), reflecting the fluid and pragmatic nature of the process.

The industrial strategy produced tangible outcomes in several sectors: a joint £1 billion long-term R&D programme for low-carbon vehicles, co-financed 50:50 by government and industry, built around an Advanced Propulsion Centre; a joint £2 billion R&D programme, similarly financed, for an Aerospace Technology Institute spanning aerodynamics, propulsion, aero-structures and advanced systems; a biomedical catalyst co-funding commercial innovation: a similar catalyst for agri-tech; supply chain mapping for most of the sectors leading to active programmes to build up UK supply chains for aerospace, automobiles, offshore wind, railways, nuclear and oil and gas; and dedicated advanced skills programmes for creative industries, aerospace, nuclear, railways, construction and the information economy. The sectoral programmes survived the 2015 Spending Review but on a more restricted basis. The industrial strategy will only succeed if it receives continuing political support and a willingness to develop long-term collaborative working of a kind that is commonplace in Korea or Germany or the Nordic countries but has long been absent from the UK.

Augmenting the sectoral work have been cross-cutting policies. The area where, arguably, the greatest progress has been made is in relation to innovation – the commercial application of new technology – where, in marked contrast to Britain's leading role in academic science, we have long lagged behind other Western countries. Work done by Tera Allas, the former chief economist of BIS, and by Jonathan Haskel and others, demonstrates both the exceptionally high economic returns from R&D spend, but also the relatively poor R&D performance of both public and private sectors (1.8 per cent of GDP spent in the UK, as against 2.8 per cent in Germany, 2.7 per cent in the USA and 4 per cent in South Korea) (Figure 11.2). Mariana Mazzucato has written eloquently of the key, catalytic role of government in triggering innovation within the private sector, from internet-based techniques to biotech.

There was cross-government acknowledgement of the broad proposition. The Chancellor extended and improved R&D tax credits. A major institutional innovation to reinforce the policy has been the Catapult centres, based loosely on the German Fraunhofer centres, and designed to promote late-stage R&D (that is, D rather than R). I launched this programme in 2010 on the back of recommendations from Hermann Hauser, the scientist and venture capitalist. At the time of writing, there were nine Catapults in operation, co-financed by government, private business and universities, with one of them, advanced manufacturing, forming a network of seven centres. Others included new offshore renewables technology, applications spinning off from the space industry, stem-cell therapy, new energy storage systems and technology for future cities. Alongside but feeding into the work of the Catapults is support for the 'Eight Great Technologies' identified by the universities and science minister, David Willetts, as key areas for British scientific research leading to commercial applications. They include robotics, new materials, space, big data, synthetic biology, regenerative medicine, energy storage and agri-science. There is now a clear sense of direction, which, however, needs strong government support to develop. The Catapults have survived the 2015 Spending Review but the grant funding support to innovative small businesses by Innovate UK is being ended, a retrograde move. I would, whatever the other constraints on public spending, double the innovation budget as a statement of intent, along with real increases in science spending in general.

Another area of qualified progress has been training. Even at an early stage of recovery, skills gaps are appearing across the economy, with chronic skills vacancies in the automotive sector, construction, professional services and agriculture. If growth is sustained, demand will rise further, accentuated by large replacement demand from an ageing labour force and the requirements of new products and process technologies. Migration will fill some of the gaps, but most will depend on domestically generated skills. A key step forward has been the expansion and heightened status of apprenticeships though sadly these have declined where the need is greatest (eg construction).

I decided to prioritize apprenticeships initially in 2010 as a way of providing a progression route for those who choose a vocational rather than academic option. I wanted to narrow the division – almost an apartheid of the mind – between the vocational and academic, based in part on the superiority over our own of the German approach to skills and training. I was also, perhaps, paying homage to my father, who was a product and champion of vocational training based on a mix of further education and work-based training half a century ago. The big increase in apprenticeships was a signature achievement of the coalition government and there was political competition to 'own' the issue.

The emphasis, rightly, shifted from quantity to quality through employer-led 'Trailblazers' setting industry standards and also to engaging SMEs, most of which do not invest in training to any degree. Indeed, under 10 per cent do so. If quantity and quality are to continue to be expanded, we need more radical solutions than the present severely rationed government subsidy. When I left office, my officials were developing a plan for a system of industry levies, reimbursable for companies that invest in training. The Conservative government is taking this initiative forward but the Treasury appears to see the apprenticeship levy (on big business) as a revenue source rather than an investment in training. And the priority is an upgrading of skills at higher levels (skill level 4 and above, the equivalent of a degree). I left behind a green paper sketching out how higher-level vocational education and training could be developed, completing a circle started by Anthony Crosland in the mid-1960s with the vision of a new generation of polytechnics. A network of national colleges was launched to develop specialist skills for, inter alia, railway projects, coding and the nuclear industry.

A serious obstacle to skill development is the lack of adequate numbers of school-leavers, students, graduates, postgraduates and teachers with STEM (science, technology, engineering and mathematics) qualifications – especially the lack of engineers at higher apprenticeship and graduate level. The international, comparative numbers for maths and science performance in schools are alarming and deteriorating. British children now lag behind not just the usual suspects in Singapore and Finland, but even Vietnam and Poland. Efforts are being made at school level to rectify these imbalances and I worked closely with the professional bodies to address the chronic shortage of engineers at all levels, and in particular the lack of women, where the UK has the lowest participation rate of any of the twenty-eight countries of the EU. The right structures are broadly in place, but there is a large gap between aspiration and supply.

There is, however, one legacy of both the coalition government and its Labour predecessor that, I worry, is neither sustainable nor very useful. That is the belief that it is both economically socially valuable to open up university education to everyone who meets fairly minimal standards, and to provide them with tuition fee loans. The Robbins Report in the 1960s set the aspiration and the coalition government finally removed residual rationing of places. The justification is that participation in higher education correlates with economic growth. I believe this may be a case of *post hoc ergo propter hoc*. There is a rampant credentialism in the professions, and the expectation that graduate nurses, primary school teachers or police officers should be better than their non-graduate counterparts is questionable. Nor does the proliferation of graduates from low-cost degree courses in business studies and law presage a surge in entrepreneurship or in the quality of justice. My primary concern is that, in a world of scarce resources and tight public spending, the creation of graduate factories diverts attention from the more pressing need for vocational training through apprenticeships and from lifelong learning in the further and adult education sectors.

There are also new structures in place to meet the access to finance issues addressed in part in the previous chapter. As stated earlier, the British Business Bank has now provided support approaching £1 billion in lending and investment, giving support to alternative finance providers such as debt funds, peer-to-peer crowd-funding lenders and supply chain finance, and launching wholesale guarantees to help expand challenger banks. The aim is to unlock $10 billion of financing mainly for early stage or

growth-oriented businesses over the next five years and to diversify the finance landscape.

In another segment of the market, the Green Investment
Bank has committed approximately £2 billion to renewable
energy, waste disposal and energy-efficiency projects, leveraging
in roughly five times that amount of private investment which
would not otherwise have been forthcoming. A third state-
financing institution, albeit without the institutional autonomy
of the two banks, the Regional Growth Fund, tries to leverage private investment mainly in regions of the UK that suffer relatively
high unemployment.

These bodies have, on most metrics of value for money, proved
their worth. Alongside other reforms of the banks, and alongside
generous tax incentives for equity investment and the emergence
of the privately financed Business Growth Fund for SME long-
term equity, there is now a healthier ecology for business finance.
But it will require time, political consensus and financial support
for the emerging system properly to lubricate the economy.

————

The further dimension of industrial strategy is to do with geogra-
phy and regional decision-making. Arguably, this is the weakest
area, and the weakness stems from ambiguity about devolution.
On the one hand there is an understandable wish, as with the
Catapult programme, to have a national strategy for innovation
in order to maximize the benefits of specialization and scale and
to avoid duplication, or, as with apprenticeships, to have a recognized brand and common standards, reflecting the fact that
many firms have branches across the country. On the other hand,
there is an equally understandable reaction against the idea that
'the man in Whitehall knows best'. In the north of England especially, there is an acute awareness of regional imbalances. These
feelings coincide with a strong push to decentralize the state, to
devolved authorities in Scotland but also within England, and to
city government on the London model.

Under the Labour government, the spatial dimension was catered for through the Regional Development Agencies (RDAs). They acquired a bad name as a result of occasional extravagance, a sense of remoteness from most businesses, and the Conservatives' dislike of regionalism. I had more mixed feelings. In the event, the coalition abolished RDAs in England, primarily in the interests of saving money. Much time and effort was spent over the ensuing five years developing a substitute. We tried business-led (in theory) Local Enterprise Partnerships (LEPs); City Deals with cities, then combined authorities; then Growth Deals with LEPs. A complex matrix was starting to evolve for economic development, with some national programmes (such as the Regional Growth Fund for major projects, and the Catapults), some devolution of decision-making (including, increasingly, skills, as well as local transport projects and housing) following Lord Heseltine's work in government; some limited devolution of financing (retaining business rates or prudential borrowing) on an 'earned autonomy' basis; varying degrees of accountability to elected authorities, with or without mayors, and unelected LEPs; and in Scotland and Northern Ireland (but not Wales), a distinct 'development corporation' model based on a design drawn up in the 1970s by Scottish Labour ministers and a team including myself.

The endless process of reinventing the wheel and the fragmented, haphazard systems of devolution – in contrast to settled arrangements in Germany, the USA, Canada and France – are a major weakness in the UK. The Conservative government is faced with a new problem: the expectation of more radical devolution within England in response to the triumph of the SNP in Scotland. The Chancellor has led the move to create more powerful combined city authorities in the north of England especially, the so-called Northern Powerhouse, with Manchester leading the way. It is too soon to judge the success of this model – and it deserves to succeed – but there are serious stumbling blocks: the lack of enthusiasm for elected mayors in overwhelmingly Labour councils; the reluctance of the Treasury to countenance serious fiscal devolution; and unhelpful moves like the postponement of an earlier decision to upgrade trans-Pennine rail routes, which had been seen as a key part of the Northern Powerhouse.

Rebalancing the economy, however, requires a lot more than following through, and financing, the industrial strategy, though that would be a big step. The adoption of a longer-term approach to investment requires cultural change, though this can be catalysed by taxation that rewards long-term rather than short-term gains, based on long-term performance. I have a lot of sympathy with those like Professor Meyer who argue that the model of shareholder capitalism – the joint-stock company – is seriously flawed, and that the constant churn of the market forces managers to act opportunistically and in a short-term way. Some countries, like Germany and Holland, or Japan and Korea, have tax and company law mechanisms for offsetting those short-term pressures. In others, like Italy and India, family ownership perpetuates long-term thinking (but creates other problems).

I sought in government to understand what precisely it was that induced this endemic short-termism and asked Professor John Kay, working with Sir John Rose (formerly of Rolls-Royce) and others, to look in detail at the problem. The team looked at the system of rewards and incentives that motivates fund managers in pension and insurance companies, who utilize long-term savings and often divert them from being channelled into long-term investment, while earning generous fees in the process. There is now, as a result, a stronger commitment from institutional investors to embrace the long-termism agenda, and various concrete steps, industry- or government-led, have resulted: an end to mandatory quarterly reporting requirements; a long-term mandate for the CMA and the Takeover Panel; a redefinition of the duties of companies to encompass long-termism; and a longer-term approach to executive pay policy.

Government has a more direct responsibility for infrastructure delivery. Big infrastructure projects, notably energy supply, require regulatory certainty and, in some cases, government guarantees and a supportive planning regime. A recurrent theme of business criticism in particular has been the delays, gaps and shortfall in high-speed broadband provision, transport congestion, delays at ports (though this is now being remedied with the new deepwater port on the Thames Estuary), hold-ups in agreeing the price or subsidy level for new power projects, and a delay of over four decades in agreeing whether and where to expand airport capacity in the south-east. (Following the report by Howard Davies for the government, there is a recommendation for Heathrow, but there are enormous political obstacles to proceeding with it.)

There is a danger of looking for 'silver-bullet' solutions. A popular demand in business circles is to remove infrastructure projects from local planning by implanting them in a quango responsible only to ministers, and not to local councils. However, there are quite legitimate local concerns that have to be addressed, about pollution, noise and other externalities. There is also often a wish to sweep aside environmental and other statutory safeguards, and the same point applies. One of my more bizarre experiences in government was hearing some captains of British business, whose politics I would normally have placed to the right of the Conservative party, promoting Chinese communism as a superior form of government to the checks and balances of our national and local democracy. Procedures, including local planning, can be made simpler and faster. The government's 2011 infrastructure plan, defining and monitoring priority projects, was designed to address those issues without importing Chinese methods.

An equally serious impediment is, however, the reluctance of government, worried about levels of public debt, to sanction public investment even when it creates valuable assets and potentially reduces debt in relation to GDP. This diffidence can lead to delays and extra costs as private investors mull political risk and seek regulatory certainty. Hopes that institutional investors, like pension funds, could step into the breach have been frustrated;

only £1 billion of the planned £20 billion had been raised by 2015. To mobilize private money, government has had to offer public sector liabilities, via guarantees. Public investment via public borrowing would have been quicker, simpler and cheaper.

––––––––

There are many strands to a joined-up approach to growth. But an absolutely key question is whether Britain remains an open economy. I discussed these issues in chapters five and six in the wider global context of how the UK and other developed countries treat the rapidly emerging economies and deal with scepticism about the merits of globalization. Here I pursue the issues in more detail.

One of the more remarkable features of UK policy-making, going back over a century, is the broad cross-party consensus in favour of free trade and a liberal economic order. There was a movement for trade protectionism in the Tory party before the First World War, led by Joseph Chamberlain, which found a favourable environment in the trade wars of the 1930s, while wartime led, of necessity, to a period of near self-sufficiency. These were, however, aberrations and certainly over the sixty years since the Second World War the prevailing orthodoxy has not been greatly different from that propounded by Peel or Gladstone. There was a brief dalliance on the left with the idea of an 'alternative strategy', including import controls, in the 1970s, but it was quickly denounced (by this author among others) and subsequently the Blair/Brown administration produced eloquent defences of globalization. At the time of writing, we are beginning to see the re-emergence of a sustained comprehensive critique of globalization directed at the TTIP negotiations, but it has yet to achieve any wider traction. There have been occasional voices on the right questioning the orthodoxy, but much of the critical energy has been devoted to attacking the European Union, mainly on the grounds that it is not free-trading enough.

This acceptance and advocacy of an open trading system has extended to free movements of capital. Britain, because of its liberal traditions, was one of the first Western countries to be faced by issues of foreign ownership of highly visible national industries, like cars, computers and consumer durables. Unlike France in particular, which felt threatened by foreign multinationals, Britain absorbed foreign investors willingly, not just through new investments but by acquisition of UK companies. Since British-based companies like Unilever, Shell (both part-Dutch) and BP were major investors overseas, the rationale for multi-market investment was already well understood. There were some doubts, for emotional as much as economic reasons, when Japanese companies moved into the car industry in the 1980s, but they were quickly banished by companies like Nissan making large welcome investments in areas of high unemployment.

The degree of foreign ownership is now so advanced that some leading commentators have expressed serious worries that the capacity for indigenous technological innovation, and for independent economic decision-making, may have been seriously depleted. Overseas-owned companies now dominate major manufacturing industries (cars, steel, cement, food production and civil aerospace), the main utilities (water, electricity generation, telecommunications and train franchises), and the information economy. Even in traditionally domestic, non-traded activities, foreign companies have become major players, as in retail (Asda, Lidl and Westfield), construction (Bouygues) and banking (Santander and Clydesdale). Even where 'British' companies – rather self-consciously – loom large, like Rolls-Royce, BAE Systems, BP, GSK, Vodaphone and BT – their share ownership is international and complex, and often their business strategy is built around global investments and supply chains.

The British, overall, seem comfortable with the idea of foreign ownership. Tata and Jaguar Land Rover, Nissan, Siemens and Airbus have become associated in the public mind with technical excellence, long-term investment, generally good employee relations and genuine corporate citizenship. Fears that foreign companies would strip the assets of UK companies, take away their know-how and abandon their UK operations in times of difficulty have not been realized in general. The UK's status as the leading destination in the EU for inward investment is a coveted one, and one of the main arguments for opposing Brexit is that major overseas investors have located here on the basis of UK access to the single market.

Nonetheless, the benefits are becoming less obvious. Between 2011 and 2014 payments to overseas owners of UK assets of all kinds rose 31 per cent to £71 billion and reverse payments from UK owned overseas assets fell by around 30 per cent to £73 billion, a key factor in the deteriorating external economic accounts. Even in the cosmopolitan UK business environment, there has been some questioning of the wisdom of unrestricted openness. The Kraft takeover of Cadbury provoked a strong reaction. There was a similar reaction to the proposed Pfizer takeover of (Anglo-Swedish) AstraZeneca, especially when it emerged that the proposed acquisition was tax-driven and would involve risks to the UK's R&D capability in life sciences. In the event, the takeover fell through – and was discouraged, including by me. But there is now greater scepticism about the merits of corporate takeovers in general, regardless of nationality, and a widely held view, almost certainly correct, that the public interest defence against major takeovers is too weak. To rectify this – to allow for a defence of national R&D capability, for example – will require agreement at European level, but narrowly focused defences should, I believe, still be used nationally. But this is not an issue of nationalism, rather a concern about the desirability of takeovers more generally.

One respect in which globalization has gone into reverse is in banking. The disastrous overseas acquisitions of RBS, the sudden withdrawal in the banking crisis of Irish and Icelandic banks, the rapid transmission of the crisis across borders post-Lehman Brothers: all of these factors have led to an emphasis on national regulation, with parallel attempts at EU-level regulation, and a focus on the supply of credit to domestic business and house-holds. But, even here, there is little crude nationalism: foreign banks are, and should be, still welcome, and the position of global banks like HSBC has been respected – though HSBC, like Standard Chartered, still trails the possibility of removing its headquarters to Asia, perhaps as a way of achieving more leverage over issues such as the taxation of bank balance sheets.

Nationalism has reared its head in one major area: immigra-tion. Immigration has been, intermittently, a significant political issue in the UK for fifty years. Indeed, it goes back much longer. Protests against Jewish refugees from Eastern Europe before the First World War led to the Aliens Act (1905) restricting admission. West Indian, then Asian migrants in the 1950s and 1960s created a strong political backlash, culminating in the infamous 'rivers of blood' speech by Enoch Powell in 1968 and the panic legisla-tion excluding British subjects of Asian origin from East Africa. Subsequent immigration panics arose over the perceived threat of Hong Kong Chinese coming to the UK, and then refugees from the former Yugoslavia and elsewhere in the 1990s.

These difficulties were not, however, about the economic consequences of net migration, but rather about the chang-ing composition of the population as mainly non-white ethnic minorities settled in the UK. In the three decades from 1960 to 1990, net immigration was actually negative overall, because immigration, averaging around 200,000 a year, was outstripped by emigration. Since immigrants were, for the most part, younger than the host population, more mobile and eager to work, the net economic impact was almost certainly positive, though there were undoubtedly pressures on services and the stock of housing in particular areas. There were important issues of identity and community, but Britain couldn't meaningfully be said to have an immigration problem until the late 1990s.

Public opinion was most hostile to immigration in the 1960s and 70s; 80 per cent thought it too high, but this fell to around 50 per cent when net immigration actually surged. Positive net migration exceeded 100,000 for the first time in 1998, and 200,000 for the first time in 2004, and it continued around that level, rising to close to 300,000 in the 2014/15 financial year. Over half of this net immigration comes from the EU, mainly Eastern Europe, which means that the issue is no longer mainly around race or culture or ethnicity, as it was in the 1960s, but focused on the impact of immigration itself. And the debate has shifted to the merits of EU membership since under the single market there is free movement of labour, as well as free capital movement and free trade in goods and services. By definition, immigration in a free labour market is uncontrolled. This was a concept that, ironically, Britain helped to create in the 1980s. Successive governments clearly underestimated the scale of response to labour market liberalization in low-wage economies still in transition from communism to capitalism. Politicians are now in the dangerous position of having to defend the whole principle of British membership of the EU and the single market, largely in response to this one issue.

Britain's recent experience of immigration is actually roughly in the middle, in terms of scale, of OECD countries as a whole. This century, foreign influxes have accounted for 7 per cent of the UK population, a little more than Holland or Italy and a little less than Germany or Sweden, and well below Spain (15 per cent), Austria (13 per cent) or Switzerland (18 per cent). The growth of the politics of identity in those countries, as well as in the UK, and of extreme anti-immigration parties based on nationalism or ethnicity, is a consequence of these changes, combined with the hardship resulting from the economic crisis.

The UK government has responded by trying to limit those elements of migration that it can control, recognizing that UK emigration and EU immigration cannot be controlled. The Conservative side of the coalition set itself a target of under 100,000 net immigration, which now appears wholly out of reach, though the new Conservative government has reasserted it. More seriously, it has pursued measures that undermine economic growth. One is to tighten the conditions around overseas students, which may have stopped some abuses but has also signalled that, in a highly competitive market, the UK is a less attractive place to study, or to work post-study, than, say, Australia or the USA. Overseas students have brought about £9 billion in earnings to the UK, and this figure will have fallen as the number of visas issued has fallen from 320,000 per year in 2010 to around 218,000 in 2014, with dramatic falls from India and Pakistan, partially offset by increases from China, Hong Kong and Malaysia. A second step has been to tighten the restrictions on Tier 2 work-related visas, which were at an annual level of 160,000 in the year to June 2014, well down on the 230,000 peak in 2006. Some of that decline is recession-related and Tier 2 visas have been under-utilized recently, but we are now moving quickly to a problem where scarce and valued personnel are being kept out by arbitrary bureaucratic hurdles.

The underlying economics of immigration starts from the proposition that net immigration will raise overall UK GDP but not necessarily GDP per head. In practice, immigration almost certainly does raise income per head, since immigrant workers (and especially migrants from the EU) tend to be younger and have higher activity rates and lower levels of unemployment than the host population. Moreover, many have the high levels of skills necessary to sustain employment. The immigrant population also generates more entrepreneurial activity than their numbers would suggest. And there is evidence that they contribute positively to the Exchequer when we net out tax receipts from benefits and other payments. There are many studies, but one intellectually respectable model suggests that a 50 per cent cut in net migration would cause GDP and GDP per capita to fall by 11 per cent and 2.7 per cent, respectively.

There is no simple mechanism to maximize the benefits of immigration and minimize the costs. What is clear is that net migration targets of the kind espoused by the Conservatives simply do not work, because the main immigration route, via the single market, does not lend itself to control, and because they have baulked at the policy of encouraging – logical in their terms – the emigration of the dependent elderly. The largely unintended consequence is that genuinely valuable people – highly skilled workers, entrepreneurs, overseas students, business visitors – tend to be squeezed out by over-zealous visa controls. It is right to have a strict set of sanctions on traffickers and other abuses, and to stop 'benefit tourism' which degrades the commitment and sense of solidarity of local people to their own benefit system. It also makes sense to track exit as well as entry so as to be better aware of trends, but managed immigration is now part of all major developed economies and we should make a virtue of it.

———

I have been at pains to stress that it is not useful to discuss economic policy in a political vacuum. In the UK, two looming and interconnected political issues will dominate the agenda, both of which are aspects of the politics of identity, and frame economic policy: Scottish nationalism and English nationalism, and how they affect relations with the European Union. EU relations are already difficult because of immigration and wider disagreements and the unsettled relationship between the members and non-members of the eurozone.

This is not the place to rehearse all the arguments for and against British membership of the EU and the various outcomes that could follow the promised referendum. We do not yet know the results of the forthcoming negotiations, or what the terms of a British exit would be if that were the referendum result. The counterfactual is difficult to define, but could be: Norwegian-style membership of the European Economic Area with access to the single market (but not the Common Agricultural Policy), with continued budget obligations and adherence to employment and financial market regulations, but with no part in making the rules; a Swiss-style bilateral arrangement, with fewer obligations and less access; or a looser relationship, including the re-establishment of some trade barriers. There is a very wide range of estimates, of costs and benefits of membership, often coloured by the people who have commissioned or carried out the study. UKIP claims that membership has net annual costs of 5 per cent of national income. My former department carried out a study that sought to capture the long-term benefits of membership, including encouraging foreign investment and stimuli to productivity growth, and came up with an estimate of net benefits of 6 per cent of GDP.

The more plausible future scenarios make full integration, including euro membership, highly unlikely, but full exclusion is also very unlikely. In practice, the issue is a little bit more Europe (broadly as in the Blair years when the UK adopted the Social Chapter, embraced enlargement and signed the Lisbon Treaty) or a little bit less (the starting point of Cameron's negotiation centring on restrictions on benefits). One study, by ING, which assumes minimum disturbance to institutional arrangements, estimates that the UK will lose around 0.5 per cent of GNP from its trend growth in each of the next two years because of uncertainty over the referendum outcome, but gain 0.5–1 per cent per annum in the two to three years following the referendum if the result is positive. If the UK votes to leave, there would be a sharp drop of another 0.5–1 per cent of GDP in the following year or two, but a net gain after two years once the new arrangements are established. That sounds as sensible an estimate as we are likely to get and discounts the more ludicrous claims that Britain, once out, will be liberated like Hong Kong or become an isolated hermit state like North Korea. There is little risk that the EU will throw up a wall of tariffs to punish a departing UK, and also virtually no opportunity for a newly freed UK to negotiate better trade deals with China, India and the rest. (Anyone suffering from that particular illusion should look at the exceedingly unflattering comparison between British export performance in those countries and that of core eurozone states like Germany, France and Italy.)

The greatest danger of a negative referendum outcome – or a

very close outcome with a 'no' vote in England – is that it will widen the growing schism within the UK, precipitating Scottish independence (and perhaps an early move to Irish unification within the EU). Whether or not that happens, a major political challenge in the next few years will be to create a new settlement with Scotland which also reflects the desire in other parts of the UK, and many parts of England, to have more decentralized government. Secessionist movements are easier to accommodate in a genuinely federal state, like Canada or India, than in a more centralized state, like Spain or the former USSR. Britain has some of the characteristics of both. Belatedly, there is a recognition that merely devolving spending decisions from a centrally determined budget decentralizes power but not responsibility. Successful federal states, the USA and Germany being the best examples, have devolved revenue-raising as well as expenditure, and borrowing powers, albeit with financial mechanisms to support regions facing structural problems and shocks, and with a wide range of common services – not least money, a single market and security. The essence of federation is a high degree of genuinely devolved decision-making over both taxation and spending, but also a generously redistributive mechanism to help regions in trouble, and some valued common functions to provide the cement to hold the union together. Getting that balance right will determine whether the UK stays together or falls apart.

We shall soon see, in real time, two major experiments taking place: one in the eurozone, as it moves from a confederal to a more federal system with sufficient cohesion to manage the stresses of economic and monetary union; the other, in the opposite direction, the move from a unitary state in the UK to a federal system able to accommodate greater diversity within an economic and monetary union. With nationalism on the loose, however, the prospects for both are in the balance.

———

Nationalism and the wider politics of identity can feed off a sense of grievance and unfairness, including inequality. The politics of inequality have a long history, going back to the French Revolution, and on some interpretations well before. But, in the wake of the financial crisis, concerns about inequality have reached a new intensity. The current enthusiasm for the writings of Thomas Piketty reflects the growth of interest in wealth and income inequalities.

One factor is the belief that globalization – the opening up of trade, investment and population flows – has widened the gap between the mobile rich and the static poor, and between capital owners and workers, especially the unskilled. A very simple model of an open economy suggests that wages will tend to converge internationally, though this makes no allowance for the impact of technology on productivity and living standards, clearly the dominant influence in recent decades. Secondly, it is a fact that the 2008 crisis and its aftermath have cut incomes and so reduced the absolute as well as the relative position of the less well-off. A third is that quantitative easing has, by boosting asset inflation (property and shares), widened wealth inequality.

The concern about inequality is not just about the perceived unfairness, but also the belief that it weakens economic performance by sapping demand and perpetuating low productivity. What concerns me here is to understand what is actually happening. The facts are somewhat surprising and do not fully accord with a convenient regressive narrative about the UK. The Gini coefficient of inequality – a measure ranging from 0, meaning total equality, to 1, meaning extreme inequality with one individual taking everything – is for the UK around 0.34, as against 0.48 for the USA. It has been roughly stable for two decades (indeed, it is lower than in 1990), after jumping sharply from 0.25 during the Thatcher years. Germany is a little more egalitarian at 0.32 but inequality has been growing there, too, over the last two decades. France has the most equal income distribution of the major economies at 0.28, having declined from the considerable height of 0.5 half a century ago. Nordic countries are all around 0.25 but growing. None of the Western economies, except for the USA, compares with the extremes of inequality of countries like Brazil (over 0.5) or Russia (now 0.45).

But much depends on how the measures of inequality are constructed. Lifetime income inequality is much lower than for annual incomes. In Britain, as in other Western countries, the share of the top 1 per cent has been growing, from 6 per cent of income in the late 1970s, having fallen steadily from over 20 per cent before 1914, up to 15 per cent now. Their share of income tax is now 28 per cent, as against 11 per cent in 1979 (and 46 per cent currently in the USA). The top 10 per cent, by contrast, have seen their share of income decline, especially since the onset of the crisis, when the lowest 10 per cent saw a rise in disposable income and the top 10 per cent a sharp fall (though there are different interpretations of this data depending on whether the income measure includes benefits and is post- or pre-tax, and whether housing costs are included and which inflation index is used). Except at the very top of the income distribution (where Britain has a transient population of stars, footballers and bankers), British income inequality is not extreme.

Much of the theoretical structural argument about inequality, as in Piketty, relates to a long-term trend of growing profit share in national income, relative to wages. That appears to be happening in other Western countries, though the story varies with the time period chosen. But it does not appear to be happening in Britain, where the labour share has been broadly stable.

A more likely area of extreme inequality is in wealth – holdings of assets – and this has almost certainly been aggravated by the asset boom (mainly in housing) leading up to the financial crisis and growing since under the influence of loose monetary policy. But again, the story is more nuanced than initially appears. Until 1990 Britain was actually one of the more egalitarian countries, with the top 10 per cent owning 56 per cent of the wealth, less than France (61 per cent), Sweden (59 per cent) or Denmark (65 per cent), let alone the USA (79 per cent) or Switzerland (71 per cent). Only Germany at 44 per cent and Canada at 53 per cent were significantly less unequal. From the early 1990s until the recent crisis, the financial assets of the wealthiest groups declined, relatively, while the housing wealth of the middle class grew substantially. The Gini coefficient of wealth inequality is now in absolute terms very high, at around 60 per cent, almost double the level of inequality of income, but it actually fell from 70 per cent in the mid-1990s to 60 per cent at the onset of the crisis.

Wealth inequality also has to be seen in generational terms. Young people are often in debt and hold few assets, in marked contrast to the middle-aged. It was recently estimated that the 25- to 44-year-old households had median wealth of around £75,000 (with 16- to 24-year-olds close to zero), while the 55- to 64-year-old group had £430,000. David Willetts has argued that the differential is widening because of the way rising house prices are creating growing barriers to entry into the housing market, as represented by growing price to income multiples, discussed in chapter nine. The sheer awfulness of housing politics threatens to make the problem worse. The Conservative government's extension of Right to Buy and Help to Buy has the effective of rewarding, and subsidizing, a small group of owner-occupiers at the expense of growing numbers trapped in the private rented sector. These regressive wealth effects have been compounded by the loss of employer-financed, secure, defined-benefit occupational pension schemes for the younger generation, and a lack of job stability which undermines the basis for long-term saving.

So what is to be done? How is it possible to reduce inequality, especially wealth inequality, without undermining recovery and economic performance? International comparative evidence from the IMF, no less, suggests that inequality reduces growth, and the likelihood that growth will last. It also suggests that (except at the extremes of these policies) redistribution does not harm growth. The econometrics is reflected in reality: the somewhat more egalitarian countries of the Western world, which have combined market dynamism with redistribution – Finland, Norway, Sweden, Denmark, Holland, Germany and Canada – have broadly outperformed the rest, and have done so without triggering the extreme financial crises that have done so much damage elsewhere, including in the UK. It will be obvious from the text that I see this group of countries, albeit with their many differences and strengths and weaknesses, as representing the kind of country I would like the UK to be.

In terms of concrete action to address the issue of inequality, one route is wage growth, especially low-wage growth through the minimum wage. As discussed in chapter eight, there was a decline in real wages after the crisis and there is a legitimate argument that depressed wages are perpetuating low productivity and weak demand. I encouraged, in office, the Low Pay Commission to plan for real increases in the minimum wage, as happened in 2014 for the first time since the crisis, but to continue to consider wider economic impacts, notably jobs. Attempts to politicize the minimum wage by setting arbitrary numbers, as the Chancellor has now done, undermine one of the most effective independent institutions. Relying on the minimum wage to reflate wages in general will not work when the gap between minimum and median, the 'bite', is lower than ever.

In any event, as the labour market tightens, wages will rise, and they will rise differentially where there are skills shortages. That, in turn, suggests the best way forward: investment by individuals, employers and the state in vocational as well as further and higher education. There is a mass of evidence to suggest that such investment earns a wage premium for the workforce and substantial economic benefits to society. The big expansion of apprenticeships under the coalition government, with improvements in quality and employer ownership, now needs to be extended, particularly for higher and advanced apprenticeships, the latter overlapping with graduate education.

Another approach to inequality is to seek to make the system of income tax more progressive. Vast amounts of political energy have been devoted to the narrow issue of where the top rate of tax should be in the band between 40 and 50 per cent. There is little political demand to raise it to over 50 per cent, as has happened in France. Nor would there be much benefit, in revenue or incentive terms, from going below 40 per cent.

An egalitarian tax agenda is often associated with extra tax on corporate income. However, companies are merely a legal form; their taxes are paid by their customers, their workforce or their shareholders. In a world in which governments compete for mobile capital by offering relatively low corporation tax, the sensible strategy for individual governments is to aim for the middle of the range, while seeking maximum cooperation between governments to minimize arbitrage. For the UK, we should be arguing for a common tax base across the EU, and ideally more widely, while minimizing tax rate competition. The Chancellor has done the opposite with a further cut in the corporation tax rate to 18 per cent. There is little evidence so far that the policy has produced benefits comparable to the revenue costs. At a national level, the UK would benefit from structural reforms that would make equity investment comparable to debt-financed investment and would reward capital investment and R&D.

The biggest challenge is the taxation of wealth, since wealth inequality is more extreme than income inequality. It is widening with current asset inflation. The top tenth of households (who own 45 per cent of wealth) had a 21 per cent increase in wealth between 2012 and 2014. In principle, wealth taxation in the form of proportional or progressive levies on property values or land values should be easy to impose since property and land are immobile, unlike people or companies. Such taxes are also favoured by economists because they do less than other taxes to distort behaviour and do not discourage work or saving. We have proxies for wealth tax in the form of capital gains tax, but it excludes owner-occupied property and addresses only capital appreciation, not the stock of capital, and inheritance tax, which is admirable in principle, as the likes of Warren Buffett and Bill Gates have argued, but easily avoided through *inter vivos* gifts.

Without doubt, a theoretically superior approach would be a land value tax, an idea that can be traced back to Adam Smith, David Ricardo, Henry George and Winston Churchill, and which has advocates on both right and left, and in the radical centre, of politics. Such taxation has the additional merit of helping to deflate volatile bubbles in land and property values, and discouraging the hoarding or inefficient use of land. It is necessary to ask why, beyond a few limited experiments, a land value tax has never been tried in over two hundred years. Practical issues of valuation and the big gains and losses of moving from our current system help to explain it. There is, however, a strong case for moving incrementally in this direction, through a land value-based approach to commercial property taxation or by trying to capture the value of land for the public in other ways: public land-banks and/or community land auctions.

There is enormous scope for arguing about the detail of tax policy, but the strategic objective, on grounds of both fairness and economic efficiency, should be to shift tax from income to assets – property and land – as well as to expenditure, provided that the latter can be applied progressively (maintaining VAT exemptions) or applied to goods that create wider social costs (carbon-based fuels, for example).

I conclude on this subject, as I did in *The Storm*, since the instability and inequalities generated by property and land markets were a major feature of the financial crisis. They lie at the heart of a distorted system of credit. They underpin a growing divide in the housing market between social classes and generations. And they cut to the heart of what it means to have a common identity, to belong to the same society. Political indifference is not sustainable.

I believe, as will be evident from this book, in an open, liberal

economy which is supportive of wealth creation and entrepreneurship and works with the grain of markets. But without a
balancing sense of fairness such a system will not be viable in the
long term. The near fracturing of the United Kingdom is but one
sign that a modern European country cannot be run indefinitely
in the interests of property owners and financiers living in one
corner of it.

Appendix

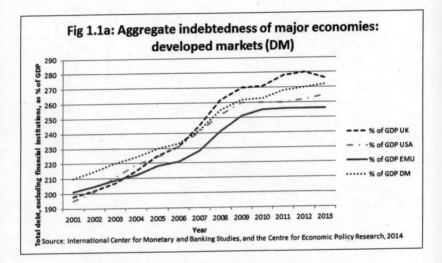

Fig 1.1a: Aggregate indebtedness of major economies: developed markets (DM)

Source: International Center for Monetary and Banking Studies, and the Centre for Economic Policy Research, 2014

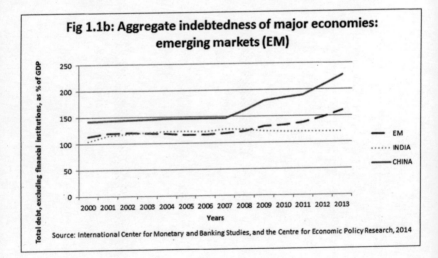

Fig 1.1b: Aggregate indebtedness of major economies: emerging markets (EM)

Source: International Center for Monetary and Banking Studies, and the Centre for Economic Policy Research, 2014

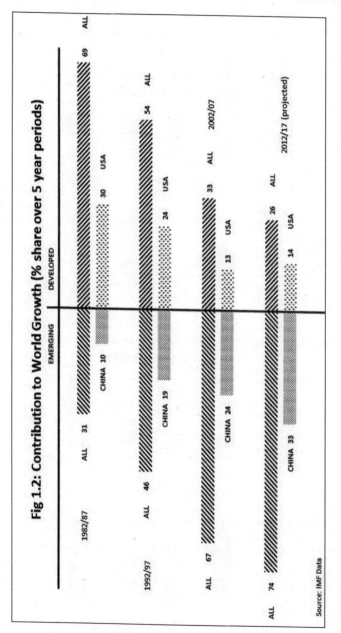

Fig 1.2: Contribution to World Growth (% share over 5 year periods)

Source: IMF Data

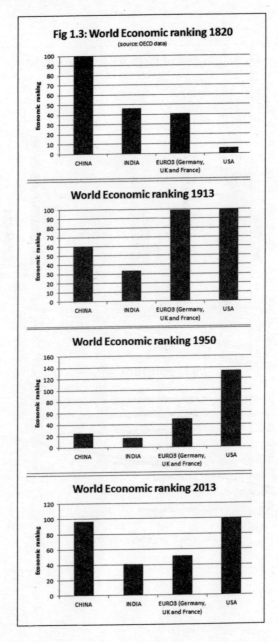

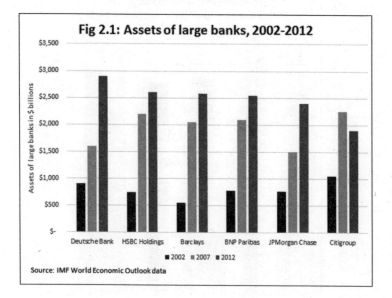

Fig 2.1: Assets of large banks, 2002-2012

Source: IMF World Economic Outlook data

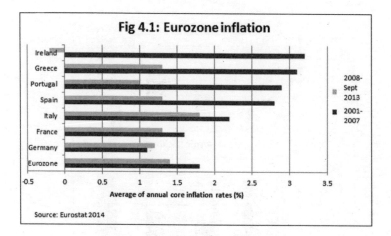

Fig 4.1: Eurozone inflation

Source: Eurostat 2014

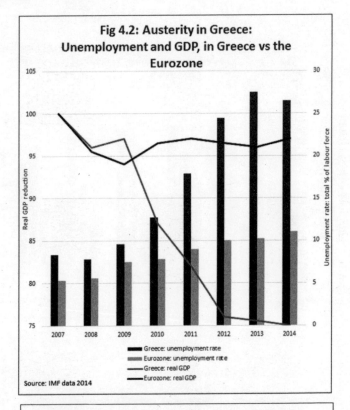

Fig 4.2: Austerity in Greece: Unemployment and GDP, in Greece vs the Eurozone

Source: IMF data 2014

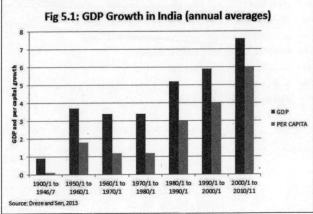

Fig 5.1: GDP Growth in India (annual averages)

Source: Dreze and Sen, 2013

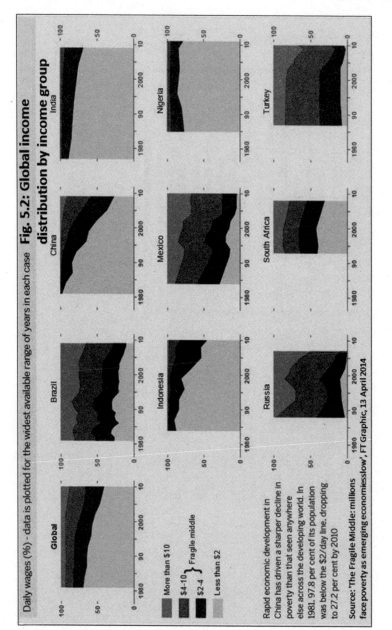

Fig. 5.2: Global income distribution by income group

Daily wages (%) – data is plotted for the widest available range of years in each case

More than $10
$4-10 } Fragile middle
$2-4
Less than $2

Rapid economic development in China has driven a sharper decline in poverty than that seen anywhere else across the developing world. In 1981, 97.8 per cent of its population was below the $2/day line, dropping to 27.2 per cent by 2010

Source: 'The Fragile Middle: millions face poverty as emerging economies slow', FT Graphic, 13 April 2014

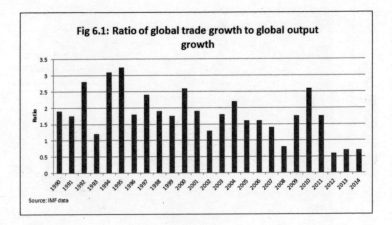

Fig 6.1: Ratio of global trade growth to global output growth

Source: IMF data

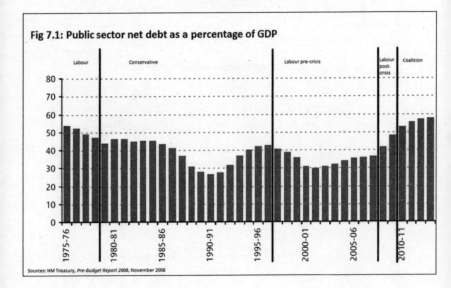

Fig 7.1: Public sector net debt as a percentage of GDP

Sources: HM Treasury, *Pre-Budget Report 2008*, November 2008

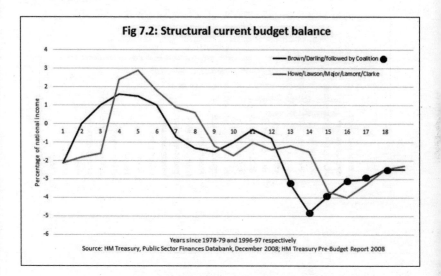

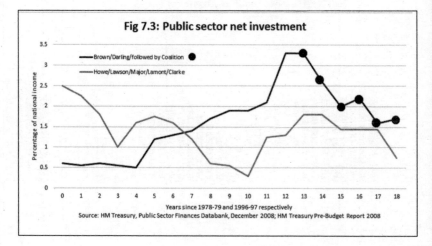

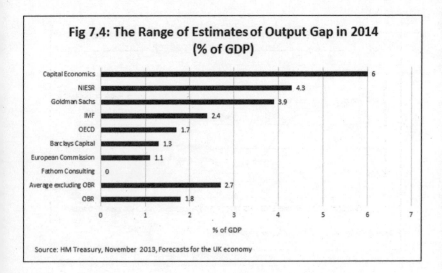

Fig 7.4: The Range of Estimates of Output Gap in 2014 (% of GDP)

Source: HM Treasury, November 2013, Forecasts for the UK economy

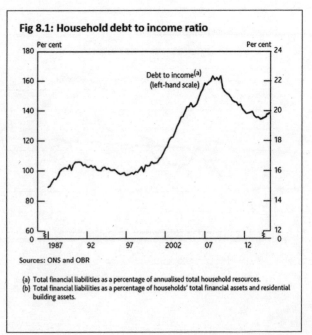

Fig 8.1: Household debt to income ratio

Sources: ONS and OBR

(a) Total financial liabilities as a percentage of annualised total household resources.
(b) Total financial liabilities as a percentage of households' total financial assets and residential building assets.

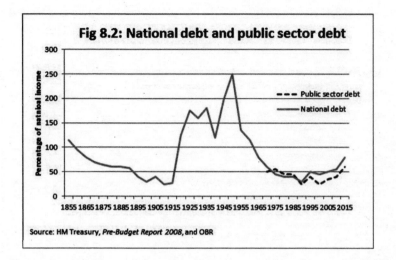

Fig 8.2: National debt and public sector debt

Source: HM Treasury, *Pre-Budget Report 2008*, and OBR

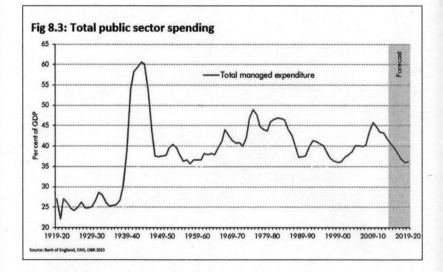

Fig 8.3: Total public sector spending

Source: Bank of England, ONS, OBR 2015

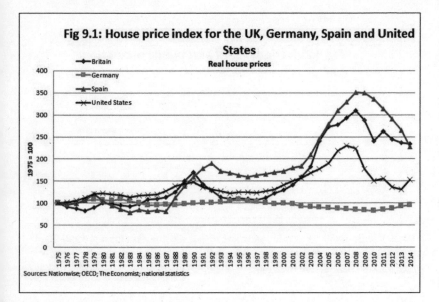

Fig 9.1: House price index for the UK, Germany, Spain and United States

Real house prices

Sources: Nationwise; OECD; The Economist; national statistics

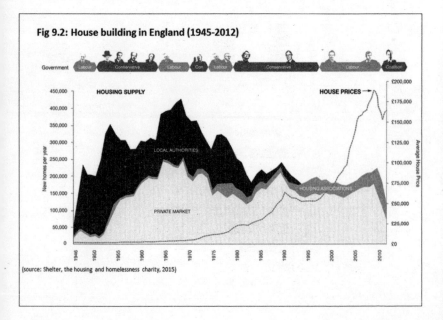

Fig 9.2: House building in England (1945-2012)

(source: Shelter, the housing and homelessness charity, 2015)

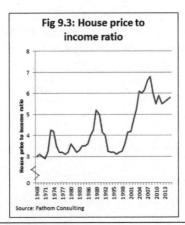

Fig 9.3: House price to income ratio

Source: Fathom Consulting

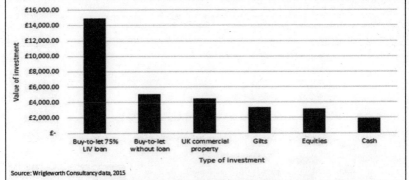

Fig 9.4: Value of a £1,000 investment in main UK asset classes, 1996–2014

Source: Wrigleworth Consultancy data, 2015

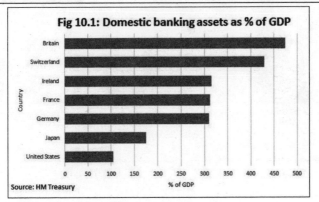

Fig 10.1: Domestic banking assets as % of GDP

Source: HM Treasury

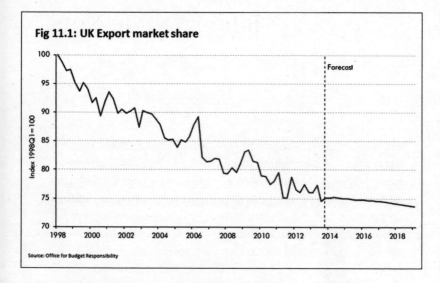

Fig 11.1: UK Export market share

Source: Office for Budget Responsibility

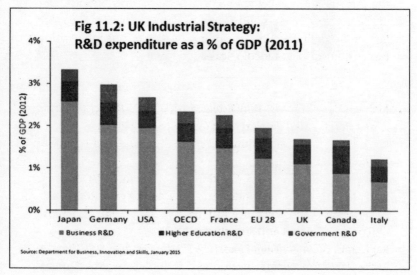

Fig 11.2: UK Industrial Strategy: R&D expenditure as a % of GDP (2011)

■ Business R&D   ■ Higher Education R&D   ■ Government R&D

Source: Department for Business, Innovation and Skills, January 2015

Bibliographic Note

This publication is a sequel to *The Storm*, written in 2009. It builds upon many of the arguments put forward there and on the economic theories that have been advanced to explain the financial crisis and its aftermath. I listed there many of the writers, ancient and modern, who had contributed to an understanding of what causes financial crises, what the consequences are, and how far the crisis has changed our concept of globalization.

Since the crisis there has been a substantial collection of literature, with *The Storm* being one of the earlier contributions. Out of the dozens of papers and books, I list below some of the more influential or interesting, including those from people writing from a quite different ideological standpoint.

———

Megnad Desai, *Hubris: Why Economists Failed to Predict the Crisis and How to Avoid the Next One* (Yale University Press)

Larry Elliott and Dan Atkinson, *The Gods that Failed* (London: Bodley Head, 2008)

Phillipe Legrain, *Aftershock* (London: Little Brown, 2010)

Paul Mason, *Meltdown* (London and Newcastle: Verso, 2009)

Robert Peston and Lawrence Knight, *How Do We Fix This Mess?* (London: Hodder and Stoughton, 2012)

Raghuram G. Rajan, *Fault Lines: How Hidden Fractures Still Threaten the World Economy* (Princeton and Oxford: Princeton University Press, 2010)

Nouriel Roubini and Stephen Mihm, *Crisis Economics: A Crash*

Course in the Future of Finance (London: Penguin, 2011)

Joseph Stiglitz, *Free Fall: Free Markets and the Sinking of the Global Economy* (New York: W. W. Norton, 2010)

Gillian Tett, *Fool's Gold* (London: Little Brown, 2009)

Adair Turner, *Economics after the Crisis: Ends and Means* (Cambridge, MA, and London: MIT Press, 2011) and *Between Debt and the Devil: Money, Credit, and Fixing Global Finance* (Princeton University Press 2015)

Graham Turner, *The Credit Crunch* (London and Ann Arbor: Pluto Press, 2008)

Martin Wolf, *The Shifts and the Shocks* (London: Allen Lane, 2014)

In **Chapter 1** I try to place current policy debate in the context of the economic ideas that have dominated thinking. There has been a welcome revival of classic texts explaining financial bubbles, notably Hyman Minsky's *Stabilizing an Unstable Economy* (Yale University Press, 1986), Charles Kindleberger and Robert Aliber's *Manias, Panics and Crashes*, 6th edn (Palgrave Macmillan, 2011) and Gary Gorton's *Misunderstanding Financial Crises: Why We Don't See Them Coming* (Oxford University Press, 2012).

One recent addition to this stable of literature has proved important and controversial because of its emphasis on government debt reduction, but it also has a good historical analysis of the impact of financial crises: Carmen Reinhart and Kenneth Rogoff, *This Time Is Different: Eight Centuries of Financial Folly* (Princeton University Press, 2009).

I have also subdivided the theoretical literature on how to respond to crises into 'monetarists', 'Keynesians' and 'Austrians' – of necessity caricaturing complex bodies of economic thinking. The dominant policy response is based on the lessons of the 1930s as concluded by Milton Friedman in Friedman and Anna Jacobson Schwarz's *Monetary History of the USA, 1867–1960* (National Bureau of Economic Research, 1963), and, crucially, as absorbed by the chairman of the Federal Reserve at the time of the financial crisis in 2008, Ben Bernanke, in the form of a pre-crisis paper *Deflation: Making Sure 'It' Doesn't Happen Here* (2002).

The best summary of Keynesian thinking is Robert Skidelsky's three-volume work, *John Maynard Keynes* (Macmillan, 1992–2001) and a contemporary book, *Five Years of Economic Crisis* (Centre for Global Studies, LSE, 2014). There is a very lucid and accessible summary of theory in Michael Stewart's *Keynes and After* (Penguin, 1967). One of the most trenchant criticisms of current policy in this tradition is Paul Krugman's *End This Recession Now* (W. W. Norton, 2012).

The original Austrian view of economics, which emphasizes the structural nature of the problem – over-investment, leading to a debt legacy, unprofitable business and the need for a purge of bad assets and the restoration of profitable business and lending – is to be found in the work of von Mises, Böhm-Bauwerk, Hayek and Schumpeter, well summarized in W. W. Rostow, *Theorists of Economic Growth from David Hume to the Present* (Oxford University Press, 1990). A strand of that thinking is the concern over 'debt deflation', as in Irving Fisher's *Debt Deflation Theory of the Great Depression* (1933) or in a contemporary setting (notably Japan) in Richard Koo's *The Holy Grail of Macroeconomics: Lessons from Japan's Great Recession* (Wiley, 2008).

Apart from 'debt deflation', the other major line of argument in relation to legacy problems of the crisis is 'secular stagnation', as in Lawrence Summers's *Strategies for Sustainable Growth* (American Economic Association, 2013). The central point is that there is a lingering, global problem of excess savings over investment, both a cause and effect of very low long-term interest rates, and requiring action to stimulate investment (through public investment financed by government borrowing). There is an excellent paper by Ryan Avent, *What Market Failures Underlie our Fears of 'Secular Stagnation'* (June 2014) which criticizes Summers and various related economic arguments, such as that of Olivier Blanchard, chief economist at the IMF, whose remedy for 'secular stagnation' is a higher target rate of inflation. For a contrasting, very positive view of the world economy, see Gerald Lyons's *The Consolations of Economics* (Faber & Faber, 2014).

––––––––

Chapter 2 reviews some of the new, post-crash thinking about banks. A good analysis is in Alistair Milne's *The Fall of the House of Credit* (Cambridge University Press, 2009); Anat Admati and Martin Hellwig, *The Bankers' New Clothes: What's Wrong with Banking and What to Do About It* (Princeton University Press, 2013); Gary Gorton, *Misunderstanding Financial Crises: Why We Don't See Them Coming* (Oxford University Press, 2012); and Andrew Haldane, *Banking on the State* (Paper at Federal Reserve of Chicago, 25 September 2009). The impact of financial crises on distorting the allocation of credit is examined in D. Jordà, M. Schularich and A. Taylor, *Financial Crises, Credit Booms and External Imbalances* (NBER Working Paper, December 2010).

Several reports summarize the policy aspects, especially in the UK, and I return to these in chapter ten:

Banking Commission Report, by David Davis, Vince Cable and John McFall (May 2010)

Final Report of the Independent Commission on Banking (The Vickers Report) (September 2011)

Report of the Parliamentary Commission on Banking Standards: *Changing Banking for Good: Conclusions and Recommendations* (12 June 2013)

Erkki Liikanen, *The Case for Structural Reforms of Banking after the Crisis* (European Commission, Brussels, October 2012).

––––––––

Chapter 3 deals with the contrasting ways in which the USA and Japan have approached post-crisis recovery. The USA is, rightly, regarded as a relative success story of the Western world – other than countries like Canada, which avoided a banking crash in the first place because of far-sighted reforms made a generation earlier under Liberal prime minister Jean Chrétien. The policies were largely based around Bernanke's monetary policy, a modest Keynesian stimulus (which critics like Stiglitz and Krugman regarded as insufficient) and rapid action to rescue banks and then write down debt under the TARP programme.

The more recent criticism of US policy has been around the idea of 'secular stagnation' (Summers) and related to it, a belief that the USA is running out of steam in terms of economic growth, as in Robert Gordon, *Is US Economic Growth Over?* (NBER Working Paper 18315, September 2012). Also in Tyler Cowen, *The Great Stagnation* (Penguin, 2011). There is a link to growing inequality in Raghuram Rajan, *Fault Lines*.

Japan's financial crisis occurred a decade and a half ago and its subsequent history of stagnation and multiplying government debt has become a case study of what to do and not to do. The Japanese experience formed the backdrop to the work of Richard Koo. There is a more comprehensive book on Japan and its economic policy in Bill Emmott's *The Sun Also Sets: The Limits to Japan's Economic Power* (Crown, 1989). The pre-crisis economic problems of Japan are discussed well in Richard Werner, *A New Paradigm in Macroeconomics* (Palgrave MacMillan, 2005).

––––––––

Chapter 4 tries to capture the recent and existential crisis in the eurozone, which I suspect is far from concluded. On the Greek crisis, among vast amounts of commentary, I found the regular columns of Wolfgang Münchau in the *Financial Times*, and those of his colleague Martin Wolf, the most plausible and convincing (essentially, very critical of the German approach). The best background is in Vicky Pryce's *Greekonomics* (Bite Back, 2012).

Much of the recent eurozone crisis was anticipated before the eurozone was formed. There was a firm warning from the analysis done then that monetary union without fuller economic union, including large fiscal transfers and close coordination of fiscal policy and attendant disciplines, would fail. Either there would be closer union or the eurozone would fragment. The history of monetary union is clear: monetary union can survive even in big and/or heterogeneous entities (Germany, the USA, Italy, Switzerland), but, without exception, they fail if there is no move to closer economic policy coordination and political union (the Latin Monetary Union, the Scandinavian Monetary Union, the Germany-Austrian Union).

The underlying theory of monetary union, and the preconditions for success, are described in R. Mundell's 'A Theory of Optimum Currency Areas', *American Economic Review*, September 1961, and developed by R. I. McKinnon in 'Optimum Currency Areas', *American Economic Review*, September 1963.

There is an excellent and balanced review of EMU (originally to assess the merits of UK entry) in David Currie's *The Pros and Cons of EMU* (Economist Intelligence Unit, January 1997, and later in an abridged version published by HM Treasury in July 1997). Other useful texts include P. de Graewe, *The Economics of Monetary Union* (Oxford University Press, 1997) and an edited volume of papers by P. Torres and F. Giavazzi (Cambridge University Press, 1993), particularly T. Bayoumi, 'Shocking Aspects of European Monetary Unification', and Paul Krugman, 'Lessons of Massachusetts for EMU'. Also T. Bayoumi and Alan Thomas, *Economic Adjustment in the United States and the European Union: A Real Story about Relative Prices and EMU* (IMF Working Paper 94/65).

One of the key issues in the literature that reverberates in the real world today is the size of the fiscal transfer mechanisms required to offset an asymmetric economic shock in a participating member. B. Eichengreen (*The Euro: Love It or Leave It*, Working Paper, 2010) estimated that in the USA 40 per cent, on average, of the revenue impact of an economic shock in an American state is offset through fiscal transfers. The MacDougall Report, one of the intellectual building blocks of EMU, estimated 20 per cent as the minimum required in EMU. The European budget is barely 1 per cent of EU GDP, and just over 2 per cent of tax receipts. David Currie, however, makes the point that what matters is not the average impact but the impact at the margin. If the European budget is targeted rather than general in its impact, it could be effective at much less than twenty times its present size. Research stressing the importance of private capital markets in offsetting regional fluctuations comes from Céline Allard et al. *Towards a Fiscal Union for the Euro Area*, IMF Discussion Paper September 2013. The inconvenient data casting doubt in the benefits of structural reform is in Schindler et al. *Jobs and Growth: Supporting The European Recovery*, IMF 2014.

Chapter 5 deals with the emerging markets and their role in the world economy. I relied heavily on Angus Maddison's *Monitoring of the World Economy, 1820–1992* (OECD Development Centre, 1995) and this magisterial work has been supplemented by another, even more ambitious, *Contours of the World Economy: 1AD to 2030AD: Essays in Macroeconomic History* (Oxford University Press, 2007). Maddison uses purchasing power parity-based measurements of GDP and I have adopted his convention (now also used by the IMF and World Bank). If traditional current exchange rate-based measurements are used, the world looks a very different place, as in Roger Bootle's essay, 'Britain Could Become the World's 4th Largest Economy within Decades', *Daily Telegraph*, 5 May 2014.

A large part of the discussion centres on China and how the world adjusts to its growth. Some of the literature referred to in *The Storm* is still relevant. Good new sources are Stephen King, *Losing Control: The Emerging Threats to Western Prosperity* (Yale University Press, 2011); Ruchir Sharma, *Breakout Nations: In Pursuit of the Next Economic Miracles* (Allen Lane, 2012); and Lawrence Edwards and Robert Lawrence, *Rising Tide: Is Growth in Emerging Markets Good for the United States?* (Petersen Institute, 2013).

There has recently been a revival of interest in India with its new and apparently more business-friendly BJP government. There is an excellent review of India's economic progress in Jean Drèze and Amartya Sen, *An Uncertain Glory: India and its Contra-*

dictions (Allen Lane, 2013). My own instinct has long been that India's potential is usually underestimated next to China's, as in the booklet I wrote for Chatham House in 1996, *China and India: The New Giants* (RIIA). The issue of whether middle income countries are succumbing to secular stagnation is dealt with in B. Eichengreen and Associates, *Secular Stagnation: The Long View* (NBER Working Paper 20836, January 2015). The Arthur Lonis theory is set out in *Development with Unrestricted Supplies of Labour,* Manchester School, 1954.

————

Chapter 6 updates from *The Storm* the experience of globalization. The interesting question during and after the financial crisis was whether the painful experience of dislocation and austerity would derail the process of international economic integration and the institutions that underpin it. I sought to address this issue, and particularly the deficit of governance, in my book *Globalisation and Global Governance* (RIIA/Pinter, 1999). Some of the key contributors to pre-crisis literature are Martin Wolf, *Why Globalization Works* (Yale University Press, 2004); Jagdish Bhagwati, *In Defense of Globalization* (Oxford University Press, 2007); and Joseph Stiglitz, *Globalization and its Discontents* (Penguin, 2003). The attacks on the globalization process from the left – that it widens inequality (well articulated in the Stiglitz book) – proved to have little political traction before or after the crisis. There has been some criticism, even in the UK, of foreign ownership of companies as in Alex Brummer, *Britain for Sale* (Random House, 2012).

What has made much more impact is a revival in large numbers of countries, including European democracies and the UK, of the politics of identity, involving a resurgence of nationalism or other dividing lines based on religion, race, language or sub-national identity. I take some pride, if no pleasure, from seeing in action what I anticipated in two Demos pamphlets: *The World's New Fissures: Identities in Crisis* (1994) and *Multiple Identities: Living with the New Politics of Identity* (2005).

There are many examples of emerging economies pre-1914 coming to grief through bad policy. Argentina is a classic case; it was much richer and more developed than Australia. Much could go wrong in China and other emerging markets, as in Daron Acemoglu and James Robinson, *Why Nations Fail: The Origins of Power, Prosperity and Poverty* (Crown Books, 2012). The model of state capitalism is discussed in A. Musacchio and S. Lazzari, *Reinventing State Capitalism* (Harvard University Press, 2014).

––––––––––

Chapter 7 is essentially a retrospective look at post-crisis economic policy in the UK. It tries to explain my own role within the debates that raged inside and outside government, defending the government in parliament to its Keynesian critics but fighting within government for some shift in that direction.

I engaged in public debate with Robert Skidelsky in the *New Statesman* initially in response to an article of his attacking austerity measures in 2010. My response was 'Keynes Would Be on our Side' (12 January 2011). He then attacked coalition claims of recovery in 'Go Left, Go Right, Go Downhill' (21 September 2012). I responded, belatedly, in 'When the Facts Change Should I Change My Mind?' (3 July 2013). His arguments are fully developed in *Five Years of Economic Crisis* (Centre for Global Studies, LSE, 2014).

I additionally sought to move the public debate through party conference speeches and occasional pamphlets such as *Moving from the Financial Crisis to Sustainable Growth* (CentreForum, 2011), in which explicit reference to the need for a fiscal stimulus via public investment had to be edited out to prevent an open split in the government. Other speeches of relevance were to the CentreForum at the Guildhall in June 2012, drawing on the work of Nicholas Crafts and others, showing that expansionary monetary policy allied to an aggressive house-building programme succeeded in promoting recovery in the UK post-1929; and a speech to the Royal Economic Society, 'Recovery and Beyond' (27 January 2014), emphasizing the work that needed to be done on economic rebalancing. Craft's important work is summarized in *Delivering Growth while Reducing Deficits: Lessons from the 1930s* (CentreForum, 2011).

A key piece of economic policy debate that continues to this day is the widely quoted assumption that the Labour government had been grossly irresponsible in fiscal policy. The arguments are summarized in David Smith, 'After Wasting Five Years, Labour Will Struggle to Rebuild Economic Credibility', *Sunday Times* and blog, 7 June 2015. Whatever the Labour government's other failings, I believe this criticism largely lacks substance.

A key debate that broke surface occasionally was a strong disagreement between the UK Treasury (and the Chancellor personally) and the IMF (in the form of the chief economist, Olivier Blanchard) which, in its annual review of the UK economy in 2012 and 2013, argued for a UK fiscal stimulus via capital spending (which I agreed with). A technical debate surrounded the measurement of the fiscal multipliers (the growth of output consequent upon a stimulus). The OBR estimated that multipliers were 0.4 for tax cuts and 1.0 for capital, but the IMF was more optimistic, using figures of 0.9 and 1.7. According to Michael Stewart in *Keynes and After* (Penguin, 1967), in the *General Theory*, the multipliers were 2 and 3, albeit under very different conditions. Essentially, based on OBR figures, the Treasury underestimated the potential and the Keynesian critics exaggerated it.

The argument continued at different levels throughout the government over whether the economy was primarily constrained by lack of demand or by supply bottlenecks of various kinds. A good analysis for the early period is in Bill Martin, *Is the British Economy Supply Constrained? A Critique of Productivity Pessimism* (Cambridge Centre for Business Research, 2011). In the same spirit, Jonathan Portes of the National Institute for Economic and Social Research consistently argued that supply constraints were exaggerated relative to weak demand, as in *Fiscal Consolidation and Growth: What's Going On?* (NIESR, 10 October 2013).

In the latter half of the government term, the issue that

increasingly dominated debate was why the recovering economy and stellar performance in employment were accompanied by depressed productivity and pay: the so-called 'productivity puzzle'. Some play down the controversy, as in John Llewelyn and Birnal Dharmesa, *UK Productivity: A Puzzle but not a Surprise* (John Llewelyn blog, 28 January 2015). Others look at the issue in terms of long-term trends: Adam Posen, *Has Trend Productivity Changed?* (NIESR and Bank of England, 29 February 2011); D. Corry, A. Valero and J. Van Reenen, *UK Economic Performance Since 1997* (Centre for Economic Performance, LSE, 2011); S. Hills, R. Thomas and N. Dimsdale, *The UK Recession in Context: What Do Three Centuries of Data Tell Us?* (Bank of England Bulletin, 2010). There is a good review in ONS, *The Productivity Conundrum, Explanations and Preliminary Analysis* (October 2012).

Among the many papers on the 'productivity puzzle', the following are of importance: Charles Goodhart of Morgan Stanley emphasizing the rise of self-employment (April 2014); the economics team at Goldman Sachs who emphasize credit supply problems (note on 13 July 2013), a view supported by Ben Broadbent, *Productivity and the Allocation of Resources* (Bank of England, 2012); and P. Goodridge, who emphasizes the importance of new forms of intangible investments in P. Goodridge, J. Haskel and G. Wallis, NESTA Working Paper 14/02, 2014.

Chapter 8 is a forward-looking account of economic policy, in particular the future of monetary and fiscal policy in the UK.

The issues around future interest rate changes and 'forward guidance' were captured in Mark Carney's speech of 28 August 2013: 'Crossing the Threshold to Recovery' (his threshold then was 7 per cent unemployment, soon overtaken by events).

The bigger issues of the Bank of England's mandate are in the *Review of the Monetary Policy Framework*, HM Treasury Discussion Paper 8588, March 2013. The concepts behind the post-1997 system were first set out in F. E. Kydland and E. C. Prescott, 'Rules

330 AFTER THE STORM

Rather than Discretion' *The Journal of Political Economy*, vol. 85, issue 3 (June 1977). The case for targeting nominal GDP rather than inflation is set out in Scott Sumner, *The Case for NGDP Targeting* (Adam Smith Institute, 2011) and earlier by Samuel Brittan and James Meade in *Measuring Internal Balances* (1978). The more conventional view is in S. Ostry, A. Ghosh and M. Chamon, *The Scope for Inflation Targeting* (IMF Staff Discussion Note, 2014) and Mervyn King, *Twenty Years of Inflation Targeting*, Sharp Memorial Lecture, LSE, October 2012.

The future of QE is well discussed in Jo Owen, *The Wrong Sort of Money: Options for Quantitative Easing* (CentreForum, May 2013) and a speech by the Governor on 'Central Bank Asset Management and Financial Markets', 20 June 2012.

There is a more wide-ranging analysis in Charles Goodhart, *The Potential Instruments of Monetary Policy*, Special Paper 219, LSE Financial Markets Group Papers (January 2013). Macro-prudential policy is discussed in *The Interaction of Monetary and Macro Prudential Policies* (IMF, 2013) and Paul Tucker, *Macroprudential Policy: Building Financial Stability Institutions* (Bank of England, 2011). The so called 'helicopter drop' is discussed in A. Turner, *Debt, Money and Mephistopheles,* (Cass Business School, February 2013).

Fiscal policy and the Treasury's 'cliff edge' theory of maximum debt levels is based on Reinhart and Rogoff, and their methodology is seriously criticized in the Konczal blog of the Roosevelt Institute, April 2003; also in R. Pullin and M. Ash, 'Why Reinhart and Rogoff Are Wrong about Austerity', *Financial Times*, 28 April 2013.

The estimates of structural deficits are widely different and are based on contrasting views of the 'output gap' (the spare capacity of the economy). The arcane issues involved are discussed in an HM Treasury paper, *Forecasts for the UK Economy* (June 2014). The figure used by the Treasury is calculated from government net borrowing + 0.5 of output gap + 0.2 of output gap in previous years.

The exchange rate issues and monetary policy were originally set out in L. Sarno and M. P. Taylor, 'Official Intervention in the Foreign Exchange Market: Is It Effective and, If So, How Does It

Work?', *Journal of Economic Literature, VA. XXXIX* (September 2001). External weakness is discussed in Ben Broadbent, *The UK Current Account* (Bank of England, 29 July 2014).

The key issue of public investment is discussed in Lawrence Summers, 'Why Public Investment Really Is a Free Lunch', *Financial Times*, 6 October 2014, and the arguments are made in the IMF World Economic Outlook, Autumn 2014. A key issue is what we mean by 'public investment', as in the Social Market Foundation's *Autumn Statement Briefing : Osborne's New Choices:* 2013.

On deficit reduction choices, I tried to set out an agenda in 2009 in a pamphlet for Reform: *Tackling The Fiscal Crisis: A Recovery Plan for the UK*. See also the Fabian Society Commission on Future Spending Choices, 2013.

On household living standards, minimum wage policy, etc., I sought to cover the ground in a speech to the Resolution Foundation, 'A Long-Term Approach to Raising Living Standards' (May 2014). See also Gavin Kelly, 'Britain Needs to Face up to its Household Debts', *Financial Times*, 3 December 2013; M. Pennycook, *What Price a Living Wage* (IPPR/Resolution Foundation, May 2012); the final report of the Living Wage Commission, *Work That Pays* (24 June 2014); The Smith Institute/Living Wage Commission, *The Living Wage: Context and Key Issues* (September 2013).

Chapter 9 seeks to integrate UK housing policy with the wider debate on the economy.

There is a historically based account of the role of house prices in destabilizing the UK economy in Fred Harrison (predicting a crash in 2010), *Boom Bust: House Prices, Banking and the Depression of 2010* (Shephard-Walwyn, 1999), and *The Inquest* (published in 2010).

There is a really excellent survey of facts and arguments around house prices and housing policy in Shelter's *The Case for Stable House Prices in England* (October 2013). The factual material comes from the English Housing Survey.

My own contributions to the debate include a speech to CentreForum at the Guildhall, June 2012: 'Building Britain out of the Slump: 80 Years On' and in a series of critical media comments from mid-2013 on rising house prices, which were dismissed by the Chancellor in September 2013 ('Prices are barely rising outside London') until they were accepted in June 2014 in his Mansion House speech, leading to new Bank of England Rules on 27 June. My specific criticism of Help to Buy was echoed more widely (p. 10 of the Shelter report and by the OECD in May 2014). There is a detailed evaluation by Dario Perkins of Lombard Street Research, 28 October 2013, and by Matthew Oakeshott, 'Help to Buy without "help to build" is potty policy', *Property Week*, 18 October 2013.

The bigger picture of housing supply and demand is contained in Kate Barker's *Review of Housing Supply* (March 2004) and her subsequent book, *Housing: Where's the Plan?* (London Publishing Partnership, 2014); and D. Dorling, *All that is Solid: The Great Housing Disaster* (Allen Lane, 2014). The collapse of social housing is charted in Peter Hall, *Good Cities: Better Lives* (Routledge, 2013).

The controversy around the green belt is covered well in Paul C. Cheshire, Max Nathan and Henry G. Overman, *Urban Economics and Urban Policy: Challenging Conventional Policy Wisdom* (Edward Elgar, 2014), and Ian Birrell, 'Why Is Green Belt so Sacrosanct?', *Independent*, 23 March 2015.

Tax reform is set out in a series of *Financial Times* articles and working papers by John Muellbauer of Nuffield College, Oxford. The history of the use of land taxation is described in Robin Harding, 'Property: Land of Opportunity', *Financial Times*, 24 September 2014.

Community land auctions were first proposed by Tim Leunig in a report, *Community Land Auctions: Working towards Implementation* (CentreForum, November 2011).

————

Chapter 10 deals with UK banking after the crash. Many of the issues have been touched on in chapter two. But several, specific to the UK, are dealt with here.

The question of the size of the banking sector was dealt with by Mark Carney in a speech on the 125th anniversary of the *Financial Times* in October 2013, and a more relaxed approach was signalled in his Mansion House speech of 10 June 2015. The critical literature pointing to the negative impact of a large banking sector is in Guillaume Bazot, *Financial Consumption and the Cost of Finance 1950–2007* (Paris School of Economics, 2014).

A critical issue, leading to the establishment of the British Business Bank, was the deficiency of bank lending to SMEs, discussed in A. Armstrong, E. P. Davis, I. Liadze and C. Rienzo, *Evaluating Changes in Bank Lending to UK SMEs over 2001–12*, NIESR Discussion Paper No.408 (February 2013). A key advocate of the argument that lack of credit was critical to poor performance was Kevin Daly, 'Four Puzzles and the Role of Credit Supply', Goldman Sachs International, May 2014; also various members of the Bank of England MPC spoke up strongly on the subject, as in Ben Broadbent's 'Rebalancing and the Real Exchange Rate' speech of September 2011, and Paul Tucker's speech in September 2013.

The gap in equity and debt funding for medium-sized companies is discussed in the CBI report, *Slice of the Pie: Tackling the Under-utilisation of Equity Finance* (2014) and the OECD 'scorecard', *Financing SMEs and Entrepreneurs* (August 2013); and *NESTA, The Rise of Future Finance: the UK Alternative Finance Benchmarking Report* (December 2013).

Radical reforms to banking are discussed in Adair Turner's *Banking at the Crossroads: Where Do We Go from Here?* (FSA, 2012); in A. Admati and Martin Hellwig, *The Bankers' New Clothes* (Princetown University Press, 2013); and Atif Mian and Amir Sufi, *House of Debt* (University of Chicago Press, 2014). The concept of 'narrow banking' is developed by J. Cochrane, Chicago Booth School of Business *Economists*, June 2014, p.78. Also Dirk Bezemer, 'Big Finance is a Problem, Not an Industry to be Nurtured,' *Financial Times*, November 2013.

Chapter 11 tries to pull together the various strands in policy designed to produce a more balanced economy. There are some excellent reviews of long-term growth policy which I largely endorse, as in the LSE Growth Commission: see Tim Besley and John Van Reenen (eds), *Investing for Prosperity: A Manifesto for Growth* (LSE Publications, 2013); also Andrew Smithers, *The Road to Recovery* (John Wiley, 2013).

I set out the rationale behind the industrial strategy in, inter alia, 'Recovery, Relative Productivity and Rebalancing' speech to Social Market Foundation, July 2014. The department's papers on this subject include *Industrial Strategy: Government and Industry in Partnership* (April 2014) and BIS Analysis Paper, *A Sectoral Approach* (September 2013); for the geographical dimension, see BIS, the Heseltine Review, *No Stone Unturned: In Pursuit of Growth* (October 2012).

The issue of short-termism in equity markets is dealt with in BIS, *The Kay Review of the UK Equity Markets and Long-Term Decision Making* (July 2012), and BIS, *Implemention of the Kay Review Progress Report* (October 2014). There is a separate report by Sir George Cox (for the Labour party), *Overcoming Short-Termism within British Business* (2013). Also A. Hughes, *Short-Termism, Impatient Capital and Finance for Manufacturing Innovation in the UK*, Centre for Business Research Working Paper No. 457.

The skills agenda is addressed in Tom Frostick (ed.), *Fit for Growth: Investing in a Stronger Skills Base to 2020* (CentreForum, 2013), and Nigel Keohane and Claudia Hupkau, *Making Progress: Boosting the Skills and Wage Prospects of the Low Paid* (Social Market Foundation, April 2014). A key document is Alison Wolf's *Review of Vocational Education* (BIS/DFEE, 2011). My views on the long-term future of further education and higher skills were set out in a speech at Cambridge University in April 2014 and in a BIS green paper in April 2015.

The arguments for investing heavily in science and innovation are made in Mariana Mazzucato, *The Entrepreneurial State* (Anthem Press, 2013), and in a speech I made to a conference she organized on 22 July 2014. The evidence base is in a BIS report, *Global Leadership in Science and Innovation* (September 2013), and also in the BIS Evidence Paper, *Our Plan for Growth: Science and Innovation* (December 2014).

The link between inequality and growth is explored in the IMF note, *Redistribution, Inequality and Growth* (April 2014). A much-quoted text is Thomas Piketty, *Capital in the Twenty-First Century* (Harvard University Press, 2014). See also John Hills, Francesca Bastagli et al., *Wealth in the UK: Distribution, Accumulation and Policy* (Oxford University Press, 2013); James Sproule (ed.), *Sharing the Spoils: How global income dispersion is measured* (Institute of Directors, June 2014). Some answers are provided in Anthony B. Atkinson, *Inequality: What Can Be Done?* (Harvard University Press, 2015). The best ways to reconcile equity with economic efficiency are discussed in the final report of the Mirlees Review, *Tax by Design* (Institute for Fiscal Studies, September 2011).

I was involved in the controversy around immigration, as in my Mansion House speech, 6 March 2014. The arguments in terms of economic impacts are summarized in *The Long-Term Impacts of Reducing Migration: The Case of the UK Migration Policy*, NIESR Discussion Paper 420 (December 2013). A more negative view is in D. Coleman and R. Rowthorn, 'The Economic Effects of Immigration into the UK', *Population and Development Review*, 30(4), (December 2004). See also Alasdair Murray, *Migration: A Liberal Challenge* (CentreForum, January 2014); Charles Clarke, *The EU and Migration: A Call for Action* (Centre for European Reform, 2011); C. Dustmann and T. Frattini, *The Fiscal Effects of Immigration to the UK*, Discussion Paper Series (Centre for Research and Analysis of Migration, UCL, 2011), and other related papers in 2010 and 2013. David Willets writes about intergenerational equality in *The Pinch* (Atlantic Books, 2010).

Acknowledgements

This book was started in government but extensively revised after the 2015 election. Speed has meant I haven't been able to cross-check or consult on many details with professional (and political) friends and colleagues. Any errors of fact and interpretation are mine alone.

My main debt is to those who helped me prepare and revise the manuscript, especially as I am still at the early stage of transition from Biro to Apple. By far the greatest burden fell on my wife, Rachel, who laboured long and hard with the text, as well as giving useful feedback and constant encouragement. My former constituency staff, Joan Bennett and Shona Priestley, also helped me (and her) considerably in the later stages of getting the book ready for publication.

I would not have been able to write the book without the experience of being a Cabinet minister for five years in the coalition government. I was directly involved in many of the controversies around UK economic management and helped to shape the outcomes in some important areas. I am grateful to Nick Clegg for giving me the opportunity to serve and to stay as Business Secretary to the end of the government.

Although they were not involved with the book itself, I was greatly helped by having a collegiate group of BIS coalition ministers and some outstandingly able, and loyal, civil servants under permanent secretary Martin Donnelly. I received particular help on economic policy matters from the department's chief economists and latterly from my economic adviser, Leo Ringer, who gave useful comments on technical aspects of the book. I am especially indebted to my special advisers, among whom Giles Wilkes was an important sounding-board on economic policy issues and played a key role in endless negotiations with the Treasury over controversial texts so as to keep me, just, on side. Emily Walch was invaluable in helping to ensure that my political and departmental speeches and comments were properly and extensively covered through the media. Mark Morris also gave me useful feedback.

Finally, I am grateful to my admirable literary agent, Georgina Capel, who gave constant encouragement to proceed with the book through its various ups and downs; and to the highly professional publishing team at Atlantic Books, led by Margaret Stead.

Index